Canada and Internatioı

Series Editors
David Carment, NPSIA, Carleton University, Ottawa, ON, Canada
Philippe Lagassé, NPSIA, Carleton University, Ottawa, ON, Canada
Yiagadeesen Samy, NPSIA, Carleton University, Norman Paterson,
Ottawa, ON, Canada

Palgrave's Canada and International Affairs is a timely and rigorous series for showcasing scholarship by Canadian scholars of international affairs and foreign scholars who study Canada's place in the world. The series will be of interest to students and academics studying and teaching Canadian foreign, security, development and economic policy. By focusing on policy matters, the series will be of use to policy makers in the public and private sectors who want access to rigorous, timely, informed and independent analysis. As the anchor, Canada Among Nations is the series' most recognisable annual contribution. In addition, the series showcases work by scholars from Canadian universities featuring structured analyses of Canadian foreign policy and international affairs. The series also features work by international scholars and practitioners working in key thematic areas that provides an international context against which Canada's performance can be compared and understood.

More information about this series at
https://link.springer.com/bookseries/15905

Gilbert Gagné · Michèle Rioux
Editors

NAFTA 2.0

From the first NAFTA to the United
States-Mexico-Canada Agreement

Editors
Gilbert Gagné
Politics and International Studies
Bishop's University
Sherbrooke, QC, Canada

Michèle Rioux
Succursale Centre-Ville
UQAM - Universite Du Quebec A
Montreal
Montreal, QC, Canada

ISSN 2523-7187   ISSN 2523-7195   (electronic)
Canada and International Affairs
ISBN 978-3-030-81696-4   ISBN 978-3-030-81694-0   (eBook)
https://doi.org/10.1007/978-3-030-81694-0

This Palgrave Macmillan imprint is published by the registered company Springer Nature
Switzerland AG
The registered company address is: Gewerbestrasse 11, 6330 Cham, Switzerland

To the memory of our mothers

Rita Gazé (1935–2016)
—Gilbert Gagné

Marie-Jeanne Rioux (1932–2016)
—Michèle Rioux

PREFACE

The idea of this book follows on two seminars entitled "Read and Understand NAFTA 2.0" held at the *Université du Québec à Montréal* (UQAM) (University of Quebec in Montreal) in February 2019. Organized jointly by the *Groupe de recherche sur l'intégration continentale* (GRIC) (Research Group on Continental Integration) and the *Centre d'études sur l'intégration et la mondialisation* (CEIM) (Centre for the Study of Integration and Globalization), both based at UQAM, the seminars grouped 12 academics and doctoral students from five of Quebec's universities, including the *Centre d'études pluridisciplinaires en commerce et investissements internationaux* (Centre for Interdisciplinary Studies in International Trade and Investment) at *Université Laval* (Laval University). Gilbert Gagné and Michèle Rioux, directors of the GRIC and CEIM, respectively, later decided to build on the seminars and to co-edit a book on the renegotiation of the North American Free Trade Agreement (NAFTA). Together with the two editors, nearly all participants in the seminars are contributors to the book. Further experts were solicited, as to cover (nearly) all key aspects of what is now known as the United States–Mexico–Canada Agreement (USMCA).

Tracing its origins to the late 1980s, the GRIC, since 1994, has been at the forefront of the study of free trade and economic integration in North America and, beyond, in the Americas. Long led by Dorval Brunelle and Christian Deblock, and since 2003 by G. Gagné, the GRIC has stood out through its publications and collaborations with various research teams sharing similar interests. Since 2000, the GRIC has been a unit of the larger CEIM, led until 2018 by C. Deblock and, since then, by M. Rioux. For now more than 20 years, the GRIC and CEIM have joined efforts in training graduate students in the study of economic integration processes in North America and the world, as well as in furthering the understanding of such processes among academics, government officials, trade union groups, and interested citizens.

For more on GRIC, consult its website: gric.uqam.ca.

For more on CEIM, consult its website: ceim.uqam.ca.

Our first thanks go to the authors: academics, legal experts, and graduate students, whose expertise was essential to analyze various, often complex, dimensions of the USMCA and their key advances/retreats from NAFTA. Thanks are also due to Éric Boulanger and Nicholas Demanche, who have worked on the formatting of the manuscript. We are as well grateful to the anonymous reviewers of the book manuscript for their comments and suggestions, and to the staff at Palgrave, in particular Anca Pusca, whose help has been much appreciated throughout the process leading to the publication of the book. The realization of the book has finally been facilitated by a grant from the *Fonds de recherche Société et culture, Québec* under the Research Team Support program. We also acknowledge the financial support received from Bishop's University and UQAM.

Centre d'études sur l'intégration
et la mondialisation

Sherbrooke, Canada   Gilbert Gagné
Montreal, Canada   Michèle Rioux
April 2021

Contents

LIST OF CONTRIBUTORS

Hamza Ali Faculty of Law, Université Laval, Quebec City, Canada

Mathieu Arès School of Applied Politics, Université de Sherbrooke, Sherbrooke, Canada

Charles Bernard School of Applied Politics, Université de Sherbrooke, Sherbrooke, Canada

Madison Black Osler, Hoskin & Harcourt LLP, Toronto, ON, Canada

Charles-Emmanuel Côté Faculty of Law, Université Laval, Quebec City, Canada

Christian Deblock Department of Political Science, Université du Québec à Montréal, Montréal, QC, Canada

Zachary Dove Politics Department, University of California, Santa Cruz, CA, USA

Delphine Ducasse Faculty of Law, Université de Sherbrooke, Sherbrooke, QC, Canada

Erick Duchesne Department of Political Science, Université Laval, Quebec, QC, Canada

Geneviève Dufour Faculty of Law, Université de Sherbrooke, Sherbrooke, Canada

Gilbert Gagné Department of Politics and International Studies, Bishop's University, Sherbrooke, QC, Canada;
Research Group on Continental Integration, Université du Québec À Montréal, Montreal, QC, Canada

David A. Gantz Center for the United States and Mexico, Baker Institute for Public Policy, Rice University, Houston, TX, USA;
James E. Rogers College of Law, University of Arizona, Tucson, AZ, USA

Michelle Hurdle Faculty of Law, Université de Sherbrooke, Sherbrooke, Canada

Sikina Jinnah Environmental Studies Department, University of California, Santa Cruz, CA, USA

Noémie Laurens Department of Political Science, Université Laval, Quebec City, QC, Canada

Nathaniel Lipkus Osler, Hoskin & Harcourt LLP, Toronto, ON, Canada

Laurence Marquis Université Laval, Quebec, QC, Canada

Jean-Frédéric Morin Department of Political Science, Université Laval, Quebec City, QC, Canada

Kimberly A. Nolan García Facultad Latinoamericana de Ciencias Sociales (FLACSO), Mexico City, Mexico

Richard Ouellet Faculty of Law, Centre for Interdisciplinary Studies in International Trade and Investment, Université Laval, Quebec City, QC, Canada

Stéphane Paquin École Nationale d'Administration Publique, Montreal, QC, Canada

David Pavot Department of Marketing, Business School on Antidoping in Sports, Université de Sherbrooke, Sherbrooke, QC, Canada

Sandra Polaski Global Economic Governance Initiative, Boston University, Boston, MA, USA;
Independent Mexico Labor Expert Board, Washington, DC, USA

Michèle Rioux Department of Political Science, Centre for the Study of Integration and Globalization, Université du Québec À Montréal, Montreal, QC, Canada

Micheline B. Somda Faculty of Law, Université de Sherbrooke, Sherbrooke, QC, Canada

ABBREVIATIONS

ACEUM	*Accord Canada-États-Unis-Mexique*
ACTA	Anti-Counterfeiting Trade Agreement
AD	Anti-Dumping
AFL-CIO	American Federation of Labor and Congress of Industrial Organizations
ASEAN	Association of Southeast Asian Nations
BIT	Bilateral Investment Treaty
BRICs	Brazil, Russia, India, China
CBO	Congressional Budget Office
CBSA	Canada Border Services Agency
CEC	Commission for Environmental Cooperation
CETA	Comprehensive Economic and Trade Agreement
CFIA	Canadian Food Inspection Agency
CFTA	Canadian Free Trade Agreement
CPTPP	Comprehensive and Progressive Agreement for Trans-Pacific Partnership
CRS	Congressional Research Service
CUSMA	Canada–United States–Mexico Agreement
CVD	(Subsidy)/Countervailing Duty
DBS	Direct Broadcasting Satellite
DSM	Dispute Settlement Mechanism
DTH	Direct-to-Home
EC	Extraordinary Challenge (Procedure)
ECA	Environmental Cooperation Agreement
EU	European Union
FCA	Fiat-Chrysler

FCN	Friendship, Commerce and Navigation
FET	Fair and Equitable Treatment
FMP	Fresh Milk Protein
FTA	Free Trade Agreement
G7	Group of Seven
GATS	General Agreement on Trade in Services
GATT	General Agreement on Tariffs and Trade
GDP	Gross Domestic Product
GHG	Greenhouse Gas
GI	Geographical Indication
GM	General Motors
GPA	Government Procurement Agreement
GRP	Good Regulatory Practice
ICSID	International Centre for Settlement of Investment Disputes
ILO	International Labor Organization
IMF	International Monetary Fund
IP	Intellectual Property
IPRs	Intellectual Property Rights
IRC	International Regulatory Cooperation
ISDS	Investor-State Dispute Settlement
ISP	Internet Service Provider
ITC	(United States) International Trade Commission
LVC	Labor Value Content
MEA	Multilateral Environmental Agreement
MFN	Most-Favored-Nation
MOU	Memorandum of Understanding
MPC	Milk Protein Concentrate
NAAEC	North American Agreement on Environmental Cooperation
NAALC	North American Agreement on Labor Cooperation
NAFTA	North American Free Trade Agreement
NAO	National Administrative Office
NFS	Non-Fat Solid(s)
NGO	Non-Governmental Organization
NME	Non-Market Economy
NT	National Treatment
OECD	Organization for Economic Cooperation and Development
PRI	*Partido Revolucionario Institucional*
PTA	Preferential Trade Agreement
RC	Regulatory Cooperation
RCC	Regulatory Cooperation Council
RCEP	Regional Comprehensive Economic Partnership
RCF	Regulatory Cooperation Forum
RTA	Regional Trade Agreement

RVC	Regional Value Chain
SMP	Skim Milk Powder
SOE	State-Owned Enterprise
SPS	Sanitary and Phytosanitary
TAA	(United States) Trade Adjustment Assistance (program)
TBT	Technical Barrier(s) to Trade
T-MEC	*Tratado entre México, Estados Unidos y Canadá*
TPA	Trade Promotion Authority
TPP	Trans-Pacific Partnership
TRIMs	(Agreement on) Trade-Related Investment Measures
TRIPS	(Agreement on) Trade-Related Aspects of Intellectual Property Rights
TRQ	Tariff-Rate Quota
UNCITRAL	United Nations Commission on International Trade Law
UNCTAD	United Nations Conference on Trade and Development
USCFTA	United States–Canada Free Trade Agreement
USMCA	United States–Mexico–Canada Agreement
USSR	Union of Soviet Socialist Republics
USTR	(Office of the) United States Trade Representative
WIPO	World Intellectual Property Organization
WTO	World Trade Organization

LIST OF FIGURES

LIST OF TABLES

CHAPTER 1

Introduction

Gilbert Gagné and Michèle Rioux

After US President Trump announced the intention of his administration
to either renegotiate or break the North American Free Trade Agreement
(NAFTA), the renegotiation officially began on August 16, 2017, and
concluded on September 30, 2018. NAFTA 2.0, henceforth known as
the United States–Mexico–Canada Agreement (USMCA) in the United
States, the Tratado entre México, Estados Unidos y Canadá (T-MEC) in
Mexico, and, in Canada, the Canada–United States–Mexico Agreement
(CUSMA) and the *Accord Canada–États-Unis–Mexique* (ACEUM), was
signed on November 30, 2018. In the United States, further negotiations were required, first between the executive and Congress, and later
with the other two parties to the USMCA, leading to a Protocol of

G. Gagné (✉)
Department of Politics & International Studies, Bishop's University,
Sherbrooke, QC, Canada
e-mail: ggagne@ubishops.ca

M. Rioux
Department of Political Science, Centre for the Study of Integration
and Globalization, Université du Québec À Montréal, Montréal, QC, Canada
e-mail: rioux.michele@uqam.ca

G. Gagné and M. Rioux (eds.), *NAFTA 2.0*,
Canada and International Affairs,
https://doi.org/10.1007/978-3-030-81694-0_1

Amendment, signed on December 10, 2019. Following its approval by the legislatures of its three states parties, the USMCA entered into force on July 1, 2020.

The renegotiation and possible termination of the NAFTA sparked a lot of concern among people, either supportive or critical of international trade agreements. This book responds to such interest and/or concern. In this introductory chapter, we return to the essentials of the NAFTA, then turn to its renegotiation, and we summarize the main elements of its successor agreement, the USMCA, while contrasting it with its predecessor, before we present the various chapters of the book.

The North American Free Trade Agreement

The NAFTA had been in place since 1994. Negotiated between June 1991 and August 1992, this preferential trade agreement (PTA) at its inception was ground breaking in many respects and viewed as a model. It then created the largest free trade area, represented the first instance of a PTA grouping both developed and developing countries, and was the most comprehensive free trade agreement (FTA) ever negotiated. The NAFTA included 22 chapters, with a preamble and annexes. Aside from trade liberalization commitments, it encompassed new topics and provisions in trade agreements, such as services, investment, telecommunications, intellectual property (IP), labor and the environment (in the latter two cases, albeit in side agreements).

The initiative for NAFTA came from Mexico's proposal in February 1990 of a comprehensive PTA with its big northern neighbor. Then, Canada joined the talks, mainly to prevent Mexico from getting a better deal with the United States, which could have undermined its privileged access to its biggest market. The United States and Canada already had a PTA, the United States–Canada Free Trade Agreement (USCFTA), negotiated between May 1986 and October 1987, in effect from 1989 to 1994, when it was superseded by the NAFTA (see Cameron and Tomlin 2000, pp. 65–68).

Nearly all tariff and most non-tariff barriers on merchandise trade had gradually been eliminated. In absolute numbers, trade among NAFTA parties has more than tripled since 1994, forming integrated production and supply chains among the three countries (Villarreal and Fergusson 2020, pp. 3–4). Total annual trilateral trade in goods and services exceeds US$1.3 trillion, which is more than US trade with the European Union (including the United Kingdom) or with the whole of Asia. The United States is by far Canada and Mexico's main trading partner, whereas the latter two have fought with China in recent years to be the US main trading partner. Canada and Mexico are also among each other's main trading partners. Yet, while Mexico's proportion of international trade as percentage of Gross Domestic Product has nearly tripled from 1994 to 2019, owing in significant part to NAFTA, such proportion has remained unchanged in Canada's case, and only slightly increased in the US case (Villarreal and Fergusson 2020, p. 4).

NAFTA is generally credited for expanding trade and economic linkages among its states parties, creating more efficient production processes, increasing the availability of lower priced and choice of consumer goods, as well as, for some trade policy experts and economists, improving living standards and working conditions. NAFTA also coincided with Mexico's trade and investment liberalization efforts, which it helped "lock in". A major exception was the energy sector, in which the Mexican government reserved the right to prohibit private investment or foreign participation. At the same time, NAFTA has been blamed for disappointing employment trends, declining average US wages, and not having done enough to improve labor standards (in Mexico) and environmental conditions (within the NAFTA zone) (Villarreal and Fergusson 2020, p. 3; see also: Brunelle 2014; Brunelle and Deblock 2004; Hufbauer et al. 2014; Scott et al. 2006).

From NAFTA 1.0 to NAFTA 2.0

The US Trump administration not only forced the renegotiation and modernization of NAFTA, its stances and objectives were also peculiar. For Trump, NAFTA was a "disaster" and the "worst agreement ever negotiated" (Villarreal and Fergusson 2020, p. 2). Some of these negotiating stances explicitly or implicitly promoted US economic sovereignty and/or curtailed long-standing American liberalization commitments. US officials even spoke of unravelling North American and global supply chains, with a view to diverting trade and investment from Canada and Mexico to the United States. For their Canadian and Mexican counterparts, such proposals were counterproductive to the spirit and mutual economic benefits of NAFTA. The latter required being modernized, not unravelled (Villarreal and Fergusson 2020, p. 2; see also Lester and Manak 2018).

The Office of the US Trade Representative (USTR), in charge of trade negotiations, published in July 2017 a summary of US objectives for the NAFTA renegotiation, which it updated in November (USTR 2017). In the latter document, unprecedented in US trade negotiations, the American side sought to "improve the US trade balance and reduce the trade deficit with the NAFTA countries," so as to "rebalance the benefits" of the agreement.[1] Other key US negotiating objectives included: (1) to promote greater regulatory compatibility, transparency, accountability and predictability; (2) to update and strengthen the rules of origin, as necessary, to ensure that the benefits of NAFTA go to products genuinely made in the United States and North America (read motor vehicles); (3) to ensure that the rules of origin incentivize production in North America as well as specifically in the United States (notably of automotive products); (4) to eliminate the Chapter 19 (unfair trade) dispute settlement mechanism; (5) on dispute settlement, to provide mechanisms for ensuring that parties retain control of disputes and can address situations when a panel has clearly erred in its assessment of the facts or the obligations that apply; (6) to provide a mechanism for ensuring that parties assess the benefits of the agreement on a periodic basis (read the "sunset" clause); and (7) through an appropriate mechanism, to ensure that NAFTA countries avoid manipulating exchange rates in order to prevent effective balance of payments adjustment or to gain an unfair competitive advantage (USTR 2017). Interestingly, there was no specific mention of the United States seeking to get rid of Canada's cultural exemption clause.

Neither Canada nor Mexico outlined their negotiating objectives as broadly as the United States. In Canada's case, Prime Minister Justin Trudeau had stated, in particular, that the Chapter 19 dispute settlement mechanism, as well as Canada's cultural exemption, were both "red lines" in the NAFTA renegotiation (Siripurapu 2018). Mexico's objectives comprised: (1) prioritizing free access for goods and services; (2) strengthening of regional energy security; (3) establishing rules of origin to guarantee NAFTA's regional benefits; and (4) bolstering NAFTA's dispute settlement mechanisms (Stargardter 2017).

Until then, various attempts to update the NAFTA had not borne fruit, despite the significant built-in agenda within the NAFTA text, with

---

[1] USTR (2017, pp. 2–3). In 2019, the US trade deficit with Canada and Mexico had increased to US$129.1 billion, up from US$74.3 billion in 2016 (Villarreal and Fergusson 2020, p. 7). Mexico accounted for nearly three-quarters of this amount.

nearly 30 committees and working groups. Some other initiatives, notably the Security and Prosperity Partnership of North America, also stumbled, in good part due to diverging priorities among the participants. Also, a significant number of provisions in the USMCA are drawn from those of the Trans-Pacific Partnership (TPP), another major US PTA initiative, in which the NAFTA parties were involved.[2] Indeed, the compressed timeline for NAFTA renegotiation, and the fact that the same negotiators from all three countries had completed the TPP in October 2015, meant that the TPP inevitably served as a starting point for "modernizing" the NAFTA (Anderson 2020, p. 157; see also Gantz 2020, pp. 5–6).

When the renegotiation was launched, the trilateral character of the NAFTA was stressed, while Canada and Mexico were to form a united front toward US threats and pressures. In the summer of 2018, Canada decided to momentarily leave the United States and Mexico work on issues supposedly specific to their bilateral relationship, officially remaining in regular touch with its counterparts and rejoining the negotiation table at the appropriate time. Yet, on August 27, 2018, the United States and Mexico rather announced that they had reached an overall agreement, putting significant pressure on Canada to join or be left out. This episode dramatically illustrated a long known reality about NAFTA. Trade and investment ties have increased substantially, but separately along the US–Mexico and US–Canada axes, with tri-national automobile supply chains as a notable exception. Political ties have evolved likewise, with the United States acting as a hub (Anderson 2020, pp. 55, 159–60).

The United States–Mexico–Canada Agreement

The USMCA is comprised of 34 chapters, a preamble, a series of annexes and side letters. It retains most of NAFTA's market opening provisions and other measures, while bringing significant changes to auto rules of origin, agricultural products, investment, government procurement and intellectual property rights (IPRs). It updates rules on services, labor and the environment, and addresses new trade issues, such as trade facilitation, digital trade, state-owned enterprises (SOEs), small- and medium-sized enterprises, anticorruption, regulatory practices and currency manipulation. The matters debated before the USMCA could be approved by the

---

[2] The TPP grouped 12 countries of the Pacific rim: Australia, Brunei, Canada, Chile, Japan, Malaysia, Mexico, New Zealand, Peru, Singapore, the United States, Vietnam.

US Congress included labor and environmental provisions, dispute settlement, IPRs, as well as steel and aluminum requirements in the motor vehicle industry rules of origin (Villarreal and Fergusson 2020, p. 13).

After initial provisions and general definitions (Chapter 1), the USMCA, as for NAFTA, has a key, long chapter on national treatment and market access, pertaining to trade in goods, with the tariff schedules of the three states parties (Chapter 2). In agriculture, NAFTA resulted in tariff elimination for most agricultural products and provided for tariff-rate quotas for certain commodities, although some remained subject to high above-quota tariffs, such as US dairy and poultry exports to Canada. NAFTA also addressed sanitary and phytosanitary (SPS) measures and other types of non-tariff barriers that could limit agricultural trade. NAFTA set separate bilateral undertakings on cross-border trade in agriculture, one between Canada and Mexico, the other between the United States and Mexico; while, as a general rule, USCFTA provisions continued to apply on trade between Canada and the United States. In USMCA, parties agreed to maintain NAFTA's market opening provisions and to add several other provisions in the agriculture and SPS chapters. The former notably includes a whole section on agricultural biotechnology (arts 3.12–3.16). The United States notably insisted on and secured further access to Canada's supply-management-restricted dairy, poultry and eggs markets. The United States also negotiated changes to the Canadian wheat grading system and to ensure national treatment for beer, wine and spirits labeling and sales (annex 3-C) (Villarreal and Fergusson 2020, pp. 16–17).

With respect to rules of origin, some key changes brought to NAFTA by the USMCA figure in an annex to Chapter 4, containing product-specific rules for different sectors, including motor vehicles and parts. The latter's tightening was to prove the most contentious issue in the USMCA negotiations. The textiles and apparel sector already received extensive protection under NAFTA, through a "made-in-North America" rule, strengthened under the USMCA (Chapter 6) (Gantz 2020, pp. 124–26). The USMCA comprises a new chapter on customs administration and trade facilitation (Chapter 7), standardizing and modernizing customs procedures throughout North America to facilitate the free flow of goods.

NAFTA had a specific chapter on energy (Chapter 6), under which Mexico notably reserved strategic activities related to the exploration of crude oil, natural gas and basic petrochemicals. Under the energy chapters of the USCFTA (Chapter 9) and NAFTA, following a "proportionality" rule, Canada could not reduce its portion of exports to the United States of specific energy goods, such as oil, relative to its total supply of such goods within the preceding three years. The USMCA does not have an energy chapter and moves some of NAFTA's energy provisions to other parts of the agreement. It has a new chapter specifically recognizing Mexico's ownership of hydrocarbons (Chapter 8), while Canada's proportionality provision has been eliminated (Villarreal and Fergusson 2020, pp. 18–19; see Gantz 2020, pp. 101–10, 119–20).

While NAFTA contained a chapter on safeguards or emergency actions (Chapter 8) and another on review and dispute settlement in anti-dumping (AD) and countervailing duty (CVD) matters (Chapter 19), the USMCA combines them into a single chapter on trade remedies (Chapter 10), with further provisions for cooperation to prevent duty evasion (arts 10.6–10.7). There are as well key improvements to the provisions on technical barriers to trade (Chapter 11), to streamline the export of goods within the USMCA region. Chapter 12 of the USMCA addresses technical standards for six specific sectors, including chemicals, information and communication technology.

NAFTA included a chapter on government procurement (Chapter 10), while the United States and Canada also have obligations under the plurilateral Government Procurement Agreement (GPA) under the auspices of the World Trade Organization (WTO). While carrying over much of NAFTA's government procurement chapter's coverage, the USMCA's corresponding chapter (Chapter 13) only applies between the United States and Mexico. It is the first US PTA, and presumably among few PTAs, not to entail procurement obligations for all parties. Public procurement opportunities between Canada and the United States are now solely covered by the WTO GPA, while those between Canada and Mexico fall under the Comprehensive and Progressive Agreement for Trans-Pacific Partnership (CPTPP), the successor to the TPP following the US withdrawal (Villarreal and Fergusson 2020, pp. 18–19; see Gantz 2020, pp. 200–04). In early 2021, the "Buy American" announcement by President Biden has cast doubt on US procurement commitments (White House 2021).

NAFTA had a chapter on investment (Chapter 11), that addressed significant barriers to investment and ensured basic protections for foreign investors, primarily through a mechanism for the settlement of disputes between investors and host states, that is, investor-state dispute settlement (ISDS). In Chapter 14 on investment, the USMCA repeats NAFTA provisions, while clarifying and/or limiting some of them in light of developments and concerns over the past two decades. A key feature pertains to the substantial revision of ISDS provisions, a most controversial aspect of NAFTA. Yet, this was not figured clearly in US renegotiation objectives for the NAFTA. Notably, ISDS no longer exists between Canada and the United States, while it will continue between Canada and Mexico under the CPTPP. Between the United States and Mexico, ISDS claims are limited under the USMCA to "direct expropriation" or to government contracts in certain heavily regulated sectors marked by the presence of SOEs (Villarreal and Fergusson 2020, pp. 21–24; see Gantz 2020, pp. 110–12).[3]

The USMCA continues NAFTA's inclusion of core obligations relating to cross-border trade in services in a specific chapter (Chapter 15). Yet, because of the complexity of services-related issues, USMCA also covers services trade in other chapters, including financial services and telecommunications, as did NAFTA. The USMCA also retains NAFTA's negative-list approach, under which all services are liberalized under the agreement unless subject to specific exceptions. As for investment, these exceptions are indicated in annexes listing "non-conforming measures" at the end of the agreement. Such approach as well implies that, unless specifically excluded, any new type of service developed after the agreement comes into force is automatically covered.

The services chapter of the USMCA is followed by one on temporary entry for business persons (Chapter 16). The latter allows professionals and other personnel to enter the territory of another party to provide services. Largely replicating NAFTA's corresponding chapter, the USMCA does not place new restrictions on the number of entrants nor expand the list of eligible professionals (Gantz 2020, pp. 207–10; Villarreal and Fergusson 2020, p. 25). NAFTA had a chapter with provisions on telecommunications (Chapter 13). In Chapter 18, the USMCA retains much of these provisions and now covers mobile service providers (see: Gantz 2020, pp. 163–66; Villarreal and Fergusson 2020, p. 26).

The digital trade chapter of the USMCA broadly covers all sectors, but explicitly excludes government procurement or provisions on data

---

[3] Claims from existing investments remain eligible for arbitration under NAFTA provisions for three years from the termination of the agreement.

held or processed by governments. Overall, Chapter 19 seeks to promote digital trade and the free flow of information, as well as to ensure an open Internet. Although the majority of digital trade-related obligations are found in this chapter, there are relevant provisions in other chapters, including financial services (Chapter 17), IPRs (Chapter 20) and telecommunications (Chapter 18). While NAFTA allowed the transfer of data in and out of a party in the ordinary course of business, USMCA strengthens that language to protect the free flow of data. Key USMCA provisions prohibit cross-border data flow restrictions and data localization requirements. Financial services firms, notably, rely on cross-border data flows and use Internet cloud services often provided by US technology companies. Other new provisions include the protection of source codes and algorithms, as well as the prohibition of forced technology transfer (Villarreal and Fergusson 2020, pp. 26–27; see also Gantz 2020, pp. 166–71).

NAFTA marked the first time a chapter on IPRs figured in a trade agreement. It notably included provisions on copyrights, trademarks, patents, trade secrets, geographical indications, industrial designs, as well as enforcement (Chapter 17). Since NAFTA predated the commercial Internet, the USMCA, in Chapter 20, contains more comprehensive obligations, notably extending enforcement to the digital environment and Internet service providers. Like NAFTA, the USMCA commits parties to provide civil, criminal and other enforcement for IPR violations. In turn, the chapter's provisions are enforceable through the state-to-state dispute settlement mechanism of the agreement (Villarreal and Fergusson 2020, pp. 27–31).

NAFTA encompassed provisions on competition policy, monopolies and state enterprises within a short chapter (Chapter 15). The USMCA has specific chapters on competition policy (Chapter 21) and on SOEs and designated monopolies (Chapter 22). The latter updates NAFTA by ensuring that SOEs compete on a commercial basis, and that the advantages SOEs receive from their governments, such as subsidies, do not have adverse trade effects.

NAFTA was the first trade agreement to include workers' rights and environmental provisions, even if in side agreements. The USMCA now incorporates such provisions into the core of the agreement in Chapters 23 and 24, respectively. It also marks an evolution toward stronger and more extensive labor and environmental provisions from those under

NAFTA. Chapter 24 is complemented by an Environmental Coopera-
tion Agreement, notably to ensure the continuity of the work of the
Commission provided for under the North American Agreement on
Environmental Cooperation.

While NAFTA included broad provisions concerning regulatory practices in several chapters, the USMCA has a new, specific chapter on
"good regulatory practices" (Chapter 28). NAFTA had a short chapter
pertaining to the publication, notification and administration of laws
(Chapter 18). The USMCA, in Chapter 29, builds upon it, with a
focus on pharmaceuticals and medical devices (Gantz 2020, pp. 210–
13). As regards administrative and institutional provisions (Chapter 30),
the USMCA replicates the minimal institutions established under the
NAFTA, namely the Free Trade Commission. The latter is composed of
government representatives of each party at the level of ministers or their
designees, and decides by consensus. It oversees any matter relating to
the implementation or operation of the agreement, including the work
of committees, working groups and other subsidiary bodies established
under the agreement. This includes a Secretariat, consisting of three
national Sections.

On dispute settlement, NAFTA encompassed three main mechanisms:
the ISDS one, under Chapter 11 on investment; unfair trade dispute resolution, under Chapter 19, providing for the review by binational panels,
instead of domestic courts, of parties' final AD and CVD determinations;
and the general or state-to-state dispute mechanism, under Chapter 20,
over the interpretation or application of the agreement. Under USMCA,
the scope of the first has been significantly reduced; the second has been
replicated in the trade remedies chapter (Chapter 10); and the third, now
under Chapter 31, has been modified, notably to prevent the possibility
for parties to block the establishment of dispute panels.

NAFTA encompassed various exceptions (Chapter 21), as for essential security and taxation measures. The USMCA's chapter on exceptions
and general provisions (Chapter 32) repeats and sometimes broadens
them, as in the case of balance of payments. It notably includes a new
provision to prevent a party from concluding a PTA with a non-market
economy, read China (Gantz 2020, pp. 214–16, 220–22). Chapter 33 of
the USMCA on currency manipulation is a key illustration of a non-trade
issue now included in a PTA. Lastly, the final provisions (Chapter 34)
notably contain a 16-year "sunset" clause, although parties may agree

to extend the agreement through periodic review procedures (see Gantz 2020, pp. 223–27).

The Book

Beyond this first chapter, consisting of the Introduction, the book comprises 15 chapters and a conclusion. Each of the chapters discusses major topics in the transition from the NAFTA to the USMCA. The conclusion, for its part, concentrates on NAFTA's impact on its three states parties, while considering whether the USMCA could do better.

The second chapter, written by Erick Duchesne, covers the 19-month period between the signing of the USMCA on November 30, 2018, and its coming into force on July 1, 2020, revolving around its ratification in its three parties. The agreement was expected to go smoothly through the Canadian and Mexican parliaments, but to face hurdles in the US Congress. Yet, it was the American tariffs on steel and aluminum that nearly derailed the enactment of NAFTA 2.0. In December 2019, a Protocol of Amendment to the USMCA was concluded, in part to address some of the concerns of the American Congress. The chapter first explains and compares the amendment and withdrawal procedures under the NAFTA and the USMCA, then turns to the context and processes of ratification in the three North American countries, to finally focus on US steel and aluminum tariffs as well as the Protocol to the USMCA.

Stéphane Paquin and Laurence Marquis, in Chapter 3, discuss the role played by Ontario and Quebec, the two largest Canadian provinces, in the NAFTA renegotiation. The chapter highlights a key dimension of the three countries belonging to the NAFTA/USMCA, namely that they all have federal systems. Yet, Canadian provinces are much more involved in trade negotiations than US and Mexican states. In order to avoid being mere implementers of international trade agreements, negotiated by Canada's central government, provinces, notably Quebec and Ontario, have become more and more involved in trade negotiations. A key reason is that international trade negotiations increasingly touch on provincial spheres of jurisdiction. Besides, Paquin and Marquis consider how the provinces' role has evolved in light of other recent Canadian PTA negotiations, namely the Comprehensive Economic and Trade Agreement (CETA)[4] and the TPP/CPTPP. Provinces were most involved in CETA negotiations, least involved in TPP/CPTPP negotiations, with a level of involvement and cooperation between the two levels of government falling in between for the USMCA negotiations. The findings are based on interviews conducted throughout and after the NAFTA renegotiation, as well as earlier CETA and TPP/CPTPP negotiations, with closely involved officials, advisors and experts from Ontario and Quebec.

In Chapter 4, Geneviève Dufour and Michelle Hurdle address agricultural issues, namely Canada's new dairy obligations under the USMCA. The dairy industry is the second largest agricultural sector in Canada, mainly concentrated in Quebec. Governed by a supply management system since the 1970s, the Canadian dairy industry had been largely exempted from PTA rules until recently. Denouncing that system as unfair, US President Trump put it at the heart of American demands in NAFTA's renegotiation. Although Canada preserved its supply management system, it gave in on several points, as it had done in CETA and CPTPP. The USMCA provisions affecting Canada-US trade in dairy products have been criticized by Canadian dairy producers, who feel they had been sacrificed.

After President Trump had stigmatized mounting US trade deficits with its two North American partners, Mathieu Arès and Charles Bernard, in Chapter 5, mention that the automotive industry was at the centre of the NAFTA renegotiation. They first describe the key features of the North American auto industry and its integrated character, before analyzing the provisions of the USMCA relating to the auto sector. The latter propose not free trade but a modern form of shared production, or a new Auto Pact, between the three North American countries. They consist of a complex and highly detailed new agreement, which figures in the Appendix to Chapter 4 of the USMCA on rules of origin. Arès and Bernard conclude that, in their final regulatory form, the auto sector provisions of the USMCA correspond to established regional value chains of North American producers. As for the dairy sector, the outcome has been a set of cumbersome provisions, amounting to an awkward form of managed trade.

---

[4] The CETA groups Canada and the European Union.

In Chapter 6, Charles-Emmanuel Côté and Hamzi Ali examine the chapter on investment in the USMCA and how it differs from NAFTA's. They ask whether it entails a new North American approach to foreign investment law and policy. Despite adaptation, the USMCA marks a continuation as regards the substantive provisions protecting foreign investors and their investments. Yet, it departs from NAFTA in procedural provisions, that is, ISDS, through significant differentiations between states parties, notably its abandonment for Canada. Also, while ISDS continues in US–Mexico relations, it is now fragmented in two regimes with a more limited scope. Thus, rather than a new approach, the USMCA would mark the end of a common North American approach to investment law and policy.

Gilbert Gagné and Michèle Rioux, in Chapter 7, consider the provisions regulating electronic commerce or digital trade within international trade agreements, the USMCA in particular, from the perspective of their main promoter, the United States. As the US government failed to secure a framework for regulating e-commerce within the WTO, from the 2000s, it concluded a series of PTAs, a path that proved much more effective in securing and furthering rules and standards on electronic commerce. The NAFTA predated the digital revolution, while the USMCA encompassed, as of late 2018, the most advanced chapter and provisions on digital trade. In view of divergences among participants, the recently resumed e-commerce negotiations under WTO auspices may still be challenging.

In Chapter 8, Nathaniel Lipkus and Madison Black stress that the USMCA captures advances in IP policy since the NAFTA, while going further in setting standards for IP protection and requiring continued harmonization efforts. They analyze the provisions of the IP chapter of the USMCA along the changes they require to Canadian IP law. Known for its balanced approach between IP protection and access, Canada has agreed to some notable expansions of IP protection under the USMCA, including to copyright term and patent term adjustments, and intercepting counterfeit or pirated goods transitioning through its territory. Like the IP chapter in the NAFTA, Chapter 20 of the USMCA may set new norms for international IP protection for decades to come.

Michèle Rioux, in Chapter 9, analyzes the provisions of Chapter 21 of the USMCA relating to competition policy and of Chapter 22 on SOEs and monopolies, while comparing them with NAFTA's Chapter 15 dealing with competition policy, monopolies and state enterprises. She first looks at NAFTA before discussing the innovations in the USMCA.

Rioux notably points out that cooperation and coordination in terms of competition policy among NAFTA parties has mostly meant alignment on the US model of trade and investment regulation. The evolution and more ambitious provisions from the NAFTA to the USMCA have also essentially resulted from competition policy cooperation and agreements within the Organization for Economic Cooperation and Development and the International Competition Network or through bilateral antitrust cooperation agreements and other informal means. She concludes on the importance of competition chapters in trade agreements, their strategic dimension and their limits as regards regional and global competition regulation.

In Chapter 10, Sandra Polaski, Kimberly A. Nolan García and Michèle Rioux discuss the path of labor governance in North America from the NAFTA to the USMCA. The North American Agreement on Labor Cooperation was a side agreement to the NAFTA, which created a framework for addressing labor rights violations within a trade context. For its part, the USMCA not only includes a specific labor chapter, but also new obligations, mechanisms and processes. The labor provisions were later central in the partial renegotiation of the USMCA, leading to a Protocol of Amendment and their further strengthening, in particular as regards enforceability.

Noémie Laurens, Zachary Dove, Jean-Frédéric Morin and Sikina Jinnah, in Chapter 11, recall that NAFTA was the first PTA to include environmental provisions, yet in a side agreement (as for labor provisions in the previous chapter). Their chapter investigates how the USMCA's environmental provisions compare with NAFTA's and the three states parties' renegotiation objectives. The USMCA encompasses the most detailed environmental (and labor) chapter of any trade agreement to date. While the USMCA reaffirms NAFTA's approach to environmental protection, it includes dozens of environmental issues that its predecessor ignored. It also brings the vast majority of environmental rules into the core of the agreement and subjects these provisions to the general, sanction-based dispute settlement mechanism under the agreement, an outcome largely consistent with the parties' negotiating objectives.

In Chapter 12, Christian Deblock discusses, from Canada's perspective, international regulatory cooperation (IRC) within three recent and major PTAs, namely CETA, CPTPP and USMCA. As public regulations, through their differences, constitute important obstacles to trade, IRC seeks to bring closer, if not to harmonize, states' regulations, procedures, methods and practices, notably through an emphasis on "good regulatory practices." Yet, each of these three PTAs advocates a different approach to regulatory cooperation. The gravity effect that weighs on Canada's trade makes the USMCA most significant. Overall, the convergence of regulatory practices and systems is expected to go in the direction of the dominant US market.

David A. Gantz, in Chapter 13, analyzes two key mechanisms included in the USMCA for the settlement of disputes; the first, available to private parties, over unfair trade remedies (NAFTA Chapter 19, USMCA Chapter 10) and the second, reserved to states parties, over the interpretation or application of the agreement (NAFTA Chapter 20, USMCA Chapter 31). Although retention of these mechanisms was not a US objective in the NAFTA renegotiation, they were essentially maintained. The first was a non-negotiable "red line" for Canada, and apparently not a critical issue for Mexico. After the United States and Mexico reached a bilateral agreement to reconduct NAFTA in August 2018, Canada was rushed to join, effectively precluding a detailed review of the mechanism. As for the second, after commenting on US ambivalence toward third-party dispute settlement, Gantz stresses that the initial mechanism in the USMCA was only slightly altered from NAFTA's, with nothing to prevent blockage of the procedure, which had plagued its history. Yet, following the Protocol of Amendment, the final version of the USMCA greatly reduces that risk.

In Chapter 14, Delphine Ducasse, Micheline B. Somda and David Pavot point out that not only does Chapter 33 of the USMCA on macroeconomic policies and exchange rate matters have no equivalent in NAFTA, it is also the first time such a chapter is included in a trade agreement. At US insistence, such inclusion is aimed to: prevent currency manipulations to gain an unfair competitive advantage; respond to the inability of the International Monetary Fund to effectively regulate competitive devaluations; and create model clauses for future PTAs. In particular, transparency and reporting provisions are subject to the dispute settlement mechanism of the agreement.

Richard Ouellet, in Chapter 15, discusses the exceptions and general provisions, contained in Chapter 32 of the USMCA, together with the review and term extension clause, figuring in Chapter 34. He hints that the USMCA is unlikely to become the 2020s gold standard for PTAs, as the NAFTA was in the 1990s. NAFTA 2.0 is not meant to be a model, essentially reflecting the particular North American context and states parties' interests or values at the time of its conclusion. The general exceptions, and those relating to essential security, indigenous peoples rights, cultural industries, as well as the provisions around information (disclosure, protection, access), non-market countries, Mexican sovereignty over hydrocarbons, not to forget the review and term extension clause, all reveal an intent for a tailor-made PTA.

In Chapter 16, Gilbert Gagné considers the treatment of cultural products under the North American trading regime. Unlike most contributions to this book, whose topics correspond to specific chapters of the USMCA, the provisions relating to cultural products mainly figure in the exceptions and annexes to the agreement. Gagné first concentrates on the rules pertaining to the cultural sector in the NAFTA, particularly the negotiation and implementation of the clause exempting Canada's cultural industries, carried over from the USCFTA, and the relevant exceptions secured by the United States and Mexico. The changes brought to the treatment of cultural products in NAFTA 2.0 are then discussed, here again, focusing on the cultural exemption clause. Canada has preserved its outright cultural exemption, including for the digital field. The US exceptions, for their part, have not varied significantly in scope and remain very limited; while Mexico's, despite a new emphasis on cultural identity, are more circumscribed.

In the Conclusion (Chapter 17), Michèle Rioux, Sandra Polaski and Gilbert Gagné first recall that, before it became outdated, NAFTA innovated in many respects and constituted a model replicated far beyond North America. They focus on the economic and social impacts of the NAFTA on Mexico, the United States and Canada, especially as regards employment. The latter impact is crucial to understand the dissatisfaction, mostly in the United States, leading to NAFTA's renegotiation. Although the overall economic effect of the NAFTA has been very small, its sectoral effects have proved more discernible. Overall, the USMCA or NAFTA 2.0 must be seen as an update and modest rebalancing of the existing North American integration model, although much less likely to be followed than NAFTA was in the 1990s.

References

Anderson, Greg. 2020. *Freeing Trade in North America*. Montreal and Kingston: McGill-Queen's University Press.

Brunelle, Dorval. ed. 2014. *L'ALENA à 20 ans: un accord en sursis, un modèle en essor*. Montreal: Éditions IEIM.

Brunelle, Dorval, and Christian Deblock. eds. 2004. *L'ALENA: le libre-échange en défaut*. Montreal: Fides.

Cameron, Maxwell A., and Brian W. Tomlin. 2000. *The Making of NAFTA: How the Deal Was Done*. Ithaca, NY: Cornell University Press.

Comprehensive and Progressive Agreement for Trans-Pacific Partnership (CPTPP), signed March 8, 2018, entered into force December 30, 2018. https://www.mfat.govt.nz/en/trade/free-trade-agreements/free-trade-agr eements-in-force/cptpp/comprehensive-and-progressive-agreement-for-trans-pacific-partnership-text-and-resources/.

Gantz, David A. 2020. *An Introduction to the United States-Mexico-Canada Agreement: Understanding the New NAFTA*. Cheltenham, UK/Northampton, MA: Edward Elgar.

Government Procurement Agreement (GPA), as amended March 30, 2012. https://www.wto.org/english/docs_e/legal_e/rev-gpr-94_01_e.pdf.

Hufbauer, Gary Clyde, Cathleen Cimino, and Tyler Moran. 2014. *NAFTA at 20: Misleading Charges and Positive Achievements*. Peterson Institute for International Economics, Number PB14–13, May. https://www.piie.com/sites/def ault/files/publications/pb/pb14-13.pdf.

Lester, Simon, and Inu Manak. 2018. The Rise of Populist Nationalism and the Renegotiation of NAFTA. *Journal of International Economic Law* 21 (1): 151–169.

North American Free Trade Agreement (NAFTA), signed December 17, 1992, entered into force January 1, 1994. https://www.nafta-sec-alena.org/Home/ Legal-Texts/North-American-Free-Trade-Agreement.

Office of the United States Trade Representative (USTR). 2017. *Summary of Objectives for the NAFTA Renegotiation*, November. https://ustr.gov/sites/ default/files/files/Press/Releases/Nov%20Objectives%20Update.pdf.

Protocol of Amendment to the Agreement between the United States of America, the United Mexican States, and Canada, signed December 10, 2019. https://ustr.gov/sites/default/files/files/agreements/FTA/USMCA/ Protocol-of-Amendments-to-the-United-States-Mexico-Canada-Agreement. pdf.

Scott, Robert E., Carlos Salas, and Bruce Campbell. 2006. *Revisiting NAFTA: Still Not Working for North America's Workers*. Economic Policy Institute, Briefing Paper #173, September 28. https://files.epi.org/page/-/old/briefi ngpapers/173/bp173.pdf.

Siripurapu, Anshu. 2018. Trudeau: Chapter 19, cultural exemptions are NAFTA red lines for Canada. *World Trade Online*, September 4.

Stargardter, Gabriel. 2017. Mexico sets out NAFTA goals ahead of re-negotiation talks: document. *Reuters*, August 1. https://www.reuters.com/article/us-

usa-trade-mexico/mexico-sets-out-nafta-goals-ahead-of-re-negotiation-talks-document-idUSKBN1AH4VW.

Trans-Pacific Partnership (TPP), signed February 4, 2016. https://www.intern ational.gc.ca/trade-commerce/trade-agreements-accords-commerciaux/agr-acc/tpp-ptp/text-texte/toc-tdm.aspx?lang=eng.

United States—Canada Free Trade Agreement (USCFTA), signed January 2, 1988, entered into force January 1, 1989. http://www.international.gc.ca/trade-agreements-accords-commerciaux/assets/pdfs/cusfta-e.pdf.

United States-Mexico-Canada Agreement (USMCA), signed November 30, 2018, entered into force July 1, 2020. https://ustr.gov/trade-agreements/free-trade-agreements/united-states-mexico-canada-agreement/agreement-between.

Villarreal, M. Angeles, and Ian F. Fergusson. 2020. *The United States-Mexico-Canada Agreement (USMCA)*. Congressional Research Service, Report R44981, July 27. https://crsreports.congress.gov/product/pdf/R/R44981/19.

White House. 2021. *Ensuring Future of America is Made in America by All of America's Workers: Executive Order, Fact sheet*, January 25. https://insidetrade.com/sites/insidetrade.com/files/documents/2021/jan/wto2021_0051a.pdf.

CHAPTER 2

Ratification and Implementation of the United–States–Mexico–Canada Agreement (USMCA)

Erick Duchesne

INTRODUCTION

Since 1994, the North American Free Trade Agreement (NAFTA) had regulated most trade relations between Canada, the United States and Mexico. Despite some deficiencies and new issues left out of the agreement, there was little political appetite to modernize NAFTA, that is, until Donald Trump came to the scene. After his election, President Trump notified Congress of his intent to renegotiate NAFTA on May 18, 2017. After seven rounds of talks that started in August of the same year, the three North American partners signed the United States–Mexico–Canada Agreement[1] (USMCA) on November 30, 2018. From that point, the political joust turned toward national territories. This chapter covers the

E. Duchesne (✉)
Department of Political Science, Université Laval, Quebec, QC, Canada
e-mail: Erick.Duchesne@pol.ulaval.ca

© The Author(s), under exclusive license to Springer Nature Switzerland AG 2022
G. Gagné and M. Rioux (eds.), *NAFTA 2.0*,
Canada and International Affairs,
https://doi.org/10.1007/978-3-030-81694-0_2

19

19 months between the signing of the USMCA and its entry into force on July 1, 2020.

The agreement was expected to sail smoothly through Canadian and Mexican parliaments, but to navigate into troubled waters in the United States. Once the document was sealed, the perceived main hurdle to the approval of the USMCA was the respect by the US Congress of the fast-track process pursuant to the Trade Promotion Authority (TPA) established by the Bipartisan Congressional Trade Priorities and Accountability Act of 2015. It turned out that it wasn't as spectacular an obstacle as expected, and it was rather the imposition of American tariffs on steel and aluminum that came close to derail the enactment of the pact. On December 10, 2019, the three countries signed a Protocol of Amendment (the Protocol) to the USMCA, in part to assuage some of the US Congress concerns. We shall address all those topics in the following pages. First, we must explain the amendment and withdrawal procedures under the USMCA, as they compare to NAFTA's. Our attention will turn thereafter to the ratification and implementation of the accord in the three domestic legislatures. We will then discuss the USMCA's Protocol of Amendment signed in December 2019, as well as issues related to the American aluminum and steel tariffs. A conclusion follows.

Amendment and Withdrawal Processes Under the NAFTA and the USMCA

The USMCA has been submitted to the same ratification and implementation of institutional practice in the three countries as was NAFTA. In particular, in the United States, both pacts were subjected to the TPA, commonly known as the "fast-track" ratification process in Congress. NAFTA's ratification in the United States led to an epic battle between Democrats and Republicans in Congress. Before sending a formal proposal to Congress, newly elected President Bill Clinton added two negotiated side agreements to NAFTA, pertaining to labor and the environment,[2] to allay the concerns of many House members. There were also some fears that the arrangement would fall through in Canada. The deal was negotiated under the Conservative government of Brian Mulroney. During the 1993 electoral campaign, the Liberal Party's leader, Jean Chrétien, vowed to tear apart NAFTA. Once voted in office, he recanted on his promise. In Mexico, President Carlos Salinas de Gortari was able to push the agreement through the Senate and NAFTA came into effect on January 1, 1994. Chapter 22 accounts for NAFTA's amendments and withdrawal. Articles 2201 and 2202 made only some vague references to the ability of all parties to agree to some adjustments or additions to the Agreement, subject to applicable legal procedures of each party. As such, there were very little possibilities that NAFTA be modified unless, as in the case of the USMCA, the parties reached an agreement that supersedes the NAFTA.[3] It is, however, Article 2205 that proved to be consequential, when President Trump threatened to resort to it before, during and after the official negotiations, including through the ratification process.[4] Article 2205 stipulates that any party may pull out of NAFTA after a six months' formal notice to the other parties. The Agreement still applies for the remaining parties.

With the qualification that an amendment would come into force 60 days after the date on which the last party has provided written notification to the other parties of the approval of the amendment, Chapter 34 of USMCA is very similar to Chapter 22 of NAFTA, in terms of any modifications to or withdrawal from the Agreement. Article 34.4 adds that the parties must concur to include into the USMCA any WTO amendment that revises a provision of the Agreement.[5] One of the most controversial provisions of the USMCA, one upon which the American negotiators insisted vigorously, pertains to its sunset clause (Article 34.7—Review and Term Extension). The sunset clause provides for an automatic termination of the USMCA after 16 years, unless the parties agree explicitly to an extension. The Agreement is subject to an assessment within the first six years of its entry into force that could lead to a renewal for another 16 years, its expiry or the withdrawal from one of the parties. The process is repeated at each fixed six-year term. If a problem arises, a period of 10 years would allow for some negotiations to revamp the treaty; otherwise the USMCA would terminate. As an example, a trilateral commission will review the USMCA in 2026 and, following the recommendations of each party, will advise its cessation or its resumption until 2042. Under the first scenario, the three signatories would have up to 2036 to reach an agreement and avoid the dissolution of the USMCA. Under the latter case, the Agreement would be reevaluated in 2032. This complex blueprint represents a compromise between the three countries, after the American negotiators had initially insisted on a strict five-year sunset clause. This provision contributes to increased uncertainties that could act as a deterrent to international investments in the region. It is, however, a far cry from the dark shadow on the USMCA that the US Trade Representative, Robert Lighthizer, had cast. The review and extension clause of the USMCA is further analyzed by Richard Ouellet in Chapter 15 of the book.

Ratification and Implementation in Mexico

The sense of urgency to conclude an agreement before President-elect Andrès Manuel López Obrador took office on December 1, 2018, played a role in the signing of the USMCA the previous day, within the framework of the G-20 meeting held in Buenos Aires. Those were legitimate concerns. After all, López Obrador had been a fierce critic of NAFTA, but he had demonstrated more openness to a renegotiation during the electoral campaign, as a show of good faith toward the Mexican business community. There were yet reasons to worry that López Obrador would push back on Trump's anti-Mexican rhetoric and his claim that overwhelming bilateral issues, including drug trafficking, illegal immigration and the construction of a border wall, be tied to an eventual bargain. Under lame-duck President Peña Nieto, Mexico reached an understanding with the United States on August 27, 2018. Canadian Deputy Prime Minister, Chrystia Freeland, joined her counterparts to sign a modified agreement in the name of her country on December 10, 2018. Upon taking office, López Obrador supported the arrangement, insisting that the USMCA would bring much-needed backing for the Mexican economy, especially on behalf of its workers, after suffering a long decline under previous governments. He praised the entry into force of the treaty, in order to attract foreign investments and provide some relief from the COVID-19 pandemic.

In Mexico, a civil law country, the ratification and implementation of international accords are subject to a unique and accelerated process, the competence of which lies within the Senate. On approval by the Senate with a majority vote, when consistent with the laws of Mexico, the treaty has force of law after a decree by its president. With a preponderant coalition supporting him in the Senate, there was little doubt that López Obrador would give his imprimatur to the bylaw, providing for the enactment of the USMCA. However, the adoption of a package of reforms to improve workers' rights had to precede its ratification. The Mexican leader had expressed his endorsement for the measures, such that American and Canadian pressures on Mexico to reinforce labor standards coincided with López Obrador Morena Party's political platform. The Mexican Senate ratified the Agreement on June 19, 2019. With the approval of all congressional coalitions and only five votes against and six abstentions, the largest tripartite trade compact in the world, which succeeded NAFTA, entered a new phase and awaited the corresponding ratifications in the US and Canadian legislatures. The Mexican legislative sanction came in the midst of the diplomatic crisis opened by Trump's tariff threats, which sought to establish a 5% duty on Mexican products as a bargaining chip to get a stronger hand on the border. That measure had been suspended when the Senators cast their ballots, but it remained a menace to harmonious business relationships between the two North American neighbors. López Obrador had repeatedly stated that his country would only ratify the USMCA if the United States lifted its Article 232 tariffs on Mexican steel and aluminum imports by that date. We will come back to this issue in Sect. 5 of this chapter. In the next segment, the exigencies of the American House of Representatives regarding Mexican labor standards will also be considered. These issues forced, not only the negotiation of the Protocol to the USMCA (see Sect. 5), but also a new vote in the Mexican Senate. The Senate approved the revised treaty by a near-unanimous support of 177–1 on December 12, 2019.

Ratification and Implementation in the United States

Ratification and implementation of NAFTA 2.0 were subject to a much more complex and uncertain process in the United States than north and south of its borders, in a political climate marked by mistrust and unpredictability. With the Congressional extension of the TPA in May 2018, both houses had until June 30, 2021, to ratify and implement the USMCA by a simple majority vote.[6] This practice, commonly referred to as "fast track", does not allow for any amendments to the bill, which does not necessarily mean that legislators cannot have an imprint on the American bargaining position. Top officials are often consulted during the negotiations and, as we have seen in the case of the USMCA, they can force the addition of side agreements. On May 30, 2019, as required by the fast-track process, the US Trade Representative informed Congress of the domestic laws that must be amended to bring them into conformity with the text of the USMCA.[7] This short document could have led us to believe that the Americans only had to make few concessions to enable the implementation of the USMCA, and that its adoption should be a mere formality. This was without counting on the high political tensions that divide the US executive and legislative branches. While the fast-track process does not require official appraisals of the agreement by congressional committees, the House Ways and Means Committee and the Senate Finance Committee can conduct "mock markups", an informal exercise to review the provisions of the text. The mock markup stage does not have a time limit on the assessment of the files, meaning that the fate of the USMCA is determined by the willingness of Congress to proceed, at its own pace, with its informal examination of the treaty. Once this step is completed, implementation of the agreement can take place within 90 days when Congress is in session.

While the implementation process appears to be fairly well framed, trade agreements, even when there is some harmony between the executive and legislative branches, always tend to generate a certain amount of frenzy in Congress, and the USMCA was no exception. Members of Congress, particularly Democratic representatives, were armed with a long list of express demands, including changes to the labor and environmental chapters. As time passed, the requirement that Canada and Mexico extend patents for biologic drugs became a deal breaker for Democrats. Republicans had their own recriminations. For many of them, USMCA proposed provisions specifying workers' rights for LGBTQ and pregnant employees were problematic.[8] The President also held an important card in his sleeves. On December 2, 2018, he announced that he would invoke Article 2205 of NAFTA to repeal this agreement after the prescribed six-month period. This was his way of saying that the choice left to the legislators was between the USMCA or no NAFTA.[9] As the ratification process progressed, Trump toned down his rhetoric and, by spring 2019, it appeared much less likely that he would resort to that subterfuge to force the Democrats' hands. After many twists and turns, the House of Representatives adopted the USMCA by a bipartisan ballot of 385 to 41 on December 19, 2019, after Democrats had reached an understanding with the Trump administration earlier in the month. Less than 30 days later, on January 16, 2020, the Senate followed suit with a positive 89 to 10 votes. On January 29, 2020, Donald Trump signed the agreement into law.

RATIFICATION AND IMPLEMENTATION IN CANADA

In Canada, the ratification and implementation of the USMCA left little room for partisan squabbles. Despite an attempt from the Conservative Party to allow more time to examine the particulars of the treaty in

February 2020, there was a relatively large consensus on the Canadian vision of the accord, especially in comparison to the initial US–Canada free trade agreement of the late 1980s.[10] This was partially due to the creation of the NAFTA Advisory Council, constituted in part of former officials from opposition parties.[11] The Canadian government would have been more ambivalent about the possibility of ratification and implementation of the deal, had Americans maintained their tariffs on aluminum and steel. Once that obstacle was cleared and with the support from the Conservatives and the New Democrats, the endorsement of the USMCA was never in doubt.

In Canada, the ratification and the implementation of an international treaty require two separate processes. The internal legislative actions with respect to ratification are expected not to exceed 21 sitting days after the Foreign Affairs Minister tables the agreement in the House of Commons.[12] The document is accompanied by an Explanatory Memorandum, which details "the obligations under the treaty; national interest; the likely economic, social, cultural, environmental and legal effects and impacts; federal-provincial-territorial implications; implementation and the costs of compliance" (Fasken 2018). Once the pact is ratified, it must navigate through Canada's legislative process to become force of law. This represents the implementation of the agreement. The introduction of a bill prompting the examination of the treaty and requiring potential amendments to existing statutes constitute the first reading of the bill. Its second reading necessitates debates, submissions to committees and voting. Once the bill returns to the House for a third and final vote, it is considered adopted in the third reading if the "yeas" prevail. It is then sent to the Senate, where the same legislative process is taking place. Finally, after the Senate approval, the bill must undergo royal assent and it then comes into force.

The government tabled the text for ratification in mid-December 2018, which meant that it could not be presented to the House for implementation before the mandatory 21 sitting days. The Liberals held some hope that the text of the agreement would receive royal assent before the October 2019 elections. Expressing some preoccupations with the American aluminum and steel tariffs, the government delayed its legislative actions. Prime Minister Trudeau finally introduced Bill C-100, titled "An Act to Implement the Agreement between Canada, the United States of America and the United Mexican States" on May 29, 2019 (first reading). The bill passed through its second reading and was referred to the House

Standing Committee on International Trade (the Committee) on June 20, 2019. When Governor General Julie Payette declared the dissolution of the 42nd Canadian Parliament on September 11, 2019, Bill C-100 died on the agenda. After the Liberals were reelected as a minority government on October 21, 2019, Deputy Prime Minister Chrystia Freeland reintroduced the bill on January 29, 2020. Bill C-4 passed its first reading without a recorded vote. It was again referred to the SCIT on February 6 after its adoption in the second reading by a vote of 275–28. Three weeks later, the Committee voted to send the bill back to the full House for a third reading, without amendments. Due to extraordinary circumstances related to the COVID-19 pandemic, Bill C-4 was implemented (third reading) without a documented vote on March 13, 2020. On the same day, the Senate passed the three readings of the bill, also without a recorded vote. The bill received royal assent from the Governor General shortly thereafter and the Canadian government notified Mexico and the United States that it had completed all its domestic requirements to implement the USMCA. This was the last step providing for the entry into force of the international pact on July 1, 2020.

Steel and Aluminum Tariffs and the Protocol of Amendment to the USMCA

In April 2017, the US Secretary of Commerce launched two investigations under Sect. 232 of the Trade Expansion Act of 1962 to examine the effects of import increases of steel and aluminum on American soil. It was alleged that such import "surges" represented a threat to US national security. Ten months later, two reports confirmed that those imports constituted a hazard to American national security. Despite heavy protests from Canadian and Mexican trade representatives, demanding an exemption from US tariffs in the context of the NAFTA renegotiation, President Trump responded to the Department of Commerce's recommendations by imposing duties of 25% and 10%, respectively, on certain steel and aluminum products, starting on March 23, 2018. Canada and Mexico were exempted temporarily from these tariffs for a limited period, ending on June 1, 2018. These actions created an immediate outrage in Canada and Mexico and led to retaliatory measures by both countries. It also tainted the fledging trade negotiations and the end of Sect. 232 tariffs became Canadian and Mexican *sine qua non* conditions for concluding the USMCA. This challenging issue did not have a direct impact on the signing of the agreement, but had a profound effect on its ratification.

On May 17, 2019, the United States announced that it had reached a settlement with Canada and Mexico to remove the Sect. 232 tariffs for steel and aluminum imports on those countries. For their part, Mexico and Ottawa agreed to eliminate all their retaliatory tariffs on American goods. The deal was associated with a monitoring review to prevent surges in imports of specific steel and aluminum products. Should the United States reimpose tariffs on those products,[13] after a non-disclosed period of consultation, retaliation by its North American counterparts would be limited to similar goods. The parties also agreed to terminate all pending WTO litigation between them regarding the Sect. 232 actions. This agreement provided the anticipated momentum toward the US congressional approval of the USMCA, as well clearing the way for ratification in Canada and Mexico. It is doubtful, however, that this bargain will end the ongoing trade dispute in the sector. Just few weeks before the entry into force of the USMCA, US Trade Representative Robert Lighthizer told the Senate Finance Committee that the Trump administration was worried about Canadian aluminum export volumes and raised the likelihood of a reimposition of tariffs on this product in accordance with Sect. 232.

As mentioned before, there remained some outstanding issues from the signing of the initial agreement in November 2018. Not surprisingly, as was the case with the ratification of the NAFTA, the main impediment to the ratification of the USMCA came from the halls of the American Congress. As detailed in previous sections, it was mainly Mexican labor standards and environmental issues that raised eyebrows in the House of Representatives. To move forward with the ratification of the treaty, the three countries negotiated over additional objects of dissension, which led to the adoption of a 27-page Protocol to the USMCA on December 10, 2019. Environmental problems and labor standards were not the only sticking points. The amended text also covers state-to-state dispute settlement, intellectual property on patents and pharmaceutical provisions, and, as expected, steel and aluminum rules of origin content for automotive products. To be certain, the revised agreement was not only the result of some legislative battles, but also of the necessary legal scrub that followed the hurried signing of the document a year earlier.

Conclusion

When the USMCA was signed in December 2018, there was a large consensus among experts that its ratification and implementation in the US Congress would face an uphill battle. These were legitimate concerns. On many occasions, there were fears that the Agreement would fall apart. Trump's impeachment proceedings did muddy the water as well. In the end, the legislative process worked and, on July 1, 2020, we entered a new era in North American economic relations.

Notes

1. In this chapter, we use the official American denomination for the agreement. The Agreement is called the CUSMA in Canada and T-MEC in Mexico. The text of the Agreement is available at: https://ustr.gov/trade-agreements/free-trade-agreements/united-sta tes-mexico-canada-agreement/agreement-between.
2. The North American Agreement on Labor Cooperation (NAALC) and the North American Agreement on Environmental Cooperation (NAAEC).
3. In a "Protocol replacing the North American Free Trade Agreement with an Agreement between Canada, the United States of America and the United Mexican States", the parties agreed, pursuant to Article 2202 of the NAFTA, that the USMCA shall supersede the NAFTA. By the date the Protocol was signed, NAFTA was suspended.
4. It is still unclear if the President held the unilateral right to pull out from NAFTA. Most experts agree that the decision would have been challenged in courts. For more details, see Murrill (2016).
5. It should be acknowledged that such an article was not included in the NAFTA since the agreement preceded the entry into force of the WTO.
6. The extension of the TPA was a saga in itself, beyond the scope of this chapter. Suffice it to say that there were fears that President Trump would not have requested the extension of "fast track" when it appeared that the Democrats were to recapture a majority in the House in the November 2018 midterm elections. Ultimately, he did request an extension in May 2018. Under the standard procedure for treaty ratification, a two-thirds majority in the Senate is required. The main drawback of such procedure is that it would have allowed for the possibility of debates, amendments and filibuster. This is, however, a procedure that cuts both ways. Fearful of any victories for President Trump, which could put the wind in his sails in anticipation of the 2020 presidential election, some Democrats floated the idea of repealing the fast-track process for ratification of the

USMCA. This drastic step would have most likely meant the death of the agreement, considering that it was very unlikely that the USMCA could have gathered a two-thirds majority vote in the Senate.

7. For a copy of the letters, see Lightizer (2019). For clarity, the President had 30 days after the signing to submit to Congress a draft bill, along with a statement of administrative action, which he did on December 13, 2019. On the same day, the USMCA Implementation Act was introduced in the House (United States House of Representatives 2019) and three days later the companion bill was introduced in the Senate (United States–Mexico–Canada Agreement Implementation Act).

8. This represents a good exemple of *ex ante* involvement of congresspersons in the nature of an international agreement. The text of the final accord was diluted with the mere mention that a party should commit to "policies that it considers appropriate to protect workers against employment discrimination on the basis of sex (including with regard to sexual harassment), pregnancy, sexual orientation, gender identity, and caregiving responsibilities …" (USMCA, art. 23.9).

9. There were a lot of speculations about what this would have meant for the future of North American trade relations and the unilateral right for the President to pull out of NAFTA. All experts agree, however, that it would have led to lengthy battles in the courts of law.

10. The Liberal Party forms a minority government. It needed the support of the New Democratic Party to defeat the Conservatives' motion. The Bloc Québécois had already rejected the USMCA, due to its insatisfaction with the May 2019 agreement on aluminum and steel that, in its view, did not provide enough support for aluminum workers in the province of Quebec.

11. For the members' list, see Global Affairs Canada (2017).

12. At this stage, there is no legal obligation to debate the agreement and the Cabinet may, if it wishes, ratify the treaty after the prescribed time has passed, without the requirement that a bill be sent to Parliament. Ratification of the agreement usually falls on the minister of Foreign Affairs.

13. Mexicans and Canadians also reserved the right to impose tariffs should meaningful surges beyond historic volumes of trade over a period of time occur.

REFERENCES

Fasken. 2018. *CUSMA / USMCA/ T-MEC—Status and Implementation in Canada, the United States, and Mexico.* December 13. https://www.fasken.

com/en/knowledge/2018/12/ott-newsletter-cusma-usmca-t-mec-status-and-implementation-in-canada. Accessed July 2, 2020.

Global Affairs Canada. 2017. *NAFTA Council Members and New Diplomatic Appointees*. https://www.canada.ca/en/global-affairs/news/2017/08/nafta_council_membersandnewdiplomaticappointees.html Accessed July 4, 2020.

Lightizer, Robert E. 2019. No Title. https://ustr.gov/sites/default/files/USMCA_SAA_Cover_Letters_5.30.19.pdf. Accessed July 5, 2020.

Murrill, Brandon. 2016. *U.S. Withdrawal from Free trade Agreements: Frequently Asked Questions*. Congressional Research Service, Report R44630. https://crsreports.congress.gov/product/pdf/R/R44630/2.

Protocol of Amendment to the United States-Mexico-Canada Agreement, signed December 10, 2019. https://ustr.gov/sites/default/files/files/agreements/FTA/USMCA/Protocol-of-Amendments-to-the-United-States-Mexico-Canada-Agreement.pdf.Accessed July 3, 2020.

Protocol replacing the North American Free Trade Agreement with an Agreement between Canada, the United States of America and the United Mexican States, signed November 30, 2018. https://www.international.gc.ca/trade-commerce/assets/pdfs/agreements-accords/cusma-aceum/cusma-000-protocol.pdf. Accessed July 2, 2020.

United States. House of Representatives, Committee of Ways and Means. 2019. *United States-Mexico-Canada Agreement Implementation Act*. H. Rept. 116–358. https://www.congress.gov/congressional-report/116th-congress/house-report/358/1. Accessed July 5, 2020.

United States-Mexico-Canada Agreement Implementation Act, S.3052, 116th Congress. https://www.congress.gov/bill/116th-congress/senate-bill/3052. Accessed July 5, 2020.

United States-Mexico-Canada Agreement (USMCA), signed November 30, 2018, entered into force July 1, 2020. https://ustr.gov/trade-agreements/free-trade-agreements/united-states-mexico-canada-agreement/agreement-between.

CHAPTER 3

Canadian Federalism and International Trade: Ontario and Quebec's Role in the Negotiation of USMCA/CUSMA/T-MEC

Stéphane Paquin and Laurence Marquis

The recent renegotiation of the North American Free Trade Agreement (NAFTA), now known as the United States–Mexico–Canada Agreement (USMCA) in the United States, the Canada–United States–Mexico Agreement (CUSMA) in Canada and the *Tratado entre México, Estados Unidos y Canadá* (T-MEC) in Mexico, touched on areas that directly

This chapter was made possible thanks to funds from the Secrétariat québécois aux relations canadiennes.

S. Paquin (✉)
École Nationale d'Administration Publique, Montreal, QC, Canada
e-mail: Stephane.Paquin@enap.ca

L. Marquis
Université Laval, Quebec, QC, Canada

G. Gagné and M. Rioux (eds.), *NAFTA 2.0*,
Canada and International Affairs,
https://doi.org/10.1007/978-3-030-81694-0_3

affect Canadian provinces' jurisdictions (labor), shared jurisdictions (environment), or are of particular interest since they could have an impact on public policy in the provinces (supply management). The government of Canada, with its progressive trade agenda, wanted to strengthen existing provisions on labor and environment, and introduce new provisions on gender and Indigenous peoples, among other things (Lilly 2018). On the defensive interests' list, Canada wanted to preserve arbitration and the dispute resolution mechanisms (Chapters 19) and the cultural exemption clause. These constitute areas of important economic and social interest for provinces. Moreover, many of the American demands during the negotiation targeted areas of provincial or shared federal and provincial jurisdiction or policy, such as government procurement, alcoholic beverages, services and investment, e-commerce, automotive, chemicals, steel and aluminum.

In addition, the Trudeau government specifically asked provincial premiers to intervene with United States state governors and interest groups in order to build consensus to support continued free trade in North America. Ontario Premier Kathleen Wynne, for example, met with 37 United States governors to promote trade in the months after US president Trump was elected (Benzie 2018). Similar efforts were made by Quebec officials. In order to help ensure that Canada "speaks with one voice" during the negotiations, the federal government coordinated closely with provinces and territories, notably through "talking points" with its provincial and territorial counterparts (Smith 2019).

It is thus relevant to consider the evolution of the provinces' role in renegotiating NAFTA. It is of particular interest to determine whether this role has evolved since negotiations of the Canada–European Union (EU) Comprehensive Economic and Trade Agreement (CETA) and the Trans-Pacific Partnership, now known as the Comprehensive and Progressive Agreement for Trans-Pacific Partnership (CPTPP). Notably, during the CETA negotiations, the provinces had unprecedented access, input, and involvement, while in working toward the CPTPP, the federal government allowed very little provincial involvement.

We will focus on the role played by Ontario and Quebec in the NAFTA renegotiation. These two provinces are the largest in Canada in terms of both Gross Domestic Product and population. In addition, the negotiations touched on areas under provincial jurisdiction that were highly sensitive in both provinces. The chapter presents findings from semi-structured interviews we conducted throughout and after the

NAFTA renegotiation with officials, advisors, and experts from Ontario and Quebec who were closely involved. In total, the interviews represent over 24 h of discussion with key players. We then compare these interviews with the many interviews we conducted during earlier CETA and CPTPP negotiations. The interview guide was approved by the Ethics Committee of the École nationale d'administration publique.

Overall, our analysis of these provinces' role in the NAFTA renegotiation reveals that in order to avoid becoming mere implementers of trade agreements negotiated by the federal government, Canadian provinces, notably Quebec and Ontario, have become increasingly involved in trade negotiations. This situation has a profound impact on the division of powers between the federal government and the provinces and confirms the multi-level nature of international trade negotiations. This situation is not linear, however. During the renegotiation of NAFTA, the relationship between federal and provincial levels reflected a situation falling between CETA and CPTPP. CETA was the zenith of federal-provincial cooperation in trade negotiations, and the EU itself requested provincial involvement. The level of sharing, participation, and discussion on every aspect of the negotiation was unprecedented. Further, it served to significantly enhance knowledge of provincial and federal trade policy officials, and required provinces and territories to work with each other. As this negotiation was not rushed, the provinces could properly articulate their strategic interests and explain the impact of proposed EU or Canadian language on their interests. For the CPTPP negotiations, the federal government seemed to deliberately pull back from the CETA approach.

We should note that there is some divergence between Ontario and Quebec on this assessment. For Ontario, the USMCA process, to some degree, resembled more closely the experience in CETA, while the Quebec team felt it was closer to a "CPTPP plus" approach. For Ontario, under the CPTPP negotiations, provinces were engaged primarily via regular updates, with relatively little consultation compared to the CETA process. In the NAFTA renegotiation, provinces and territories were involved more significantly than in CPTPP, even though the provinces were excluded from the actual negotiating table where they had been welcome during CETA for areas of provincial or shared federal-provincial jurisdiction and had daily meetings with federal negotiators during each negotiation round. Quebec found relations with Ottawa more difficult, especially near the end of negotiations. The Québec government was not informed or involved in final decisions, and did not have much input into federal government strategy.

The role played by Ontario and Quebec in the NAFTA renegotiation in comparison with CETA and the CPTPP is first considered through the cooperation between federal and provincial levels, and, later, the challenges toward the end of negotiations.

The renegotiation of the North American Free Trade Agreement (NAFTA)

There are two main reasons for provincial involvement in trade negotiations. The first is that, while the federal government has constitutional responsibility for international trade and can negotiate in areas of exclusive provincial jurisdiction, it cannot compel provinces to implement ratified trade agreements. In Canada treaties do not have a direct impact on subnational domestic law; they must be implemented at both the federal and provincial level, making provincial "buy-in" essential (Cyr and de Mestral 2017, p. 596). Second, in this new era of "deep integration," all spheres of government activity, including matters under the sole jurisdiction of substate governments, come under the purview of at least one and often several chapters of these types of trade agreements. International trade negotiations address issues such as services, public procurement, public monopolies and state corporations, regulatory cooperation, public health, cultural diversity, subsidies, treatment of investors, investor-state dispute settlement (ISDS), agriculture, labor mobility, environment and climate change, etc. Trade agreements today have greater impact on areas under provincial jurisdiction than in the past. It is therefore not surprising that Canadian provinces are protective of areas under their authority in trade negotiations (Paquin 2006, 2010, 2013, 2017; Kukucha 2008, 2013, 2016).

As the federal government became increasingly aware of its limitations through the 1970s and 1980s, it developed a number of mechanisms for consultation between federal and provincial governments. For trade negotiations, the most important intergovernmental mechanism is known as the "C-Trade" forum (Kukucha 2016; Paquin 2013). C-Trade is regularly convened by the federal government together with officials from provinces and territories to review ongoing trade policy issues and exchange views.

In order to make their positions clear and increase their influence in negotiations, Quebec and Ontario retained the services of experienced advisors, and appointed chief negotiators for the NAFTA renegotiation to lead engagement with the federal government. Ontario appointed a high-ranking official to act as chief negotiator. John Gero, a trade specialist and Canada's former ambassador to the World Trade Organization, was also appointed as special advisor. In Quebec, the government has preferred to appoint chief negotiators from outside the public administration. Its strategy of appointing public figures who are "politically connected" is justified by the fact that political pressure must often be exerted on federal ministers and even the Prime Minister, and that negotiators need rapid responses from the office of the Premier of Quebec during the negotiation.[1] For CETA, Pierre-Marc Johnson, former Quebec Premier, was selected; for the softwood lumber dispute, former Canadian ambassador in Washington, Raymond Chrétien was chosen; for the NAFTA renegotiation, Raymond Bachand, strategic advisor at the Norton Rose Fulbright law firm and former Quebec minister of Finance, was named chief negotiator in July 2017. The appointment of chief negotiators is not a new strategy. During the free trade negotiations with the United States in the late 1980s, the Ontario government had retained the services of Robert Latimer, a former federal official, while the Québec government had recruited Jake Warren, who had served as Canadian negotiator during the Tokyo Round (Hart et al. 1994, p. 138). Interestingly, according to a representative of the government of Quebec, no province designated an external chief negotiator for the TPP negotiations.[2]

Cooperation between federal and provincial levels

During the NAFTA renegotiation, the level of cooperation between federal and provincial negotiators fell somewhere between that experienced during CETA and CPTPP negotiations (see Paquin 2013, 2017; Kukucha 2016). During the CETA negotiations, the provinces played an important role at virtually all stages of negotiations. Importantly, they provided contributions in formulating the federal negotiating mandate.

---

[1] This article is based on Stéphane Paquin, "Means of Influence, the Joint-Decision Trap and multilevel trade negotiations: Ontario and Québec and the renegotiation of NAFTA compared" Journal of International Economic Law, December 2021.

[2] Anonymous interview in Québec and Toronto in October 2017 and March 2018.

During preparation, the provinces were consulted about their key issues of concern and interest. In addition, they had secure access to negotiating texts and were extensively consulted throughout. Quebec, for example, presented over 150 position papers or strategic position briefs.[3] In addition, more "than 275 meetings between federal negotiators and their provincial and territorial counterparts, many meetings involving provinces and territories with common interests, and bilateral meetings in camera between a province or territory and federal negotiators" were held. Quebec's CETA chief negotiator, Pierre-Marc Johnson, had over 12 face-to-face bilateral meetings with the chief EU negotiator, Mauro Petriccionne (Johnson et al. 2015, p. 30).

During the CETA negotiations, the government of Canada also concluded the TPP, which later became the CPTPP, after the withdrawal of the United States and the negotiation of a new agreement in early 2018. Canada was not part of these negotiations until 2012, almost four years after discussions began. This particular context influenced the scoping exercise, but above all the drafting of the negotiation mandate. Indeed, Canada joined negotiations in a defensive perspective to ensure that an agreement was not concluded without Canada. This contrasts with the offensive role Canada assumed in CETA. Unlike CETA, the issue of provincial participation in negotiations was never raised by countries already participating in the TPP.

According to Quebec and Ontario representatives, the CETA model of active participation by the provinces was not reproduced in the TPP negotiations.[4] For instance, the provinces were not consulted on strategic issues in advance of Canada's participation in the negotiations. Nor did provinces have access to the negotiating tables, and federal-provincial consultation and information mechanisms were limited to C-trade meetings and updates during and following CPTPP negotiating rounds.

The level of provincial intervention at these meetings was not considered to be very high by officials from Quebec. In addition, during the rounds of negotiations, negotiating texts were often presented to the provinces at the last minute; comments were invited, but no real reaction was allowed and the time for analysis was often insufficient. The

[3] Anonymous interview, June 2014.

[4] Anonymous interviews in Quebec City in October 2017, April and October 2018, and in Toronto in March and October 2018.

same approach was used for briefings after rounds of on-site negotiations and during C-Trade meetings. However, a Quebec representative noted that provincial participation was important in the CPTPP negotiations because of work that had already been done under the CETA. In other words, some of the work done by the provinces during the CETA negotiations was also undertaken, though with less direct involvement, in the CPTPP. A federal government representative pointed out that C-Trade meetings were much better organized than they had been in the past.[5] The federal government thus seems to consider that the participation by the provinces was optimized, and not necessarily reduced.

As with the TPP negotiations, provinces were not invited to the negotiating tables during the NAFTA renegotiation. The provinces rather received regular updates and provided their views to the federal government; they did not have access to the Canada–US–Mexico tripartite negotiations. However, they were consulted closely in areas of strong economic interest (i.e., Ontario for automotive rules of origin) or shared/specific jurisdiction (i.e., alcoholic beverages, state-owned enterprises, labor, and environment). Frequent consultations between federal and provincial teams were held at special meetings focused on the renegotiation, rather than at the usual C-Trade meetings. The provinces were also invited to participate in strategy meetings prior to negotiation rounds, as well as in monthly debriefing sessions. Provinces with specific interests had good access to chapter negotiating leads. At the NAFTA renegotiation round held in Montreal, for instance, approximately 12 such meetings were held, according to an Ontario representative.[6]

Representatives from Ontario, Quebec and all other provinces were present at each round of the NAFTA renegotiation. These were important opportunities to meet with (1) federal negotiators regarding provincial interests; (2) stakeholders from various sectors (e.g., agriculture, autos, pharmaceuticals, etc.); and (3) representatives of other provinces in order to work with them on specific issues. Even though no formal negotiation rounds were held after March 2018, Quebec and Ontario remained in regular contact with the federal government at both official and

[5] Anonymous interview, Montreal, August 2016.

[6] Anonymous interview in Quebec City in October 2017, April and October 2018, and Toronto in March and October 2018.

political level. Throughout the renegotiation, both provinces also had a representative in Washington.[7]

The provinces were given an opportunity to participate in discussions affecting all issues within their areas of competence. Negotiating texts were circulated, and all parties respected confidentiality protocols. During negotiation rounds, the provinces participated in a nightly briefing on the day's progress. With the great volume of information required for USMCA, C-Trade meetings gave way to separate meetings specifically dedicated to these negotiations. Provinces were not only consulted, but they were also given the opportunity to provide input, which was considered. In contrast to TPP negotiations, where provinces were not consulted in an in-depth manner due to the rapid pace of the process—or were only belatedly consulted—federal-provincial-territorial engagement during NAFTA renegotiations was seen to be more extensive and inclusive.[8]

During NAFTA renegotiations, provinces also met among themselves to discuss specific issues in order to prepare for rounds.[9] These meetings came together somewhat organically and informally, most often instigated by the province at the helm of the Council of the Federation, or held in parallel with negotiation rounds. Meetings on NAFTA's renegotiation were held at the Council of the Federation in Alberta, as well as alongside the NAFTA round held in Montreal in January 2018.

Views from Ontario and Quebec differ somewhat on the overall process for the NAFTA renegotiation. The level of trust between federal and provincial teams appears to have been high, at least at the beginning of the negotiation. Ontario, under the Liberal Wynne government and at least initially under the Conservative Ford government, was generally seen to be supportive of a "Team Canada" approach in NAFTA renegotiation.

For Ontario, cooperation between the federal and provincial levels was seen as closer to the approach used in the CETA negotiations than under the CPTPP negotiations: provinces were consulted early and often on key

---

[7] Anonymous interview in Quebec City in October 2017, April and October 2018, and Toronto in March and October 2018.

[8] Anonymous interview in Quebec City in October 2017, April and October 2018, and Toronto in March and October 2018.

[9] Anonymous interviews in Québec in October 2017, April and October 2018, and Toronto in March and October 2018.

issues of concern to their economic and social interests. Quebec representatives, on the other hand, considered the USMCA process closer to that experienced in the CPTPP. Federal-provincial collaboration was excellent on issues such as public procurement and rules of origin. Yet, according to one Quebec official, the overall quality of the relationship depended on the personality of individual civil servants and was not related to intergovernmental relations.[10]

Toward the end of the NAFTA renegotiation, the federal-provincial-territorial official-level process de-intensified. This was due to the fact that, following Round 7 in April 2018, NAFTA renegotiations were held primarily between ministers and chief negotiators from the three NAFTA countries. In August and September 2018, all meetings took place in Washington, chiefly at the political level. With the looming deadline of September 30 to submit the text to US Congress so that it would be approved in time for signature by the outgoing Mexican president, the pace of negotiations between Canada and the United States intensified. There was thus much less opportunity and time for provinces to provide input.

While CETA's negotiations are often described as remarkable for their inclusion of the provinces at negotiating tables, what is mentioned less often is that, by the end of discussions, only federal negotiators remained at the table. A similar approach to the end-game process was repeated in the NAFTA renegotiation. The federal level remained in charge of final decisions,[11] and all final decisions on sensitive issues were decided at the federal ministerial level or higher, without direct input from provinces. As communication was primarily among ministers in the final weeks, updates and consultations with provinces and territories became less frequent during this time. According to a senior Quebec official, the last few weeks of the negotiations were, to say the least, "problematic".[12] The final decisions were made in the middle of Quebec's elections, where the issue of supply management in agriculture was central.[13] Quebec representatives were, by the end of negotiations, more critical of the federal approach.

[10] Anonymous interview in Québec, October 2018.

[11] Anonymous interviews of Quebec and Ontario officials in October 2018.

[12] Anonymous interview of Quebec officials in October 2018.

[13] Anonymous interview of Quebec officials in October 2018.

"The strategy didn't work. At some point, we should ask ourselves why," said one high-level Quebec representative.[14]

Ontario focused its concerns less on the process and more on the negotiating outcome, particularly regarding supply management and tariffs on steel and aluminum. The absence of public concerns around the process may in part be attributed to the high level of provincial involvement fostered by Canada's NAFTA chief negotiator, Steve Verheul, who was also the chief negotiator for the CETA negotiations. The Canadian chief negotiator was therefore familiar with the new federal-provincial relationship established during CETA. In addition, the difference between federal-provincial relations during CETA and USMCA, on the one hand, and TPP/CPTPP, on the other, could be explained by the fact that the EU insisted on provincial involvement in the CETA negotiations, the EU's most important offensive interest in those negotiations being public procurement, undertaken by provincial and municipal governments in Canada (Paquin 2013).

CLOSING THE DEAL

Ontario and Quebec reacted strongly to the conclusion of the USMCA deal. They publicly protested the final content of the agreement. The principal elements denounced by the provinces were concessions in supply management, including opening 3.6% of Canada's dairy market to the United States and cancelling Class 6 and 7 milk products (see Chapter 4 of the book), as well as the maintenance of tariffs on steel and aluminum that went against American promises to remove them.[15]

Elections were also held in Ontario and Quebec during the NAFTA renegotiation. Both provinces saw a change in government, with the election of Doug Ford's Progressive Conservative Party and François Legault's Coalition Avenir Québec (CAQ). While there was a consensus in Ontario to sustain a Team Canada approach to negotiations during the election campaign, in Quebec the NAFTA renegotiation became a central issue, especially over the dairy concessions. During the election campaign, the leaders of all political parties in Quebec were strongly opposed to any concession on supply management. All party leaders participated in a press

---

[14] Anonymous interview of Quebec officials in October 2018.

[15] Anonymous interviews in Québec and October 2018 and Toronto in October 2018.

conference organized with the *Union des producteurs agricoles* (Agricultural Producers' Union) in Longueuil. Philippe Couillard of the Liberal Party, Jean-François Lisée of the Parti Québécois and Manon Massé of Québec Solidaire were on location. François Legault of the CAQ also voiced his support for supply management and strong opposition to any dairy concessions (Messier 2018).

Philippe Couillard, then Premier of Quebec, told reporters several times during the campaign that there would "be serious political consequences" if Ottawa made concessions on dairy and supply management. When a journalist asked him, "how far are you ready to go?," the Premier responded with the reknown "Just watch me," famously used by Pierre Elliott Trudeau at the beginning of the 1970 October Crisis in Quebec. Philippe Couillard even went as far as to say that he would impose Québec's "veto" on USMCA and stated that no compromise was possible (Paquin 2018). While Quebec does not, in fact, have a vetos, the province's ability to refuse to implement the agreement in its field of jurisdiction is absolutely real. At one point, the issue became so heated that the Financial Times reported that Canada was thinking of waiting until after the Quebec election on October 1 to annonce the deal with the United States (Blackwell 2018). The USMCA agreement was announced on September 30, the night before Quebeckers went to the polls. After the election, François Legault, the new Premier of Quebec, stated that he would "look at every option with specialists to see what can be done [to oppose the deal]." The Quebec Parliament could refuse to "approve the deal" and make the necessary changes to Quebec laws and regulations to implement the deal (Foisy 2018; Paquin 2018).

In Ontario, the reaction of Doug Ford, the new premier of Ontario was also negative. Doug Ford held views somewhat similar to the Quebec Premier, but instead of talking about blocking the deal, he immediately called for compensation (McGillivray 2018). Although minister Freeland has promised compensation to the agricultural sector, no specific numbers have been provided, and negotiations are currently ongoing even at the time of writing this article. Provinces were still waiting, when the USMCA was annonced, for the compensation promised by the Canadian government fot the concession made during the CPTPP negotiations. This compensation was finally included in the March 2019 federal budget, which proposed up to $3.9 billion in support for farmers under supply management (Canada 2019, p. 190).[16]

The relationship between Ontario Premier Ford and Canadian Prime Minister Trudeau has been, to say the least, difficult. Tensions arose over the carbon tax and the Charter of Rights and Freedoms soon after the election of Doug Ford (Delacourt 2018). Regarding trade negotiations with the United States, the Ontario Premier's attitude changed over time. In June 2018, Doug Ford publicly stated that "we stand shoulder to shoulder with the Prime Minister and our federal counterparts" and "we are going to stand united. I know all provinces should be standing united with our federal counterparts" (Benzie 2018). In October 2018, Ford stated that Ottawa left out many key sectors in the new agreement, telling 600 supporters in a political rally in Etobicoke that "the new deal leaves too many Ontario families and businesses out in the cold. The Trudeau Liberals left out Ontario farmers, they left out Ontario's steelworkers and aluminum workers" (Benzie 2018).

Intergovernmental Affairs Minister in Ottawa, Dominic LeBlanc, responded to the comment, stating that Premier Ford had fully supported Canada's negotiating position, in public and in private. He also stated that: "Just days before the deal was concluded, the premier was briefed in detail in Washington, D.C., including about the modest changes to the supply management sector". Simon Jefferies, Doug Ford's press secretary, answered that "the more we study this deal, the more concerned we are that the federal government threw hard-working Ontario farmers, and steel and aluminum workers under the bus". The Ontario government

---

[16] Bill C-4, Canada–United States–Mexico Agreement Implementation Act—February 18, 2020—Privy Council Office—Canada.ca—Canada.ca: "On January 23, 2020, premiers issued a press release stating their unanimous support for the Agreement and calling for its implementation as soon as possible, including the commitment by the federal government to provide full and fair compensation for supply managed farmers and processors", available at: https://www.canada.ca/en/privy-council/corporate/tra nsparency/briefing-documents/parliamentary-committees/standing-committee-internal-trade/bill-c-4-canada-united-states-mexico-agreement-implementation-act-february-18-2020.html. Impatience has steadfastly grown for compensation with delays from the federal government. On October 29, 2020, it was reported that "Dairy farmers received a first payment of $345 million in 2019, before the federal election, but haven't heard about the remainder of the promised $1.75 billion over eight years." Karen Briere, "Dairy sector impatient on trade compensation, 29 October 2020," https://www.pro ducer.com/news/dairy-sector-impatient-on-trade-compensation/.

is also very concerned about Canada's ability to negotiate future PTAs (Benzie 2018).

Requirements for implementation mechanisms for international trade agreements are different in every province in Canada. Most legislative modifications resulting from new provisions in the USMCA will have to be made at the federal level, be it the dismantling of Class 6 and 7 products under supply management, or increasing the term in patent laws to comply with new obligations. The situation under CETA was different, as the agreement included areas under exclusive provincial jurisdiction, such as procurement and regulations on services and investment, for example. In that case, the federal government had requested that the provinces indicate their support for CETA and describe measures they would take to implement the agreement. Although there is no legal obligation to proceed in this manner, this was done specifically to avoid future issues with the provinces. No such commitment was requested from the provinces for the new NAFTA.[17]

Conclusion

Since the mid-2000s, the government of Canada has negotiated several new-generation trade agreements, notably CETA, CPTPP and USMCA, that have a significant impact on the interests or jurisdiction of Canadian provinces. This situation has a profound impact on the division of powers between the federal government and the provinces and confirms the multi-level or "de facto shared practice" nature of trade negotiations. Indeed, in order to avoid becoming mere implementers of trade agreements negotiated by the federal government, Canadian provinces, notably Quebec and Ontario, have become increasingly involved in trade negotiations. Trade negotiations are a regular occurrence in today's global context, and questions around the role of Canadian provinces in these negotiations are likely to resurface. It is also in the interest of the Canadian federal government in having provinces "buy into" commitments and being comfortable if the expectation is that provinces will comply, particularly as these agreements cover provincial measures. Ensuring provincial interests are satisfied only makes for a better overall agreement, even if it takes longer to negotiate, both for Canada, the provinces and

[17] Anonymous interview with Ontario officials, October 2018.

our trading partners. Provinces also have more expertise in certain aspects covered by trade agreements because the industries (e.g., alcohol, softwood, energy) are located on their territory. This is why the EU was able to negotiate such deep procurement commitments from Canadian provinces.

It is true that the status of Canadian provinces in CETA negotiations set a historic precedent. We also see, in the new NAFTA and CPTPP negotiations, that the provinces had an important role. Ontario and Quebec have expressed some concern about the government of Canada's attitude toward information sharing and openness to provincial input in the CPTPP negotiations. However, Canadian provinces are still much more involved in trade negotiations than are US and Mexican states. Quebec and Ontario may have different views on relations between provinces and the federal government during the NAFTA renegotiation, but the fact remains that their role was more important than during the TPP/CPTPP negotiations, during trade negotiations with India or South Korea (Paquin 2017; Kukucha 2016). Thus, the CETA negotiations helped improve intergovernmental trade negotiation processes.

While Quebec and Ontario expected to build off of CETA, they were completely caught off guard when the federal government reverted back to a less transparent/cooperative approach during the CPTPP negotiations. This was a source of contention between provinces and the federal government. But Canadian provinces are also partly responsible for the way CPTPP negotiations were handled, notably because they were less interested than they had been for CETA.

The views of Quebec about the NAFTA renegotiation may also reflect public opinion in the province. According to an Angus Reid Institute survey (2018) conducted two weeks after the USMCA agreement was announced, Quebec respondents have the least favorable assessment of the new NAFTA. Indeed, 58% were "disappointed/very disappointed" with the new deal, compared to 40% of respondents in Ontario. Approval of the agreement was higher in Ontario (39% of respondents approved) than anywhere else in Canada; only 27% of respondents in Quebec said they approved.

Many of the opinions expressed by representatives of the Quebec government can also be explained by the impact of NAFTA renegotiation on Quebec. During the renegotiation, Bombardier, which was heavily funded by the governments of Quebec and Canada, sold the C-series to Airbus after punitive tariffs were announced by the Trump administration.

Tariffs on steel and aluminum, as well as dairy concessions, particularly affect Québec. The fact that the Canadian government agreed to concessions on dairy products that clearly went against the will expressed during an election campaign by all party leaders represented in the National Assembly of Québec is an element that has to be taken into consideration.

Ultimately, there was no relationship between the level of federal consultation with Quebec and the result of negotiations. More consultation would not have changed the result. In its final decisions, the federal government was faced with a limited choice set. In the end, despite all the drama, Ontario and Quebec preferred to have the resulting agreement than no agreement at all. This explains why Ontario and Quebec are now talking about compensation and not about renegotiation or legal contestation.

References

Angus Reid Institute. 2018. *USMCA: Canadians ambivalent about 'New Nafta', feeling bruised by the U.S.* October 23. http://angusreid.org/usmca-new-nafta/. Accessed April 10, 2019.

Benzie, Robert. 2018. NAFTA talks: a priority for Premier-designate Doug Ford. *The Star*, June 12. https://www.thestar.com/news/queenspark/2018/06/12/nafta-talks-a-priority-for-ford.html. Accessed April 10, 2019.

Blackwell, Tom. 2018. Canada may hold off until after Quebec election as U.S.-Mexico drafting two-way trade deal. *Financial Times*, September 20.https://business.financialpost.com/news/u-s-mexico-drafting-final-text-of-two-way-trade-deal-but-canada-may-wait-until-after-quebec-election-on-oct-1. Accessed April 10, 2019.

Bouvier-Auclair, Raphael. 2016. L'accord de libre-échange Canada-EU est signé. *Radio-Canada*, October 30. https://ici.radio-canada.ca/nouvelle/811713/canada-ue-libre-echange. Accessed April 10, 2019.

Canada. Department of Finance. 2019. *Investing in the Middle Class. Budget 2019*. Ottawa : Department of Finance. https://www.budget.gc.ca/2019/docs/plan/budget-2019-en.pdf. Accessed April 10, 2019.

Comprehensive and Progressive Agreement for Trans-Pacific Partnership (CPTPP), signed March 8, 2018, entered into force December 30, 2018. https://www.international.gc.ca/trade-commerce/trade-agreements-accords-commerciaux/agr-acc/tpp-ptp/text-texte/toc-tdm.aspx?lang=eng.

Comprehensive Economic and Trade Agreement (CETA), signed October 30, 2016, entered provisionally into force September 21, 2017. https://www.international.gc.ca/trade-commerce/trade-agreements-accords-commerciaux/agr-acc/ceta-aecg/text-texte/toc-tdm.aspx?lang=eng.

Cyr, Hugo, and Armand de Mestral. 2017. Treaty-Making and Treaty Implementation in the Canadian Federation. In *The Oxford Handbook of the Canadian Constitution*, ed. Peter Oliver, Patrick Macklem and Nathalie Des Rosiers, 595–620. Oxford : Oxford University Press.

Delacourt, Susan. 2018. Ottawa worried Ford's Washington visit could impact NAFTA talks. *The Star*, September 18. https://www.thestar.com/opinion/star-columnists/2018/09/18/ottawa-worried-fords-washington-visit-could-impact-nafta-talks.html. Accessed April 10, 2019.

Foisy, Philippe-Vincent. 2018. Le Québec peut-il bloquer le nouvel ALENA?. *Radio-Canada*, October 6. https://ici.radio-canada.ca/nouvelle/1128175/alena-quebec-bloquer-nouvel-accord-aeumc-libre-echange-canada-etats-unis. Accessed April 10, 2019.

Gerbet, Thomas. 2018. Environnement: les Premières Nations se sentent trahies; Québec s'excuse. *Radio-Canada*, March 16. https://ici.radio-canada.ca/nouvelle/1089443/premieres-nations-autochtones-trahis-gouvernement-couillard-excuses-trudeau-ottawa-quebec-melancon-environnement. Accessed April 10, 2019.

Giovannetti, Justin. 2018. Ontario retaliates against New York State's Buy American provisions. *TheGlobe and Mail*, April 2. https://www.theglobeandmail.com/canada/article-ontario-retaliates-against-new-york-states-buy-american-legislation/.

Hart, Michael, Bill Dymond, and Colin Robertson. 1994. *Decision at Midnight: Inside the Canada-US Free Trade Negotiations*. Vancouver: UBC Press.

Johnson, Pierre Marc, Patrick Muzzi, and Véronique Bastien. 2015. Le Québec et l'AECG. In *Un nouveau pont sur l'Atlantique: l'Accord économique et commercial global entre l'Union européenne et le Canada*, ed. Christian Deblock, Joël Lebullenger and Stéphane Paquin, 47–60. Québec: Presses de l'Université du Québec.

Kukucha, Christopher. 2008. *The Provinces and Canadian Foreign Trade Policy*. Vancouver: UBC Press.

Kukucha, Christopher. 2013. Canadian sub-federal governments and CETA: Overarching themes and future trends. *International Journal* 68 (4): 528–535.

Kukucha, Christopher. 2016. Provincial/Territorial Governments and the Negotiations of International Trade Agreements. *IRPP Insight* 10: 1–16.

Lévesque, Céline. 2015. Les rôles et responsabilités des provinces canadiennes dans le cadre de procédures d'arbitrage entre investisseurs et État fondées sur des traités économiques. *Revue Québécoise De Droit International* 28 (1): 107–155.

Lilly, Meredith. 2018. International Trade: The Rhethoric and Reality of the Trudeau Government's Progressive Trade Agenda. In *Justin Trudeau and*

Canadian Foreign Policy: Canada Among Nations, ed. Norman Hillmer and Philippe Lagassé, 125–144. New York: Palgrave Macmillan.

McGillivray, Kate. 2018. Ford Gets His Wish For Federal Compensation Of Farmers Affected by USMCA. *CBC News*, October 1. https://www.cbc.ca/news/canada/toronto/usmca-ford-1.4845481. Accessed April 10, 2019.

Messier, François. 2018. Les chefs font front commun sur la gestion de l'offre, puis s'attaquent mutuellement. *Radio-Canada*, August 31. https://ici.radio-canada.ca/nouvelle/1121063/alena-upa-gestion-offre-jean-francois-lisee-pq-philippe-couillard-plq-manon-masse-qs. Accessed April 10, 2019.

North American Free Trade Agreement (NAFTA), signed December 17, 1992, entered into force January 1, 1994, suspended July 1, 2020. https://www.international.gc.ca/trade-commerce/trade-agreements-accords-commerciaux/agr-acc/nafta-alena/fta-ale/index.aspx?lang=eng.

Office of the Premier of Ontario. 2017. Premier's Statement of U.S. Release of NAFTA Negotiating Objectives. *Ontario Newsroom*. July 17. https://news.ontario.ca/opo/en/2017/7/premiers-statement-on-us-release-of-nafta-negotiating-objectives-1.html.

Paquin, Stéphane. 2006. Quelle place pour les pronvinces canadiennes dans les organisations et les négociations internationales du Canada à la lumière des pratiques au sein d'autres fédérations? *Administration Publique Du Canada* 48 (4): 447–505.

Paquin, Stéphane. 2010. Federalism and compliance with international agreements: Belgium and Canada compared. *The Hague Journal of Diplomacy* 5 (1–2): 173–197.

Paquin, Stéphane. 2013. Federalism and the Governance of international trade negotiations in Canada: Comparing CUSFTA with CETA. *International Journal* 68 (4): 545–552.

Paquin, Stéphane. 2017. Fédéralisme et négociations commerciales au Canada: l'ALE, l'AECG et le PTP comparés. *Études Internationales* 48 (3–4): 347–369.

Paquin, Stéphane. 2018. Le Québec ne possède pas de droit de veto sur l'ALENA. *Le Soleil*, August 28. http://www.stephanepaquin.com/le-quebec-ne-possede-pas-de-droit-de-veto-sur-lalena/. Accessed April 10, 2019.

Skogtad, Grace. 2012. International Trade Policy and the Evolution of Canadian Federalism. In *Canadian federalism : performance, effectiveness, and legitimacy*(3rd ed.), ed. Herman Bakvis and Grace Skogtad. Don Mills: Oxford University Press.

Smith, Joanna. 2019. Ottawa Wanted All of Canada Speaking with One Voice on NAFTA: Emails. *CBC News*, May 4. http://www.cbc.ca/news/politics/nafta-emails-verheul-1.4648786. Accessed April 10.

Swanson, Ana, and Ian Austen. 2018. Canada Attacks U.S. Tariffs by Taking Case to the World Trade Organization. *The New York Times*,

January 10. https://www.nytimes.com/2018/01/10/us/politics/canada-us-tariffs-wto.html. Accessed April 10, 2019.

United States—Canada Free Trade Agreement (USCFTA), signed January 2, 1988, entered into force January 1, 1989, suspended January 1, 1994. https://www.international.gc.ca/trade-commerce/assets/pdfs/agreem ents-accords/cusfta-e.pdf.

United States—Mexico—Canada Agreement (USMCA), signed November 30, 2018, amended December 10, 2019, entered into force July 1, 2020. https://www.international.gc.ca/trade-commerce/trade-agreements-accords-commerciaux/agr-acc/cusma-aceum/text-texte/toc-tdm.aspx?lang=eng.

CHAPTER 4

Canada's New Dairy Obligations Under USMCA and the Associated Implications for Canadian Dairy Producers and Processors

Geneviève Dufour and Michelle Hurdle

The dairy industry is the second largest agricultural sector in Canada. In 2018, it contributed C$6.64 billion to the Canadian economy and generated more than 42,000 jobs (Canada 2020). Quebec is Canada's main milk-producing province, representing 36% of Canadian revenues from dairy production (PLQ, n.d.a).

A supply management system has governed the Canadian dairy industry since the 1970s. It acts on three levels: it controls the production of dairy products, establishes minimum selling prices and controls imports (PLQ, n.d.b). For this reason, Canada imposes significant tariff peaks on imported dairy products.[1] This system provides Canadian producers with stability by ensuring a balance between supply and demand in Canada.

G. Dufour (✉) · M. Hurdle
Faculty of Law, Université de Sherbrooke, Sherbrooke, Canada
e-mail: Genevieve.Dufour2@USherbrooke.ca

© The Author(s), under exclusive license to Springer Nature Switzerland AG 2022
G. Gagné and M. Rioux (eds.), *NAFTA 2.0,*
Canada and International Affairs,
https://doi.org/10.1007/978-3-030-81694-0_4

Quotas are set annually for each producer, avoiding milk surpluses, which would have to be sold at loss (Heminthavong 2018).

The preferential trade agreements (PTAs) concluded recently, i.e., the Comprehensive Economic and Trade Agreement (CETA) and the Comprehensive and Progressive Agreement for Trans-Pacific Partnership (CPTPP), have opened up a major gap in this system since Canada has agreed to grant tariff-rate quotas (TRQs) to its partners, allowing a certain quantity of dairy products to enter duty free.

Canada's supply management system has come under increasing criticism since the late 1990s.[2] Critics see it as a subsidy system, supporting both domestic production and exports.

US President Donald Trump has used this system to convince Americans that the trade game with Canada was unfair (Ouellet and Messier 2017, p. 130). On April 18, 2017, during a visit to Wisconsin, President Trump attacked the North American Free Trade Agreement (NAFTA), targeting Canadian dairy regulations:

> We are going to stand up for our dairy farmers in Wisconsin ... and that demands really immediately fair trade with all of our trading partners, and that includes Canada, because in Canada some very unfair things have happened to our dairy farmers ... It's another typical one-sided deal against the United States ... NAFTA has been very very very bad for our country, it's been very very very bad for our companies and for our workers and we are going to make some very big changes or we are going to get rid of NAFTA for once and for all (Trump 2017, 12:24).

For Donald Trump, Canadian dairy regulations were responsible for the loss of jobs and income in the US dairy industry (Macdonald 2020, p. 155; Paquin 2019, pp. 207–211). The Canadian dairy sector was then at the heart of the American demands in NAFTA's renegotiation (USTR 2017, pp. 4, 6–7). Canada was under great pressure to facilitate access to its market for American farmers (Jones and Stone 2018).

Under NAFTA, Canada had largely exempted its dairy industry. The Canada–US agricultural provisions were based on the United States–Canada Free Trade Agreement (USCFTA), which granted full market access for most agricultural products, except dairy products (Debailleul 2006, p. 244). For Canada, the protection of its supply-managed sectors, along with securing a better access to the US market, were priorities in USCFTA and NAFTA negotiations. For the US, it was the protection of feed grains and its sugar production (Debailleul 2006, pp. 244–245; Villareal and Fergusson 2020, pp. 4–5). Mexico's priorities were to secure better access to both markets and obtain a transition period (Debailleul 2006, p. 245). Therefore, the pressures on Canada's supply management system in NAFTA talks were not a central focus, as they were in its renegotiation (Villareal and Fergusson 2020, pp. 1–5; Dey 2017, pp. 13–14; Debailleul 2006, p. 223).

In the face of US pressures, Canada had to give in on several points in NAFTA's renegotiation. The United States–Mexico–Canada Agreement (USMCA) provides for new provisions affecting Canada–US trade in dairy products. These provisions have been widely criticized by Canadian dairy producers who felt they had been sacrificed (CBC News 2018) for the benefit of the Canadian economy, including Ontario's auto sector (EDC 2018).

Article 3.A.3 of USMCA provides for four new obligations, essentially incumbent on Canada regarding dairy products. It grants new market shares to US dairy producers (I), abolishes milk classes 6 and 7 (II), quantitatively caps Canadian exports of certain products (III) and imposes considerable transparency obligations (IV). This chapter provides an analysis of these new obligations and the associated implications for Canadian dairy producers and processors.

New Market Shares

USMCA grants duty-free access to a certain quantity of US dairy products entering Canada. Fourteen categories of dairy products[3] are affected, for a total market opening of 3.59% by 2024 (PLQ, n.d.b). USMCA anticipates a significant annual increase in these quantities, especially in the first six years. By the sixth year, Canada will have increased its import quotas by 500% (USMCA, Ch. 2, Appendix 2-CAN, arts 5–18)[4] and then will have to grant an annual increase of 1% until the 19th year.[5] For US dairy farmers, it represents a gain of about US$70 million, a 10% increase (Livingston International).

It was to be expected that Canada would offer concessions in the dairy sector to its major trading partner considering those made in recent PTAs. But this access is well above the CETA (1.4%) and CPTPP (3.1%) (PLQ, n.d.b). More importantly, in this case, distance cannot be a factor in limiting the importation of fresh products.

With these three PTAs, Canada has agreed to open up 8.4% of its market, representing more than C$450 million in losses for Canadian producers, or C$41,000 per farm. Nearly 800 million liters of milk will no longer be produced by Canadian farmers. Once CETA, CPTPP and USMCA are fully implemented, Canada will import approximately 18% of its milk production, an annual loss of C$1.3 billion for producers alone (PLQ, n.d.b).

Despite this opening of 3.59%, Canada succeeded in preserving its supply management system, which was a priority (Global Affairs Canada 2017). Nevertheless, Canadian producers will have to adapt to greater influx of US products, causing them to fear an imbalance between supply and demand and an accumulation of surpluses.

Canada has negotiated reciprocal access to the US dairy market, but the benefits are likely to be modest. First, the US government heavily subsidizes dairy farmers, making the US dairy market more difficult for Canadian products to access. In 2015, the US government provided US$22.2 billion in subsidies to its dairy sector (GCS 2018, p. 7). Therefore, the US dairy industry is in a chronic situation of overproduction (Paquin 2019, p. 211), making it more difficult for Canadian producers to compete with US products on the American market, as their prices are generally lower (Mussell 2019, p. 2). Second, USMCA prohibits the export of subsidized agricultural products (art. 3.4).[6] But products under supply management are considered to be subsidized (Mussell 2019, p. 6). Third, the Pasteurized Milk Ordinance of the US Food and Drug Administration provides basic standards for milk hygiene and the "Grade A" requirements for milk products. However, the US has not yet entered into an equivalency agreement with Canada. Without this certification, dairy products cannot be imported into the US, except for cheese, ice cream and butter (CFIA 2018). Therefore, export opportunities for Canadian dairy products to the US are more limited and complicated.

Undoubtedly, these new American shares in Canada's dairy market are one of the most controversial consequences of USMCA. The abolition of milk classes 6 and 7, however, is largely responsible for Canadian dairy producers' anger.

Abolition of Milk Classes 6 and 7

By January 2021, Canada must eliminate milk classes 6 and 7, including their associated prices and ensure that products and ingredients covered by these classes are reclassified and appropriately priced (USMCA, art. 3.A.3.3–4). Essentially, USMCA provides that the price of non-fat solids (NFSs)[7] will be based on the US price (USMCA, art. 3.A.3.5).

Since their creation in 2017, milk classes 6 and 7[8] allowed Canadian producers to lower their NFS price despite the minimum one imposed under the supply management system. Their purpose was to mitigate the impact of similar imported US products and give a competitive Canadian option to dairy processors (Hufbauer and Jung 2017, pp. 5–6; Mussell 2019). Their creation was a response to tariff misclassification that allowed importing countries to circumvent Canadian import limits (PLQ, n.d.c).

In order to control imports, Canada imposes up to 300% tariffs on imported dairy products (CBSA 2020). Yet, incongruously, some NFSs are not considered dairy products by the Canada Border Services Agency (CBSA) but ingredients, creating a loophole in Canada's supply management system (Lampron 2016). Therefore, since the late 1990s, NFSs, especially milk protein concentrates (MPCs), have been entering Canada duty free. MPCs are used by dairy processors to replace Canadian fresh milk protein (FMP) in the manufacture of dairy products (PLQ, n.d.c).

In 2008, Canada introduced compositional standards for cheese, which require a minimum percentage of FMP (caseins) in the manufacture of cheese, thus limiting the addition of MPCs (CFIA 2013). However, in 2013, diafiltered milk[9] and its different classification by the CBSA and the Canadian Food Inspection Agency (CFIA) rendered these standards obsolete (PLQ, n.d.c; Groleau 2016). While the CBSA considers diafiltered milk as an ingredient, the CFIA considers it as fresh milk. Therefore, as an ingredient, diafiltered milk, mostly from the US, enters Canada duty free, but as fresh milk, it circumvents Canadian compositional standards (Lampron 2016).

Consequently, US diafiltered milk competes directly with Canadian NFSs and fresh milk. Dairy processors use diafiltered milk to achieve the minimum fresh milk requirement for cheese production, rather than in the allowable percentage of ingredients. Thus, Canadian NFSs, subject to supply management (relatively higher) prices, could not find buyers from processors (Lampron 2016).

This misclassification has been widely criticized by Canadian dairy producers, who calculate annual losses at C$231 million (Lampron 2016). For years, producers had been trying to draw the Canadian government's attention to the misclassification and on better control of US NFS imports, especially diafiltered milk (Groleau 2016; The Canadian Press 2016). Then, in 2016, Canadian dairy producers concluded a private agreement with dairy processors, leading to the creation of milk classes 6 and 7 in 2017. These classes made it possible to dispose of Canadian NFS stocks on markets (Heminthavong 2018).

For the US, these milk classes have rendered the exportation of dairy products, namely diafiltered milk, more complex, resulting in significant financial losses. While in 2016 US exports of diafiltered milk to Canada represented US$102 million, they dropped to US$32 million in 2018 (USDA, n.d.). Therefore, their abolition was a priority for the Trump administration in NAFTA renegotiations (USTR 2017, p. 4).[10] For Canada, it may lead to a surplus of NFSs. However, the concession to cap Canadian exports may make it impossible for Canadian producers to export these surpluses.

Canadian Export Caps

USMCA requires Canada to self limit its exports around the world in three categories of dairy products. Exports of skim milk powder (SMP) and MPCs, taken together, must not exceed 55,000 tons in year 1, and 35,000 tons in year 2. Before the Agreement entered into force, Canada exported 75,000 tons of these products annually (PLQ, n.d.b). Canadian exports for infant formulas[11] are also limited to no more than 13,333 tons in year 1 and 40,000 tons in year 2. These export caps will then increase by 1.2% per subsequent dairy year.[12] Above these thresholds, set for one dairy year, Canada will be subject to significant export charges (USMCA art. 3.A.3.8–9). In other words, Canada has agreed to include, in a PTA, clauses restricting its freedom to trade with the rest of the world for certain dairy products.

While this type of self-limiting clause was relatively common in the 1970s and 1980s, it is no longer the case today and it sets a precedent for Canada (Bernier 1974, pp. 50–54; Jones 1984, pp. 82–85). Such limitations are contrary to the Agreement on Safeguards (WTO 1994a), but they appear to be part of US negotiating technique under the Trump administration (Pethokoukis 2017, pp. 38–39). Guided by the America First Doctrine, the Trump administration imposes quotas strongly resembling self-limiting export measures on other countries in order to protect US producers (Fidler 2017, pp. 13–15; Schneider-Petsinger 2017, p. 14; Paquin 2019, p. 209).

The lawfulness of this type of clause in PTAs is questionable. Indeed, free trade areas are permitted under WTO law only as an exception regime.[13] Consequently, to form a free trade area, states must comply with a series of rules. In particular, free trade areas cannot limit a country's ability to trade with non-parties (WTO 1994b, art. XXIV.4).[14]

Therefore, USMCA poses significant barriers to trade between Canada and third countries. Since USMCA imposes export tariffs for any quantity exceeding the threshold set in a dairy year, Canada will either avoid exporting these products or will impose a surtax that will increase their price. USMCA appears to be inconsistent with GATT Article XXIV.

In the coming months, USMCA is expected to undergo a review by the Committee on Regional Trade Agreements (RTA) of the World Trade Organization (WTO) (WTO, n.d.b). This process begins as soon as members notify the RTA and is normally completed within one year.[15] USMCA was notified on September 16, 2020 (WTO, n.d.c). WTO members may then require explanations of the provisions' impacts on international trade. Following the review, a report is submitted to the WTO Council for Trade in Goods, which may impose measures on the RTA's states parties.

Independently, under the WTO dispute settlement mechanism, a WTO member could bring a complaint against Canada and the US regarding Article 3.A.3.8 and challenge its lawfulness under Article XXIV of the GATT. However, a WTO dispute settlement proceeding against the United States appears to be quite ineffective in the context of the Appellate Body crisis.[16] Canada remains vulnerable as a party to the WTO Multi-Party Interim Procedure for the Appellate Review of Trade Disputes.

Nevertheless, Canada has made a conventional commitment to respect Article 3.A.3 and must comply with it. Otherwise, it could face a complaint under the general dispute settlement mechanism provided for by USMCA (Ch. 31). To this end, USMCA also establishes a Committee on Agricultural Trade (art. 3.7.2.c).

In sum, these three new obligations could have a major impact on the production of cream-based products and on the way Canadian dairy producers will be able to dispose of their NFS surpluses. Following Canada's concessions, Canadian dairy producers will produce less milk, and thus less fat. At the same time, the Canadian dairy sector is experiencing a period of unprecedented growth since 2015, particularly for high-fat products. Agriculture and Agri-Food Canada forecasts an increase in demand of 1.2% annually until 2027 (AAFC 2018, p. 12).

Therefore, dairy farmers must produce more fat, resulting in an equal increase of SNF (AAFC 2018, p. 12.). However, the demand for Canadian NFSs from dairy processors has decreased significantly in recent years due to strong competition from similar US products, such as diafiltered milk (FCC 2016, p. 3). In this regard, the abolition of milk classes 6 and 7 cancels the incentives created for dairy processors to choose Canadian products and Canadian producers risk facing NFS surpluses.

Transparency Obligations

Finally, Article 3.A.3 provides for extremely specific transparency obligations (art. 3.A.3.10–13). First, Canada must notify the US at least one month prior to any changes that would increase tariffs to allow sufficient time to consider the proposed change. This obligation includes any changes to the classification of dairy products and price classes (USMCA, art. 3.A.3.12).

Second, Canada must share raw data such as milk utilization by class and month, quantities sold, etc. For example, Canada is required to provide the US with monthly data on its global exports of SMP, MPCs and infant formula (USMCA, art. 3.A.3.13). USMCA also requires Canada to publish information on regulations pertaining to the pricing of milk classes, including milk components (art. 3.A.3.10–11).

The Trump administration had made greater transparency a central requirement in NAFTA renegotiation (USTR 2017, p. 10). These transparency obligations are intended to prevent a new agreement between dairy processors and producers that would circumvent the abolition of milk classes 6 and 7 and the export cap. Ultimately, the publication of Canadian export data will allow US authorities to assess whether Canada complies with USMCA provisions. In order to monitor the implementation of these new obligations, Canada has agreed to discuss any issues related to this monitoring mechanism at the request of the United States (USMCA, art. 3.A.3.15).

Conclusion

The United States and Canada will review USMCA dairy provisions five years after its date of entry into force and every two years thereafter to assess whether they should be withdrawn or modified (art. 3.A.3.16).

Evidently, the milk sector has borne the brunt of NAFTA's renegotiation. Yet, the United States had a net trade surplus of C$445 million in dairy products with Canada in 2016 (PLQ, n.d.b). Nevertheless, President Donald Trump had made it one of his hobbyhorses, strongly criticizing Canada's supply management system as an unfair practice that has put US farmers out of work (Fidler 2017, pp. 9–10). For Trump, a renegotiation of the dairy sector was essential to woo his constituents in dairy-producing states.

USMCA entered into force on July 1, 2020. However, the Canadian government had intended an effective date of August 1, 2020, to coincide with the new dairy year. Therefore, instead of having 12 months under the export ceilings set for the first year, Canadian dairy producers and processors had only a few weeks to reorganize for the new dairy year (McCarten 2020). August 1, 2020, marked the beginning of the second dairy year under the terms of USMCA, involving a significant reduction in export ceilings for certain dairy products. It resulted in a reduction of nearly 40% in Canadian dairy exports, representing an additional C$100 million in losses (DFC 2020a).

In 2019, the Trudeau government promised C$1.75 billion in financial compensation over eight years to Canadian dairy producers to offset market losses (DFC 2020b). Dairy farmers called on the Canadian government numerous times to announce the payment schedule for USMCA, CETA and CPTPP (DFC 2020c). On November 28, 2020, the government announced this payment schedule through direct payments to farmers over three years, renewed its commitment on compensation for dairy farmers and processors for USMCA, and underscored the government's firm commitment not to sacrifice any more supply-managed market share in future trade agreements (AAFC 2020).

On December 9, 2020, barely five months after USMCA entered into force, the US announced it was challenging Canada's allocation of dairy TRQs. The US is accusing Canada of assigning too much of its quotas to processors, therefore limiting the access of US farmers and producers to the Canadian market (USTR 2020). Consultations will be held to resolve these concerns, under Article 3.A.3.15 of the USMCA. If they fail, the US may request the establishment of a dispute settlement panel (USMCA, Ch. 31). Canada's trade minister responded that Canada is meeting its obligations.

Without a doubt, the coming into force of USMCA represents a major reorganization for the Canadian dairy industry, not only for production, processing and marketing, but also in terms of systematic data collection in order to meet transparency obligations. Canadian farmers will have to find new strategies to face US competition as well as changes in Canadian consumption of dairy products and to make their surplus NFSs profitable, all in an exceptional context where COVID-19 has already had significant impacts on the dairy sector (PLQ 2020).

Notes

1. Some dairy products reach tariff peaks around 300% (CBSA 2020).
2. For dispute settlement cases concerning Canada and measures affecting the import of milk and the export of dairy products, see WTO (1997a, 1997b). Since the Doha Ministerial Conference in 2001, agriculture has been one of the central topics of discussion at the WTO. Since then, WTO members have been conducting negotiations to reform trade in agricultural products with the objective of reducing agricultural support and protection under the 1995 Agreement on Agriculture, the implementation of which is overseen by the Committee on Agriculture. Canada's dairy policy is regularly questioned and revised by WTO members at meetings of this Committee (WTO, n.d.a).
3. Specifically, milk, cream, skim milk powder, butter and cream powder, industrial cheeses, cheeses of all types, milk powders, concentrated or condensed milk, yogurt and buttermilk, powdered buttermilk, whey powder, products consisting of natural milk constituents, ice cream and ice cream mixes, and other dairy products.
4. These articles provide for the total quantities to be imported duty free for each of the 14 dairy product categories for the 19 years following the coming into force of the USMCA. The agreement provides that the TRQs will be phased in over five years through six equal increases, and then, after the sixth year, the quantities will increase at a fixed annual growth rate of 1% for the following 13 years. See also USTR (2018).
5. Note that for whey powder, the situation differs from the other categories. USMCA anticipates that the TRQs will be eliminated after the tenth year (USMCA, Ch. 2, Appendix 2-CAN, art. 15.a).
6. It will also be for Canada under WTO rules in 2021 following the full implementation of the Decision adopted at the Nairobi Ministerial Conference (WTO 2015).
7. Specifically, milk protein concentrates (HS040490), skim milk powder (HS040210) and infant formula or infant milk (HS190110).

8. Milk class 6 was established in Ontario, then class 7 extended class 6 nationally in February 2017, following an agreement between Canadian dairy producers and processors regarding the prices of certain milk products and milk ingredients (DFO 2016).
9. Diafiltered milk is a liquid protein concentrate containing 15% milk protein and does not require rehydration (PLQ, n.d.c).
10. Concerns on these two milk classes have been raised a few times by WTO members such as Australia and New Zealand (WTO 2016, 2018).
11. Infant formulas contain more than 10% cow's milk solids (HS190110).
12. Under the terms of USMCA, a dairy year is between August 1 and July 31 of the following year.
13. Indeed, free trade areas establish preferential regimes between the states that conclude them, which run counter to the principle of the most-favored-nation treatment. Article XXIV of the General Agreement on Tariffs and Trade (GATT) is an exceptional regime.
14. GATT Article XXIV.4 has been interpreted by the WTO Appellate Body as stating the purpose of a customs union, but can be applied to that of a simple free trade area: "A customs union should facilitate trade within the customs union, but it should *not* do so in a way that raises barriers to trade with third countries" (WTO 1999, para. 57).
15. Due to the COVID-19 pandemic, and despite the notification of five RTAs, the Committee was unable to meet.
16. Since November 2019, the Appellate Body's work has been blocked due to the refusal of the United States to appoint members.

References

Bernier, Ivan. 1974. Les ententes de restriction volontaire à l'exportation en droit international économique. *Canadian Yearbook of International Law* 11: 48–86.

CBC News. 2018. 'Our government sold us out': Critics at Ontario agricultural fair fearful of USMCA. *CBC News*, October 6. https://www.cbc.ca/news/canada/hamilton/ontario-dairy-farmers-usmca-1.4853756.

Dairy Farmers of Canada (DFC). 2020a. *CUSMA implementation: The dairy sector was also misled by the federal government*. April 29. https://dairyfarmersofcanada.ca/en/cusma-implementation-dairy-sector-was-also-misled-federal-government.

Dairy Farmers of Canada (DFC). 2020b. *When promises are no longer enough*. July 14. https://dairyfarmersofcanada.ca/en/when-promises-are-no-longer-enough.

Dairy Farmers of Canada (DFC). 2020c. *Dairy farmers remind Trudeau government that 'promise made is promise to be kept.'* October 20. https://

dairyfarmersofcanada.ca/en/dairy-farmers-remind-trudeau-government-pro
mise-made-promise-be-kept.
Dairy Farmers of Ontario (DFO). 2016. *Dairy farmers of Ontario to implement on April 1, 2016 Ontario's milk ingredient class in regulation 753.*
February 16. https://www.milk.org/Corporate/PDF/News-IngredientStrat
egy_20160216.pdf.
Debailleul, Guy. 2006. ALENA et agriculture: Accord de libre-échange ou
intégration économique autour des États-Unis? *Le Déméter*, 207–280.
https://cdn.ca.yapla.com/company/CPYeQ23lLcPYvZ9GTj339cZ7/asset/
files/alena_et_l_agriculture_accord_de_libre_echange_ou_integration_econ
omique_autour_des_etats_unis_.pdf.
Dey, Sujata. 2017. *Mémoire sur la renégociation de l'Accord de libre-échange
nord-américain.* Presented by the Council of Canadians to Global Affairs
Canada and the House of Commons Standing Committee on International
Trade, July 17. https://www.noscommunes.ca/Content/Committee/421/
CIIT/Brief/BR9162410/br-external/CouncilOfCanadians-9694763-f.pdf.
Fidler, David P. 2017. President Trump, trade policy, and American grand
strategy: From common advantage to collective carnage. *Asian Journal of
WTO Health Law and Policy* 12 (1): 1–31.
Grey, Clark, Shih and Associates, Limited (GCS). 2018. *Congress Thumbs its nose
at WTO and the Doha Round: U.S. federal and state subsidies to agriculture.*
Study prepared for Dairy Farmers of Canada. http://www.greyclark.com/
wp-content/uploads/2018/02/US-Subsidies-Post-2014-Farm-Bill-FEB-
2018.pdf.
Groleau, Marcel. 2016. Importations de lait diafiltré: le gouvernement du
Canada doit bouger rapidement. *L'Union des producteurs agricoles.* March
30. https://www.upa.qc.ca/en/opinions/2016/03/importations-de-lait-dia
filtre-le-gouvernement-du-canada-doit-bouger-rapidement/.
Heminthavong, Khamla. 2018. *Canada's supply management system.* Library
of Parliament, no. 2018-42-E, November 30. https://lop.parl.ca/static
files/PublicWebsite/Home/ResearchPublications/BackgroundPapers/PDF/
2018-42-e.pdf.
Hufbauer, Gary Clyde, and Euijin Jung. 2017. *NAFTA renegotiation: US
offensive and defensive interests vis-à-vis Canada.* Peterson Institute for International Economics, Policy Brief 17-22, June. https://www.piie.com/sys
tem/files/documents/pb17-22.pdf.
Jones, Jeffrey, and Laura Stone. 2018. U.S. escalates pressure on Canada
for dairy concessions in NAFTA talks. *The Globe and Mail*, September
9. https://www.theglobeandmail.com/business/article-us-escalates-pressure-
on-canada-for-dairy-concessions-in-nafta-talks/.
Jones, Kent. 1984. The political economy of voluntary export restraint agreements. *Kyklos* 37 (1): 82–101.

Lampron, Pierre. 2016. What is diafiltered milk? *Dairy Farmers of Canada.* May 4. https://dairyfarmersofcanada.ca/en/dairy-in-canada/dairy-news/what-dia filtered-milk.

Livingston international. *USMCA: Understanding North America's new trade deal.* https://view.livingstonintl.com/usmca/p/1. Accessed September 8, 2020.

Macdonald, Laura. 2020. Stronger together? Canada-Mexico relations and the NAFTA re-negotiations. *Canadian Foreign Policy Journal* 26 (2): 152–166.

McCarten, James. 2020. Canada's dairy industry will lose $100M if CUSMA takes effect in July. *Global News Canada,* April 28. https://globalnews.ca/news/6880811/usmca-canada-dairy-losses-plett/.

Mussell, Al. 2019. Milk supply management after CUSMA: An economic policy analysis. *WCDS Advances in Dairy Technology* 31: 25–33. https://wcds. ualberta.ca/wp-content/uploads/sites/57/2019/05/p-025-036-Mussell-WCDS-2019-Milk-Supply-Management-After-CUSMA.pdf.

Ouellet, Richard, and Maxence Messier. 2017. Renegotiating NAFTA under a Trump presidency: Tweak, tear or think again? A legal perspective from Québec. *Québec Studies* 64 (1): 123–140.

Paquin, Stéphane. 2019. Négocier avec Trump: l'Alena 2.0. In *Fin du leadership américain?* edited by Bertrand Badie and Dominique Vidal, 207–213. France: La Découverte.

Pethokoukis, James. 2017. How Trump views trade: It's more than economics. *The International Economy* 36 (1): 36–39.

Les Producteurs de lait du Québec (PLQ). 2020. *COVID-19—Milk producers are still on the job.* April 5. https://lait.org/en/covid-19-les-producteurs-de-lait-fideles-au-poste/.

Les Producteurs de lait du Québec (PLQ). n.d.a. *Profile and impact of milk economy.* https://lait.org/en/the-milk-economy/profile-and-impact-of-milk-economy/. Accessed September 8, 2020.

Les Producteurs de lait du Québec (PLQ). n.d.b. *Supply management and trade agreements.* https://lait.org/en/the-issues/trade-agreements/. Accessed September 8, 2020.

Les Producteurs de lait du Québec (PLQ). n.d.c. *Imported milk ingredients - our dairy farms are in danger.* https://lait.org/wp-content/uploads/2016/04/fiche_IMPORTATIONS_ANG.pdf. Accessed January 15, 2021.

Schneider-Petsinger, Marianne. 2017. *Trade policy under president Trump: implications for the US and the world.* The Royal Institute of International Affairs, November. https://www.chathamhouse.org/sites/default/files/pub lications/research/2017-11-03-trade-policy-trump-schneider-petsinger-final. pdf.

The Canadian Press. 2016. Farmers say Ottawa must better enforce milk requirements in cheese products. *Winnipeg Free Press,* April 12. https://

www.winnipegfreepress.com/canada/dairy-farmers-say-ottawa-must-enforce-tariffs-on-milk-products-entering-from-us-375434561.html.

Trump, Donald. 2017. President Donald Trump full speech from Kenosha, Wisconsin Snap-on Tools headquarters 4/18/2017. *ABC News*. Streamed live on April 18, 2017. YouTube video, 25:48. https://www.youtube.com/watch?v=vDaid4Hh1gA%3E.

Villareal, M. Angeles, and Ian F. Fergusson. 2020. *The United States-Mexico-Canada Agreement (USMCA)*. Congressional Research Service, Report R44981, July. https://fas.org/sgp/crs/row/R44981.pdf.

OFFICIAL DOCUMENTS

Agriculture and Agri-Food Canada (AAFC). 2018. *Medium term outlook for Canadian Agriculture 2018—International and domestic markets*. http://publications.gc.ca/collections/collection_2018/aac-aafc/A38-1-4-2018-eng.pdf.

Agriculture and Agri-Food Canada (AAFC). 2020. *Government of Canada announces investments to support supply-managed dairy, poultry and egg farmers*. November 28. https://www.canada.ca/en/agriculture-agri-food/news/2020/11/government-of-canada-announces-investments-to-support-supply-managed-dairy-poultry-and-egg-farmers.html.

Canada. 2020. *Canada's dairy industry at a glance*. Last modified August 27, 2020. https://dairyinfo.gc.ca/eng/about-the-canadian-dairy-information-centre/canada-s-dairy-industry-at-a-glance/?id=1502465180911. Accessed December 1, 2020.

Canada Border Services Agency (CBSA). 2020. *Chapter 4 - T2020-2*. Last modified June 18, 2020. https://www.cbsa-asfc.gc.ca/trade-commerce/tariff-tarif/2020/html/02/ch04-eng.html.

Canadian Food Inspection Agency (CFIA). 2013. *Cheese composition standards verification*. Last modified August 30, 2013. https://www.inspection.gc.ca/food-safety-for-industry/archived-food-guidance/dairy-products/manuals-inspection-procedures/product-inspection/cheese-composition/eng/1377615610542/1377617519591?chap=0.

Canadian Food Inspection Agency (CFIA). 2018. *United States of America—Export requirements for milk and dairy products*. Last modified March 9, 2018. https://www.inspection.gc.ca/exporting-food-plants-or-animals/food-exports/requirements/usa-milk-and-dairy-products/eng/1519396364559/1519396365078.

Comprehensive and Progressive Agreement for Trans-Pacific Partnership (CPTPP), signed March 8, 2018, entered into force December 30, 2018. https://www.international.gc.ca/trade-commerce/trade-agreements-accords-commerciaux/agr-acc/tpp-ptp/text-texte/toc-tdm.aspx?lang=eng.

Comprehensive Economic and Trade Agreement (CETA), signed October 30, 2016, entered provisionally into force September 21, 2017. https://www.int ernational.gc.ca/trade-commerce/trade-agreements-accords-commerciaux/ agr-acc/ceta-aecg/text-texte/toc-tdm.aspx?lang=eng.

Export Development Canada (EDC). 2018. *How USMCA offers stability for Canada's auto sector*. October 24. https://www.edc.ca/en/article/usmca-sta bility-for-auto-sector.html.

Farm Credit Canada (FCC). 2016. *The Canadian dairy sector looking forward*. Spring. https://www.fcc-fac.ca/content/dam/fcc/about-fcc/reports/fcc-ag-economics-the-canadian-dairy-sector.pdf.

Global Affairs Canada. 2017. *Address by Foreign Affairs Minister on the modernization of the North American Free Trade Agreement (NAFTA)*. August 14. https://www.canada.ca/en/global-affairs/news/2017/08/address_by_f oreignaffairsministeronthemodernizationofthenorthame.html.

North American Free Trade Agreement (NAFTA), signed December 17, 1992, entered into force January 1, 1994. https://www.international.gc.ca/trade-commerce/trade-agreements-accords-commerciaux/agr-acc/nafta-alena/fta-ale/index.aspx?lang=eng.

Office of the United States Trade Representative (USTR). 2017. *Summary of objectives for the NAFTA renegotiation*. July 17. https://ustr.gov/sites/def ault/files/files/Press/Releases/NAFTAObjectives.pdf.

Office of the United States Trade Representative (USTR). 2018. *United States-Mexico-Canada trade fact sheet. Agriculture: Market access and dairy outcome of the USMC agreement*. https://ustr.gov/trade-agreements/free-trade-agreements/united-states-mexico-canada-agreement/fact-sheets/mar ket-access-and-dairy-outcomes. Accessed September 8, 2020.

Office of the United States Trade Representative (USTR). 2020. *United States takes action for American dairy farmers by filing first-ever USMCA enforcement action*. December 9. https://ustr.gov/about-us/policy-offices/ press-office/press-releases/2020/december/united-states-takes-action-ame rican-dairy-farmers-filing-first-ever-usmca-enforcement-action.

United States—Canada Free Trade Agreement (USCFTA), signed January 2, 1988, entered into force January 1, 1989. http://www.international.gc.ca/ trade-agreements-accords-commerciaux/assets/pdfs/cusfta-e.pdf.

United States Department of Agriculture (USDA). n.d. *Dairy Data*. Last modified January 14, 2021. https://www.ers.usda.gov/data-products/dairy-data/.

United States-Mexico-Canada Agreement (USMCA), signed November 30, 2018, entered into force July 1, 2020. https://ustr.gov/trade-agreements/ free-trade-agreements/united-states-mexico-canada-agreement/agreement-between.

WTO. 1994a. Agreement on Safeguards. signed April 15, 1994, entered into force January 1, 1995. https://www.wto.org/english/docs_e/legal_e/25-safeg.pdf.

WTO. 1994b. General Agreement on Tariffs and Trade (GATT), annexed to the Marrakesh Agreement establishing the World Trade Organization, signed April 15, 1994, entered into force January 1, 1995. https://treaties.un.org/doc/Publication/UNTS/Volume%201867/volume-1867-I-31874-English.pdf.

WTO. 1997a. *Canada—Measures affecting the importation of milk and the exportation of dairy products.* WT/DS103//R (Panel report), May 19, 1999; WT/DS103/AB/R (Appellate Body report), October 13, 1999. https://www.wto.org/english/tratop_e/dispu_e/cases_e/ds103_e.htm. Accessed September 8, 2020.

WTO. 1997b. *Canada—Measures affecting dairy exports.* WT/DS113//R (Panel report), May 17, 1999; WT/DS113/AB/R (Appellate Body report), October 13, 1999. https://www.wto.org/english/tratop_e/dispu_e/cases_e/ds113_e.htm. Accessed September 8, 2020.

WTO. 1999. *Turkey—Restrictions on imports of textile and clothing products.* WT/DS34/AB/R (Appellate Body report), October 22, 1999. https://www.wto.org/english/tratop_e/dispu_e/cases_e/ds34_e.htm.

WTO. 2015. *Export competition: Ministerial decision of 19 December 2015.* WT/MIN(15)/45; WT/L/980.

WTO. 2016. *Canadian dairy policy top of agenda for farm committee.* September 14. https://www.wto.org/english/news_e/news16_e/agcom_16sep16_e.htm.

WTO. 2018. *WTO members agree on timetable to review use of Bali tariff quota mechanism.* February 20. https://www.wto.org/english/news_e/news18_e/agcom_23feb18_e.htm.

WTO. n.d.a. *Agriculture news archive.* https://www.wto.org/english/news_e/archive_e/ag_arc_e.htm. Accessed September 8, 2020.

WTO. n.d.b. *The committee on regional trade agreements.* https://www.wto.org/english/tratop_e/region_e/regcom_e.htm. Accessed September 8, 2020.

WTO. n.d.c. *2021 Regional trade agreements: Database.* http://rtais.wto.org/UI/PublicShowRTAIDCard.aspx?rtaid=1087. Accessed September 8, 2020.

CHAPTER 5

Make America Great Again: A New Auto Pact for the North American Car Industry?

Mathieu Arès and Charles Bernard

On July 1, 2020, after long and difficult negotiations, the United States–Mexico–Canada Agreement (USMCA) entered into force. The auto sector was at the heart of this renegotiation of the North American Free Trade Agreement (NAFTA). From the very start of his election campaign, candidate Donald Trump made the sector a central pillar of his *Make America Great Again* platform, adopting Ross Perot's famous *Giant Sucking Sound*. Along the way, he took every opportunity to accuse Mexico of stealing American jobs, something only an impenetrable wall could stop. The evidence he presented: trade deficits with Mexico had grown from US$47.8 billion in 2009 to US$101.4 billion in 2019 (US Census Bureau 2020a), and were now second only to China (US Census Bureau 2020b). This discourse held great appeal to autoworkers. Many observers credit Trump's narrow election victories in the industrial states around the Great Lakes—and thus his entry into the White House—to

M. Arès (✉) · C. Bernard
School of Applied Politics, Université de Sherbrooke, Sherbrooke, Canada
e-mail: Mathieu.Ares@USherbrooke.ca

© The Author(s), under exclusive license to Springer Nature
Switzerland AG 2022
G. Gagné and M. Rioux (eds.), *NAFTA 2.0*,
Canada and International Affairs,
https://doi.org/10.1007/978-3-030-81694-0_5

autoworker support. While accusations against Canada were less acerbic, President Trump nevertheless used national security to justify imposing, through Section 232 of the US Trade Expansion Act, tariffs of 25% on steel and 10% on aluminum, and did so in the middle of NAFTA renegotiations and just days before the 2018 Group of Seven (G7) Summit in Charlevoix, Canada. Prime Minister Trudeau took offense, and President Trump reacted by abruptly leaving the summit. However, in May 2019, the United States agreed to exempt Canada and Mexico from the measure in order to re-energize NAFTA renegotiations, though it preserved the right to re-impose tariffs at a later date (Swanson 2020), and, in fact, did so in August 2020. Also in the name of national security, the American President went so far as to threaten imposition of a 25% tariff on vehicles and parts unless Mexico, but also Canada, made major concessions in negotiations (Isidore 2019).

In its final form, the USMCA reflects the priority given to the auto sector: Appendix 4-B on rules of origin is entirely dedicated to the sector. We maintain that, for the automotive production sector, this complex and highly detailed new agreement proposes not free trade, but a modern form of shared production between the three partners. The USMCA reflects tight integration of automotive production at regional level and, in direct violation of the World Trade Organization (WTO), a form of regional protectionism. This chapter is divided into three parts. The first presents the key features of the North American auto industry, notably its integrated character. The second analyzes the provisions and rules of the USMCA pertaining to the auto sector. The final part concludes that, in their final regulatory form, auto sector provisions correspond to established regional value chains (RVC) of North American producers.

MADE IN NORTH AMERICA: THE NORTH AMERICAN AUTO INDUSTRY

The auto sector is without a doubt the star player in North American economic integration. The regionalization of automotive production began with the US–Canada Auto Pact of 1965. While it greatly facilitated trade between Canada and the United States, it consisted primarily of shared production between the two countries. The Big Three (Ford, General Motors [GM], Chrysler—now Fiat-Chrysler [FCA]) undertook to produce in Canada at least the number of vehicles that could be absorbed by the Canadian market. That brought economies of scale through specialization in factories on both sides of the border, even as it offered Canadians a wider range of models, significantly increased the competitiveness of Canadian factories and energized a sector that had been in decline (Reinsch et al. 2019, p. 7). The Big Three's presence in Mexico dates back to the mid-1920s (Klier and Rubenstein 2017). However, national protectionism and the pursuit of import substitution policies after World War Two limited foreign producers' ability to export vehicles to Mexico. This promoted local manufacturing, most often based on older technologies, a trend epitomized by the Volkswagen Beetle. The quality of vehicles thus produced remained well below international standards. In response, Mexican authorities gradually eased border controls, going so far as to promote exports in 1983 and, in 1989, set local content requirements at just 36%. The establishment of manufacturers was facilitated by the re-export program and free-trade zone along the Mexico–United States border (IMMEX-maquiladoras). Thus, in Canada as well as in Mexico, NAFTA, which fit directly into a Lockean contractual model, simply established a common set of rules for an auto sector that already had well-established value chains at regional level.

Each vehicle is composed of about 10,000 parts and components produced by various manufacturers. Depending on the model, these components represent an estimated 71–77% of the value of a vehicle, with the rest being profits, labour costs, research and development, etc. (Reinsch et al. 2019, p. 13). The industry is typically divided into three sectors. Tier 1 includes the big manufacturers that design vehicles, produce and assemble their main elements and assure quality control as well as distribution. Tier 2 companies produce complex modules, such as seats, brakes or dashboards, which they sell to Tier 1 manufacturers. Tiers 1 and 2 are supplied with simple parts by Tier 3 suppliers (Reinsch et al. 2019, p. 2). Moreover, the value chains and spatial distribution of suppliers to North American producers directly correlate with per capita income and market size, and inversely correlate with distance and exchange rate. Transport costs and rules of origin encouraged most global manufacturers to locate in North America, as NAFTA gave them tariff-free access to North American markets.

In Canada in 2018, the auto sector accounted for some 125,000 direct jobs, 10% of manufacturing gross domestic product (GDP) and 23% of trade in manufacturing (Invest in Canada 2018). In Mexico that year, the sector provided almost 137,000 direct jobs and accounted for 17.7%

Table 5.1   US automobile trade (billion US$) (2019)

	New passenger vehicles and light trucks		Automobile parts		Trade balance
	Exports	Imports	Exports	Imports	
Canada	23.2	38.8	29.1	17.0	(3.5)
Mexico	2.9	58.4	33.1	60.9	(83.3)
World	58.8	197.8	85.4	115.8	(169.4)

Source US Department of Commerce (n.d.)

of manufacturing GDP and 33.7% of manufacturing exports (Figueroa-Hernández et al. 2018, table 2). Finally, in the United States, automotive production employed about 1 million people and made up 12.5% of manufacturing GDP (Statistica 2020).

Table 5.1 illustrates the intensity of trade integration. First, it reveals the centrality of the United States. In comparison, and recognizing that transit through the United States means the volume of trade between Canada and Mexico is generally under-estimated, bilateral trade between Canada and Mexico in motor vehicles and auto parts was only C$8.7 billion in 2018 (León 2019, pp. 3–4), compared to US$108.1 billion between Canada and the United States, and US$155.3 billion between Mexico and the United States. It is also noteworthy that more than half of the vehicles exported from Canada and Mexico to the United States were made by FCA, GM and Ford (Schultz et al. 2018, p. 4). Table 5.1 also reveals the scale of value chains in North American auto production. Seen as a proportion of the total value of new vehicles, trade in parts and components between Canada and the United States represents 74.4% of total value, while between Mexico and the United States it is 153.3%. Obviously, the extent of trade in parts and components considerably increases trade volume statistics. It is estimated that a part generally crosses North American borders six to eight times prior to final assembly and sale to the consumer. Almost 63% of the added value of a vehicle assembled in Canada and exported to the United States is therefore of American origin (Scotia Bank, n.d.). And while the Trump administration claims that there is barely 18% American content in vehicles imported from Mexico, representatives of the Big Three, using a more reliable methodology, estimate that about one third of the added value of a vehicle exported from Mexico to the United States involves parts and components coming from the United States (AAPC 2017). Finally, there is consensus in the literature that American manufacturers use more inputs produced in North America than do manufacturers originating from outside the NAFTA zone (Reinsch et al. 2019, p. 14). Table 5.1 clearly reveals why American manufacturers have been Canada and Mexico's main allies in opposing the Trump administration's protectionist ambitions. The imposition of tariffs or quotas would be disastrous to the American auto industry, dealerships and consumers. Depending on the scenario, the imposition of tariffs would increase the price of vehicles sold in the United States by between US$980 and US$6,875 (Schultz et al. 2018).

"Ben Laden Is Dead, GM Is Alive" (Biden 2012, 23:42).

The automotive industry radically transformed after the great recession of 2009. Table 5.2 illustrates the extent of these changes. First, despite the fact that production levels regained their pre-crisis levels of about

Table 5.2 North American car and commercial vehicle production (selected years 1990–2019) (in millions of units and North America as a percentage of world total)

	Canada	Mexico	USA	North America (N-A)	World Production (% made in N-A)
2000	2.96	1.94	12.80	17.70	58.37 (30.2)
2005	2.69	1.68	11.95	16.32	66.72 (24.5)
2006	2.57	2.05	11.26	15.88	69.22 (22.9)
2007	2.58	2.10	10.78	15.46	73.27 (21.1)
2008	2.08	2.17	8.67	12.92	70.73 (18.3)
2009	1.49	1.56	5.71	8.76	61.76 (14.2)
2010	2.07	2.34	7.74	12.15	77.58 (15.7)
2011	2.14	2.68	8.66	13.48	79.88 (16.9)
2012	2.46	3.00	10.34	15.80	84.24 (18.8)
2013	2.38	3.05	11.07	16.50	87.60 (18.8)
2014	2.39	3.37	11.66	17.42	89.78 (19.4)
2015	2.28	3.57	12.10	17.95	90.78 (19.8)
2016	2.37	3.60	12.20	18.17	94.98 (19.1)
2017	2.20	4.07	11.19	17.46	97.30 (18.2)
2018	2.02	4.10	11.31	17.43	95.63 (18.2)
2019	1.92	3.99	10.88	16.79	91.79 (18.3)

Source OICA (2019)

17 million vehicles for the whole of North America, it represents a mature sector where production does no more than replace used vehicles. The bulk of new demand is now in emerging economies, which means the North American share of global production is falling, from around 30% in 2000 to just over 18% in 2020. As well, automotive technology has expanded significantly: the main innovations are now around embedded electronics, where international competition, especially with Asia, is particularly fierce. Last but not least, a revolution is underway as electric vehicles gain popularity, forcing manufacturers to make massive investments not only in research and development, but also in their assembly lines, with the abandonment of many parts (bloc engines, reservoirs, cooling systems, etc.). In this context, Tesla has leapt ahead, overtaking the Big Three combined in market capitalization (AFP2020). Perhaps more important to our immediate concerns are the internal changes induced by these developments.

The crisis of 2009, when only 5.71 million vehicles were produced in the United States, profoundly and lastingly affected the spirit of the industry and its employees. As seen in Table 5.2, the drop in the United States was steeper than in Canada or Mexico. Although the sector slowly recovered in subsequent years, Mexico saw the strongest increase, from about 2 million to 4 million vehicles, while production in the United States only recovered to pre-crisis levels. Canada was the real loser in this profound restructuring of the industry, with the loss of almost 1 million vehicles. In fact, Mexico was able to position itself as a low-cost player in the production line, whether for assembly or for the production of parts and components. Production costs in Mexico were 91% of those in the United States (and less than costs in China at 96%). Canada's production costs, at about 115% of US ones, were clearly uncompetitive (Sirkin et al. 2014, p. 3). Mexico's competitive advantage regarding investment was also clear. Since the advent of the NAFTA in 1994, the number of light vehicle assembly factories grew from 9 to 17, while dropping from 59 to 49 in the United States, and from 14 to 10 in Canada (UAW 2017). Mexico became especially attractive to European and Asian manufacturers, and almost 90% of new investments were from companies outside the NAFTA zone. It is therefore not surprising that candidate Trump's protectionist discourse resonated so strongly with American auto sector workers.

From NAFTA to USMCA

In line with the alarmist tone that has defined his approach to commercial diplomacy, President Trump quickly pointed to NAFTA's chapter on automobiles as exemplifying the inequalities of North American economic integration. An analysis of the new rules for the automotive sector under the USMCA clearly reveals protectionist American, if not North American, ambitions. The regulatory changes touch on three main aspects: an increase in the regional value thresholds in vehicle production, expansion of tracing controls and the addition of workers' wages and use of North American aluminum to rules of origin.

Sectorial rules of origin serve as a legal definition of criteria that must be met before a product can be exported and benefit from the USMCA's preferential tariffs (EDC 2017). Put simply, for the automobile manufacturing sector under NAFTA, these rules represented the level, set at 62.5%, of North American content that allowed a vehicle to benefit from preferential treatment in the free trade zone. These criteria structured the supply chains in vehicle production over the decades and, as described above, enabled Mexico to position itself as a low-cost producer for the whole of North America. The sector was also inevitably affected by the movement of capital, notably an increase in foreign investment and the relocation of some American and Canadian production and activity to Mexico. The gradual exodus of American production towards partner economies even as the United States consumed the vast majority of automobiles was central to the US President's critique of NAFTA's rules of origin (Chatzky et al. 2020). President Trump stressed that overly permissive rules of origin not only favoured America's partners in the agreement, but also opened the door to the North American vehicle market to major players from outside NAFTA (Hufbauer and Jung 2017).

Tightening the rules was meant to ensure that the advantages flowing from the North American free trade area fell primarily to signatories, a position that Canada largely supported. The initial demand for a minimum US content of 40% was unacceptable to Mexico and Canada and abandoned during negotiations. However, in the Appendix to Chapter 4, the USMCA details increase to various thresholds of RVC that must be met to benefit from the absence of tariffs. Chapter 4 stipulates that passenger vehicles and light trucks, with a few exceptions, must have 66% RVC in 2020, 69% in 2021, 72% in 2022, and 75% in 2023, along a four-year calendar following the agreement's entry into force on

July 1, 2020. For heavy vehicles, RVC is set at 70% (Articles 3 and 4 of Appendix 4-B). These levels apply to finished vehicles ready for sale, and take into account that a vehicle is the sum of engine, brakes, suspension, frame, etc.

The new agreement adds a level of complexity by separating individual components into three categories: principal, complementary and core. The RVC required for each part depends on its categorization as well as the type of vehicle into which it is to be incorporated. This addition is extremely important, as it contrasts with the tracing lists in NAFTA.[1] Tracing lists were put in place to ensure that firms prioritized North American materials and content, the same preoccupation behind the USMCA's rules of origin. The form and scope of USMCA measures are quite different, however. In the earlier agreement, producers had to rely on a list to determine whether a part or component was considered to *originate* in North America (Rubin 2017). If the part was on the list, it had to meet criteria for RVC to benefit from preferential tariffs. If the component was not on the list, it was recognized, de facto, as North American and the manufacturer could integrate it into vehicles without restrictions. By forcing producers to conduct meticulous evaluations of the origin of parts, tracing lists added a considerable administrative burden. As tracing lists were rarely updated after the NAFTA negotiation period, tracing lists also reflected an archaic view of vehicle manufacturing. Many components that are now essential to vehicle production were not on the list, with computerized parts (GPS, touch screens, etc.) a prime example. Companies could therefore take advantage of this regulatory gap to obtain either very competitive prices outside North America, or niche expertise, notably for sophisticated technological components. Modernizing tracing was a priority for the American government as a way to expand the scope of new rules of origin (USITC 2019). In Article 4.10 of Appendix 4-B, presentation of the three categories of parts signals an important transition from the rigid tracing list approach in NAFTA to a much more encompassing and comprehensive model. The vast majority of vehicle components must now, under the USMCA, be evaluated for RVC (Gantz 2019). Table 5.3 provides a summary of American proposals

---

[1] The concept of traceability remains central to rules of origin as the process of evaluating regional content. The tracing list, on the other hand, refers to a NAFTA measure that does not appear in the USMCA.

Table 5.3 US initial requests and Appendix 4-B provisions

US initial requests	*Ch. 4 Appendix provisions*
Rules of origin: Preferential tariffs (0%) • Between 62.5 and 85% of RVC per vehicle, engine and transmission system • Between 60 and 85% RVC for components on a 29-category list • Between 50 and 72.5% RVC for components not otherwise covered	Rules of origin: Preferential tariffs (0%) • 62.5–75% RVC in 2023 for light and passenger vehicles • 60–70% RVC in 2027 for trucks and heavy vehicles • Possibility for producers to use an *alternative staging regime*, which would allow them to reach the RVC threshold on a more permissive time frame. However, this regime could only apply to a maximum 10% of a producer's total production in the year preceding the agreement's entry into force
Tracing measures: • A list of 29 categories of components not in NAFTA, including steel, aluminum and textiles	Tracing measures: • Three categories of components: core, principal and complementary • 75% RVC for core components (engine, batteries, transmission) • 70% RVC for principal components (brakes, exhaust systems) • 65% RVC for complementary parts (lighting, locks, switches)
Production sharing: • American production of at least 50% of components of vehicles assembled in Mexico and Canada	Production sharing: • No concession on this point. However, the implementation of a labour value threshold of US$16/h can be seen as way to stimulate American and Canadian production
New rules of origin labour value content (LVC) requirement: • A portion of production on each vehicle must be handled by workers earning a wage of at least US$16/hour	New rules of origin LVC requirement: • 30% LVC in 2020, increasing to 40% in 2023 for light and passenger vehicles • 45% LVC in 2020 for heavy vehicles and trucks • Minimum 25% LVC in the manufacturing sector, while spending on "technology" and assembly cannot surpass 10 and 5%, respectively, of the LVC total

Source Holmes (2018) and Johnson (2019)

around regional value and the measures finally adopted by the three USMCA signatories.

Many observers expected that the auto industry would find it challenging to implement the USMCA's new provisions. The significant increase in RVC and tight deadline to meet requirements demand rapid adjustment to the supply chains of a great many automakers, especially given the common practices they had developed under NAFTA (Johnson 2019). As stated earlier, parts involved in vehicle manufacture could cross the borders of commercial partners multiple times: from design work in California to moulding in the American Rust Belt, assembly in Monterrey and finishing touches south of Toronto. The potential discrepancy between multiple modifications to a same piece, and the more draconian regional content thresholds, risk causing short-term planning problems for manufacturers (Anson et al. 2015). As well, the higher regional value needed to benefit from USMCA treatment creates important barriers to foreign, mainly Asian and European, firms entering the North American market. It is hard to tell whether, in the near future, these new administrative constraints will really serve as an incentive for foreign competitors to invest and, thus, lead to the creation of new North American manufacturing jobs (Johnson 2019).

While these changes aim to promote workers and manufacturers across the USMCA zone, the two major innovations in terms of rules of origin carry a palpable pro-American bias. The agreement includes two new dimensions: requirements regarding labour value content (LVC) and traceability rules that extend to a greater number of parts and components. On this last point, conflict between Canada and the United States makes steel and aluminum a special case.

A key element of the USMCA is the inclusion of a wage clause. Bolstered by union demands, President Trump made this a *sine qua non* of any agreement. For American and Canadian autoworker unions, Mexico's hourly wages at barely US\$2.30/hour in 2015—fully 90% less than the average auto sector wage in the United States—constituted an unfair competitive advantage, akin to social dumping (Covarrubias Valdenebro 2020), that distorted the distribution of production capital in North America (Catoire 2014). The new agreement stipulates that, for a vehicle to be recognized as North American, between 40 and 45% of its manufacture must be undertaken by workers earning at least US\$16/hour (Sosnow and Kirby 2018). The assessment of labour value is actually tailored to the type of vehicle and component produced. For example, wage expenses related to technological elements in a vehicle are no longer counted after they reach 10% of the total costs of production. Remuneration of work in the area of production may complicate or even distort calculations of labour value in automobile production. Similarly, Article 7 of the Auto Appendix specifies that at least 25% of the required 40% LVC come from the manufacturing sector. The United States administration sold this new rule of origin to the public as an effective way to raise American factory worker wages (Chatzky et al. 2020). Implementation of the rule of origin also appears as an attempt to harmonize wage disparities and indirectly reduce the attractiveness of the Mexican auto sector for investors thinking about relocating.

On the other hand, a report by the International Monetary Fund (IMF), looking at the agreement's potential benefits to the three partner economies, paints a darker picture of this new rule of origin. The authors consider that two factors could create effects quite opposite to the expectations of the US government. The first is that, given the higher wages in Canada and the United States, many manufacturers' supply chains already meet the LVC criteria. Despite American ambitions, it would be surprising if the agreement's LVC thresholds had a significant impact on investments in the Mexican auto sector (Burfisher et al. 2019). The second factor is more revealing: the commercial incentive of USMCA preferential tariffs is highly affected by LVC thresholds as well as RVC. Achieving these levels significantly increases costs for producers established in Mexico. For this reason, many manufacturers may prefer to seek most-favored-nation tariffs rather than bend to the rules of origin in the USMCA. The IMF model predicts that wages in Mexico might increase from US$3.40/hour to about US$5/hour, a boost of 50%, but this emphasizes just how few exported vehicles will meet the new criteria for wages at US$16/hour (Burfisher et al. 2019).

The second major innovation in the auto sector is the new requirement for use of North American steel and aluminum in manufacturing. In order for a vehicle, whether heavy or light, to be traded at USMCA tariffs, 70% of the aluminum or steel used to make it must originate in the North American market. Like the increase in regional content, this change seeks to strengthen the position of American producers within auto sector supply chains. As the world's biggest importer of steel and aluminum, the United States hoped to gradually transform this dependence into more jobs and production of metals needed by the manufacturing sector. The steel industry, once a backbone of the American economy, suffered a severe contraction with massive job losses over the last century, from some 650,000 steelworkers in 1950 to about 140,000 today. The American steel sector has, for many years, faced fierce competition from Southeast Asia, Brazil and its neighbours (McBride 2018). This desire to bring the steel sector back to life dates from before the Trump administration. Any number of past presidents, both Republican and Democrat, have enacted tariffs on steel and aluminum, to the delight of thousands of American workers (McBride 2018).

The increase in the proportion of North American steel and aluminum required in vehicle production was introduced in the same spirit as other changes to rules of origin. And the anticipated effect is likely to be the same: privileging North American steelworkers will lead to an increase in costs that will, in time, increase consumer prices for vehicles (Dziczek et al. 2018). As stated in the introduction, the atmosphere around negotiations on rules of origin became much more charged following the American threat to impose a 25% tariff on Canadian exports of steel and aluminum. Uncertainties around commercial relations between the three partners may become a defining factor in the decisions of producers, managers and investors. However, for Canada, the side letter signed in 2018 allows for some optimism as it guarantees, in the event tariffs are applied, the exemption of 2,600,000 light vehicles and almost $32 million in auto parts (Canada 2019). In fact, it is even possible that Canada and Mexico might gain a comparative advantage if the United States increases tariffs on competitors outside the USMCA. If that were to happen, the WTO would probably have something to say.

Conclusion

In this era of globalized production, recourse to protectionist measures like those President Trump has sought to impose is illusory and even counterproductive. To promote employment and growth, the state must help the national production apparatus insert itself into value chains that are now global. However, the auto sector is particular in that high transport costs privilege short distances and production at regional scale. In line with market logic, what NAFTA did was to redeploy North American production to Mexico's benefit as the zone's low-cost producer. With the tightening of rules of origin and the introduction of a high-wage clause, the USMCA reveals the United States' desire to rebalance in its favour the benefits of the free trade area. As well, the USMCA moves away from a liberal Lockean logic where market forces decide the winners and introduces a kind of obligation of results, in the form of an employment floor through the calculation of the wage clause, as high wages are concentrated before and after direct manufacturing production, that is, in phases concentrated in the United States and, to a lesser extent, Canada.

The USMCA can therefore be seen as a compromise between parties around sharing production, which only marginally changes North American manufacturers' supply chains. By enlarging the range of parts and inputs, it can be seen as a form of protectionism at regional scale, so that European and Asian manufacturers are the ones that will suffer higher costs as a result of the agreement, as they usually import more parts and components from outside the zone. Also, as an auto sector advisor very close to the Mexican negotiating team stated: "after worrying it would lose an important part of its auto production, Mexico came to see that, to a certain extent, its role as low-cost producer was confirmed, as most Mexican production already met the new rules of origin!"[2] Mexico could not let such a deal go by. It is therefore not surprising that Mexico broke away from Canada and concluded a separated bilateral agreement with the United States on August 27, 2018. The auto sector was hardly a central focus in the marathon negotiations that followed and finally led Canada to join the USMCA on October 1, 2018, agreeing with American positions, except in the case of steel and aluminum.

References

AFP. 2020. Tesla pèse plus lourd que le big three de l'automobile. *Les Affaires*, January 30. https://www.lesaffaires.com/bourse/nouvelles-econom iques/tesla-pese-plus-lourd-que-le-big-three-de-l-automobile/615573.

American Automotive Policy Council (AAPC). 2017. *U.S. auto parts content in Mexico's motor vehicle production.* http://www.greyclark.com/wp-content/uploads/2017/10/AAPC_US-Auto-Parts-Content-in-Mexicos-Motor-Veh icle-Production.pdf.

Anson, José, Olivier Cadot, Antoni Estevadeordal, Jaime de Melo, Akiko Suwa-Eisenmann, and Bolormaa Tumurchudur. 2015. Rules of origin in North–South preferential trading arrangements with an application to NAFTA. *Review of International Economics* 13 (3): 501–517. https://doi.org/10.1111/j.1467-9396.2005.00520.x.

---

[2] Interview with the authors, Mexico City, March 2019.

Biden, Joseph Jr. 2012. Vice President Biden 2012 acceptance speech. Clipped from Democratic National Convention, day 3. *C-SPAN*, September 6. Clipped by user burgess, June 15, 2016. C-SPAN video, 38:51.

Burfisher, Mary E., Frederic Lambert, and Troy Matheson. 2019. *NAFTA to CUSMA: What is gained*. International Monetary Fund Working Papers, no. 19/73. https://www.imf.org/en/Publications/WP/Issues/2019/03/26/NAFTA-to-USMCA-What-is-Gained-46680.

Canada. 2019. *U.S. Section 232 side letters summary*. Last updated July 18, 2019. https://www.international.gc.ca/trade-commerce/trade-agreements-accords-commerciaux/agr-acc/cusma-aceum/article-232.aspx?lang=eng.

Catoire, Serge. 2014. Les chaînes de valeur dans l'industrie automobile. *Annales des Mines - Réalités industrielles* (2): 53–59. https://doi.org/10.3917/rindu.142.0053.

Chatzky, Andrew, James McBride, and Mohammed Aly Sergie. 2020. *NAFTA and the USMCA: Weighing the impact of North American Trade*. Council on Foreign Relations. Last updated July 1. https://www.cfr.org/backgrounder/nafta-and-usmca-weighing-impact-north-american-trade.

Covarrubias Valdenebro, Alex. 2020. Mexico competitive advantage in NAFTA: A case of social dumping? A view from the Automotive Industry. *International Journal of Automotive Technology and Management* 20 (3): 239–257.

Dziczek, Kristin, Michael Schultz, Benerard Swiecki, and Yen Chen. 2018. *NAFTA briefing: Review of current NAFTA proposals and potential impacts on the North American automotive industry*. Ann Arbor: Center for Automotive Research. https://www.cargroup.org/wp-content/uploads/2018/04/nafta_briefing_april_2018_public_version-final.pdf.

Export Development Canada (EDC). 2017. *Rules of origin: The top 3 things exporters need to know*. December 8. https://www.edc.ca/en/article/rules-of-origin.html.

Figueroa-Hernández, Ester, Luis Enrique Espinosa-Torres, and Lucila Godínez-Montoya. 2018. Importancia de la industia autonomitriz en México. *Revista De Desarrollo Económico* 5 (17): 1–11.

Gantz, David A. 2019. *The United States-Mexico-Canada agreement: Tariffs, customs, and rules of origin*. Baker Institute for Public Policy, Report 02.21.19.https://www.bakerinstitute.org/media/files/files/6ee1ade5/bi-report-022119-mex-usmca.pdf.

Holmes, John. 2018. *NAFTA and the automotive industry*. 61st Annual EDCO Conference presentation. https://automotivepolicy.ca/wp-content/uploads/2018/05/holmes-presentation-edco-february-2018-1.pdf.

Hufbauer, Gary Clyde, and Euijin Jung. 2017. *NAFTA renegotiation: US offensive and defensive interests vis-à-vis Canada*. Peterson Institute for International Economics, Policy Brief 17-22, June, https://www.piie.com/

publications/policy-briefs/nafta-renegotiation-us-offensive-and-defensive-int
erests-vis-vis-canada.

International Organization of Motor Vehicle Manufacturers (OICA). 2019.
2019 Production statistics. https://www.oica.net/category/production-statis
tics/2019-statistics/.

Invest in Canada. 2018. *Canada's competitive advantages: Automotive
Sector.* https://www.international.gc.ca/investors-investisseurs/assets/pdfs/
download/vp-automotive.pdf.

Isidore, Chris. 2019. Why Mexico is so important to the American Auto industry.
CNN Business, May 31.

Johnson, Jon R. 2019. *Bumper to bumper: Will the CUSMA rules of origin make
America's auto industry great again?* C.D Howe Institute, July 3. https://
www.wita.org/atp-research/cusma-rules-america-auto-industry/

Klier, Thomas H., and James M. Rubenstein. 2017. Mexico's growing role in the
auto industry under NAFTA: Who makes what and what goes where. *Federal
Reserve Bank of Chicago: Economic Perspectives, 41*(6).

León, Andrés. 2019. *Canadian trade and investment activity: Canada–Mexico.*
Library of Parliament, no. 2019-519-E, August 28. https://bdp.parl.ca/sta
ticfiles/PublicWebsite/Home/ResearchPublications/TradeAndInvestment/
PDF/2019/2019-519-e.pdf.

McBride, James. 2018. *The risks of U.S. steel and aluminum tariffs.* Council
on Foreign Relations, March 8. https://www.cfr.org/backgrounder/risks-us-
steel-and-aluminum-tariffs.

Reinsch, William Alan, Jack Caporal, Madeleine Waddoups, and Nadir Tekarli.
2019. *The impact of rules of origin on supply chains. USMCA's auto rules as a
case study.* Center for Strategic & International Studies, April.

Rubin, Jeff. 2017. *How has Canadian manufacturing fared under NAFTA? A
look at the auto assembly and parts industry.* Centre for International Governance Innovation, CIGI Papers No. 138, August.https://www.cigionline.
org/sites/default/files/documents/Paper%20no.138web_1.pdf.

Schultz, Michael, Kristin Dziczek, Benerard Swiecki, and Yen Chen. 2018. *Trade
briefing: Consumer impact of potential U.S. Section 232 tariffs and quotas on
imported automobiles & automotive parts.* Center for Automotive Research
(CAR). https://www.autonews.com/assets/PDF/CA116391719.PDF.

Scotia Bank. n.d. *The North American auto sector. A NAFTA case study.* https://
www.scotiabank.com/corp/downloads/NAFTA_infograph_AutoSector.pdf.

Sirkin, Harold L., Michael Zinser, and Justin R. Rose. 2014. *The shifting
economics of global manufacturing: How cost competitiveness is changing worldwide.* Boston: The Boston Consulting Group https://image-src.bcg.com/
Images/The_Shifting_Economics_of_Global_Manufacturing_Aug_2014_t
cm9-185726.pdf.

Sosnow, Clifford, and Peter E. Kirby. 2018. L'AEUMC: premier coup d'œil sur les principaux enjeux controversés. *Fasken Bulletin*, October 4. https://www.fasken.com/fr/knowledge/2018/10/the-usmca-a-first-look-at-key-con tentious-issues.

Statistica. 2020. *U.S. motor vehicle and parts manufacturing gross output from 2005 to 2019 (in billion U.S. dollars)*. https://www.statista.com/statistics/258075/us-motor-vehicle-and-parts-manufacturing-gross-output/.

Swanson, Ana. 2020. 'Like a Bad Horror Movie': U.S. weighs reinstating Canadian aluminum tariffs. *The New York Times*, June 23. https://www.nytimes.com/2020/06/23/business/economy/usmca-canada-aluminum-tariffs.html.

The International Union, United Automobile, Aerospace and Agricultural Implement Workers of America (UAW). 2017. *UNIFOR-UAW statement on auto and the re-negotiation of NAFTA*. July 11. https://uaw.org/unifor-uaw-sta tement-auto-re-negotiation-nafta/.

United States Census Bureau. 2020a. *Trade in goods with Mexico*. https://www.census.gov/foreign-trade/balance/c2010.html.

United States Census Bureau. 2020b. *Top trading partners—December 2019*. https://www.census.gov/foreign-trade/statistics/highlights/top/top 1912yr.html#def.

United States Department of Commerce. n.d. *Automotive team: Industry trade data*. https://legacy.trade.gov/td/otm/autostats.asp.

United States International Trade Commission (USITC). 2019. *U.S.-Mexico-Canada trade agreement: Likely impact on the U.S. economy and on specific industry sectors*. April. https://www.usitc.gov/publications/332/pub4889.pdf.

United States-Mexico-Canada Agreement (USMCA), signed November 30, 2018, entered into force July 1, 2020. https://ustr.gov/trade-agreements/free-trade-agreements/united-states-mexico-canada-agreement/agreement-between.

CHAPTER 6

The USMCA and Investment: A New North American Approach?

Charles-Emmanuel Côté and Hamza Ali

INTRODUCTION

The United States–Mexico–Canada Agreement (USMCA) includes a chapter devoted entirely to foreign investment within North America. This is not surprising given the previous existence of the landmark Chapter 11 in the North American Free Trade Agreement (NAFTA), dealing comprehensively with the same topic. While Chapter 14 of the USMCA is a continuation of the substantive protection afforded to foreign investment by the NAFTA, it does depart significantly from its predecessor regarding investor-state dispute settlement (ISDS). It introduces significant differentiations between the United States, Mexico and Canada regarding ISDS. In doing so, the USMCA partakes in a global trend in recent treaty practice seeking to reform ISDS, questioning even its very existence (UNCTAD 2020, pp. 113–114). Indeed, two recent major treaties leave out ISDS altogether, namely the Regional

C.-E. Côté (✉) · H. Ali
Faculty of Law, Université Laval, Quebec City, Canada
e-mail: Charles-Emmanuel.Cote@fd.ulaval.ca; Hamza.Ali.1@ulaval.ca

© The Author(s), under exclusive license to Springer Nature Switzerland AG 2022
G. Gagné and M. Rioux (eds.), *NAFTA 2.0*, Canada and International Affairs,
https://doi.org/10.1007/978-3-030-81694-0_6

Comprehensive Economic Partnership (RCEP) and the European Union (EU)–China Comprehensive Agreement on Investment, both of which having in common to include China. Moreover, Canada and Mexico already embraced the new investment court system proposed by the EU in the Comprehensive Economic and Trade Agreement[1] (CETA), and in the draft EU–Mexico association agreement,[2] which differs from previous ISDS.

NAFTA contributed to the creation of a uniform North American approach to investment law and policy, which spread across the globe through subsequent US and Canadian bilateral investment treaties (BITs). The North American approach was improved incrementally in response to issues raised by investment disputes. This fine tuning aimed at striking the right balance between foreign investment protection and the right to regulate for legitimate purposes such as health or environment protection. The North American approach culminated in the investment chapter of the Comprehensive and Progressive Agreement for Trans-Pacific Partnership[3] (CPTPP), which was once hailed as the possible new "gold standard" for investment agreements (Alvarez 2016). Despite the fact that the United States eventually rejected the Trans-Pacific Partnership (TPP), the unique influence of the North American approach, especially of US treaty practice, is unquestionable (Alschner and Skougarevskiy 2016, p. 353). This begs the questions as to why and to what extent the USMCA departs from this approach, and whether it represents a new one or rather the end of a uniform North American approach to investment law and policy.

The first section of this chapter will briefly examine the creation of a North American approach to investment law and policy by the NAFTA. The origins, content and legacy of NAFTA Chapter 11 will be summarized, including the controversy raised by the use of its ISDS provisions. The second section will compare the new USMCA Chapter 14 with NAFTA Chapter 11, in order to assess its impact on the North American approach. Key aspects of the renegotiation will be analyzed, as well as the substantive and ISDS provisions of Chapter 14.

NAFTA Chapter 11 and the Creation of a North American Approach

The Origin of NAFTA Chapter 11

The United States, Mexico and Canada had a contrasted history with foreign investment law and policy until they announced in 1990 a plan to negotiate a continental free trade agreement (FTA), including an investment chapter (Lantis 2008, p. 33). After initial bilateral talks between the United States and Mexico, Canada decided to step in the negotiation. The United States–Canada Free Trade Agreement (USCFTA) was used as a starting point in the negotiation, which was mainly a process of adapting this treaty to accession by Mexico (Fraser and Garcia 1994, pp. 373–375; de Mestral 1998, p. 254). However, the three countries had different objectives in terms of investment policy (de Mestral 1998, p. 253).

The United States had launched its BIT program in the early 1980s, joining the movement started two decades earlier by European capital-exporting countries (Vandevelde 1988). However, US BITs contained more detailed and liberalization-oriented provisions. They also built on a pioneer network of Friendship, Commerce and Navigation (FCN) treaties developed in the aftermath of World War II, which included robust protection for US investments abroad (Vandevelde 2017). The USCFTA already included an investment chapter, which was a first for Canada, but its provisions were less protective than those of US BITs and it did not foresee ISDS (Raby 1990). The need to prevent discrimination against US investments in Mexico was even greater, because of Mexico's traditional support of the Calvo doctrine and the troubled history of US investments in Mexico (de Mestral 1998, p. 294). No investment agreement had ever existed between the two countries and resort to diplomacy and mixed claims commissions had been necessary in the past (Feller 1935).

Until the NAFTA, Mexico had never signed an investment treaty. At the time of the USCFTA negotiation, Mexico was trying to recover from the 1982 debt crisis. The Mexican government undertook series of reforms, which included easing restrictions on foreign investment (Robert 2000, p. 26). In 1990, foreign investment was much needed by Mexico to stimulate economic growth and to pay its external debt (Robert 2000, p. 27). In negotiating a trade agreement with the United States, Mexico hoped to attract more US investment (de Mestral 1998, p. 253). Strong investment protection was also a bargaining chip to gain access to the North American market through trade liberalization (Robert 2000, p. 28; de Mestral 1998, p. 294).

The position of Canada regarding foreign investment was initially different from that of the United States. Until the signature of the USCFTA, Canada refrained from entering into any international agreement that would have limited its right to legislate concerning foreign investment (Côté 2012, pp. 271–276). The scale of US property in the Canadian economy was a highly controversial issue and several measures were taken to respond to this situation. In addition to closing sensitive economic sectors to foreign investment, Canada set up a restrictive screening mechanism for foreign investment. This mechanism was successfully challenged at the General Agreement on Tariffs and Trade (GATT) Council by the United States, and it was replaced by a lighter one.[4] Signature of the USCFTA marked a radical change for Canada, as it led to the launch of its own program of foreign investment promotion and protection agreements (FIPAs) (Leckow and Mallory 1991; Paterson 1991).

A North American Approach to Investment Law and Policy

The resulting NAFTA Chapter 11 established a common North American approach to investment law and policy that would be echoed in subsequent US and Canadian treaty practice, culminating with the CPTPP. This approach combined previous US BIT practice with the nascent Canadian FIPA one, as well as Chapter 16 of the USCFTA. The result is a distinctive approach, far more detailed and complex in its legal drafting than its European counterpart, but also more liberalization-oriented in terms of policy (Thomas 1999; VanDuzer 1998). This could be observed both in terms of substantive protection offered to foreign investors and their investments, and of settlement of investment disputes.

The scope of application of Chapter 11 was broadly defined by a definition of investment in the form of an exhaustive list of economic operations based on the notion of enterprise (art. 1139). It offered protection at the pre-investment stage in applying the most-favored-nation (MFN) and national treatment (NT) clauses to the establishment or the acquisition of investment (arts 1102–1103). This came to be a landmark feature of the North American approach to investment treaties, as opposed, for instance, to European BITs that never apply at the pre-investment stage.

Financial services and cultural industries were largely exempted from the purview of Chapter 11 (arts 1101.3 and 2106).[5] All the exceptions provided by NAFTA, regarding national security, taxation measures or balance of payments, were applicable to Chapter 11, allowing justification of potential breaches of the substantive protection of foreign investors (arts 2102–2104). However, general exceptions for health or environmental measures were not made applicable to Chapter 11, omitting to protect the right of the state to regulate for such purposes (art. 2101).[6]

The legal protection offered to foreign investors and their investments by Chapter 11 could be distinguished between provisions that were subject to reservations and those that were not. The MFN clause belonged to the first category and was new in US–Canada relations, since it was not provided by the USCFTA (art. 1103). It was completed by the NT clause, the performance requirements clause and the key personnel clause (arts. 1102, 1106–1107). The last two clauses also became typical of the North American approach, dealing, respectively, with trade-related investment measures and nationality requirements for senior management and boards of directors. All these provisions were subject to reservations filed by each state party, either to grandfather existing measures or to carve out sensitive sectors of the economy (art. 1108). Important enough, no blanket grandfathering was allowed for federal measures, which needed to be specifically listed in order to be protected. However, the initial intention of doing the same with subnational measures was abandoned, and the temporary general grandfather clause became permanent through an exchange of letters between the parties (Côté 2012, p. 283).

The second category of provisions included the fair and equitable treatment (FET) clause, with a reference to the minimum standard of treatment of customary international law that led to controversies in arbitral practice (art. 1105). The USCFTA did not contain a FET clause. This category also included the expropriation clause, covering explicitly both direct and indirect expropriation, as well as the clause on freedom of transfer of funds, both of which were previously subject to a blanket grandfather clause in the USCFTA(NAFTA, arts 1109–1110; USCFTA, art. 1607). A timid affirmation of the right of the state to regulate to protect the environment was also provided, but with the important caveat that such environmental measures had to be consistent with the substantive protection guaranteed by Chapter 11 (NAFTA, art. 1114).

NAFTA introduced for the first time ISDS in North American relations, since the USCFTA only contemplated state-to-state settlement for investment disputes. Moreover, it was the first time that ISDS was made applicable between industrialized countries, simultaneously with the Energy Charter Treaty between European countries. However, Canada and the United States had already started to include ISDS in their respective treaty practice. Chapter 11 took on their approach to ISDS, establishing a very complete set of highly technical provisions. A clear and unconditional consent to arbitration was provided by states parties, offering investors the choice between three different arbitration rules, namely the International Centre for Settlement of Investment Disputes (ICSID) Convention, the Additional Facility Rules of ICSID or the UNCITRAL Arbitration Rules (arts 1120, 1122).[7] Many innovative provisions supplement the ISDS regime in Chapter 11. First, investors must file a notice of intent to submit a claim to arbitration before actually filing a claim (art. 1119). Second, a state facing multiple claims in similar disputes may request their forced consolidation into one common case (art. 1126). Finally, NAFTA allowed states parties to adopt an interpretation of the provisions of Chapter 11 binding on arbitral tribunals, an important innovation aiming to respond to the risk of incoherent interpretations by various arbitral tribunals (art. 1131.2). Despite these important provisions taking stock of the particular nature of ISDS, transparency of the procedure as an issue was totally ignored by NAFTA.

NAFTA Chapter 11 Legacy and Controversies

The first case brought under Chapter 11 concerned an allegedly environmental measure adopted by Canada in *Ethyl Corporation v Canada*.[8] This claim of indirect expropriation and the settlement that ensued alarmed civil society and governments both in North America and beyond about the potential use and abuse of ISDS to defeat public policy measures. The fear of a "regulatory chill" appeared, according to which Chapter 11 would deter governments to adopt such measures. Frivolous notices of intent to submit claims, huge damage requests, broad interpretations of state obligations, conflicting arbitral awards, or lack of transparency of the procedure all fueled the controversy about Chapter 11 (Côté 2017). This situation triggered a series of responses by states parties to improve NAFTA itself, or the North American approach in subsequent treaty practice. In 2001, the North American Free Trade Commission issued a binding interpretation of Chapter 11, in order to clarify the meaning of the FET clause (NAFTC 2001). Arbitral tribunals and governments enhanced the transparency of ISDS in Chapter 11, by opening hearings to the public, affirming the power of tribunals to accept *amicus curiae* briefs, or publishing arbitral awards and other documents related to cases (VanDuzer 2007).

Canada and the United States faced numerous claims under Chapter 11, while Mexico was expected to be the prime target.[9] This belief was ill-advised, given the scale of investment flows between the two industrialized countries, and the powerful legal remedy offered by ISDS. During the lifespan of NAFTA, between 1994 and 2020, Canada faced 29 claims by US investors, losing or settling in favor of the investors in seven cases, in which it had to pay a total of US$180 million in damages, while five cases are still pending. As for Mexico, 24 cases were brought against it by US and Canadian investors, including seven that are still pending and five in which it lost and had to pay a total of US$186 million in damages. The United States never lost any of the 17 cases that were brought against it by Canadian investors and, in only one case, by Mexican investors.

Chapter 11 deeply impacted the subsequent investment treaty practice of all three NAFTA parties with third countries, which in turned expanded the North American approach to all corners of the world. Chapter 11 acted as the de facto model FIPA for Canada from 1994 (Côté 2012, pp. 294–298). As for Mexico, it marked the launch of its program of investment agreements, with a first BIT with Spain signed in 1995, where the influence of NAFTA is also palatable, but to a lesser extent. The North American approach was gradually adapted to new challenges and controversies identified in the multiple claims that arose under Chapter 11 against all three countries. Substantive protection provisions were circumscribed to avoid expansive interpretation, while the transparency of ISDS was consolidated. The 2004 US model BIT and the 2004 Canadian model FIPA codified this incremental evolution that aimed to set a better balance between investor protection and the right to regulate for legitimate public policy objectives. Yet, the matrix of Chapter 11 and of the North American approach was not discarded.

USMCA Chapter 14: The End of the North American Approach?

Renegotiating NAFTA *Chapter 11*

The long-awaited modernization of the NAFTA was precipitated by the US Trump administration, which engaged in the renegotiation of the agreement in 2017, including Chapter 11 (Marcoux 2019, pp. 260–268). Since the conclusion of NAFTA and up to 2017, the US position had always been in favor of including robust ISDS provisions in FTAs and BITs negotiated with other countries (Gantz 2020, p. 14).[10] However, the Trump administration was skeptical about the ISDS regime as it viewed it as a violation of US sovereignty and an encouragement of US companies to move their facilities abroad (Lester 2018). The aborted US$15 billion dispute brought by TransCanada Corporation, concerning the construction of the Keystone XL pipeline between Alberta and the Gulf of Mexico, shed light on the exposure of the United States to claims by Canadian investors against environmental measures.[11] According to the US chief negotiator, the alternative to the inclusion of mandatory ISDS should be state-to-state dispute settlement and the option for investors to include arbitration provisions in their contracts with host states (Lester 2018). This position was somehow reflected in a document issued by the Office of the United States Trade Representative stating the objectives of the renegotiation of the NAFTA as aiming to provide "meaningful procedures for resolving investment disputes, while ensuring the protection of US sovereignty and the maintenance of strong US domestic industries" (USTR 2017, p. 9).

On the Canadian side, renegotiation of the investment chapter was heavily influenced by the Canadian experience with ISDS. The Canadian government was mostly worried about its right to regulate given that the ISDS regime costed Canadian taxpayers more than C$300 million in damages and legal fees (Canada 2018). The Canadian negotiating strategy aimed at ensuring that investment provisions allow governments to regulate in the public interest. A proposal by the United States to eliminate ISDS in the new agreement was thus met favorably by Canada. It would remove the threat of claims against domestic measures through a system that some viewed as more favorable to foreign investors' interests than to public policy considerations (Canada 2020; Adès and Larouche-Maltais

2019, p. 20). Both Canadian and US governments have hence welcomed the elimination of ISDS from the USMCA (Gantz 2020, p. 49).

In the case of Mexico, the proposal to abolish ISDS needed to be mitigated both for domestic and diplomatic reasons (Perezcano 2019, pp. 9–12; Côté 2018, p. 439). First, the outgoing Peña Nieto's administration wanted to keep ISDS in a series of key sectors of the economy where it had conducted liberal regulatory reforms, in order to embed them in international law to prevent their repeal. Second, the controversial history of the protection of US property in Mexico probably led to keeping a minimum form of ISDS between the two countries.

Continuation in Terms of Substance

As result of the renegotiation, the USMCA still includes an investment chapter. Chapter 14 reproduces the state of the art of latest US and Canadian investment agreements, and of the CPTPP investment chapter in particular (Côté 2018, p. 433). This means that many new provisions are included to re-balance the language of NAFTA Chapter 11 in order to protect the right to regulate for legitimate public policy objectives. All the substantive provisions of Chapter 11 are thus to be found in Chapter 14 of the USMCA, as they evolved in subsequent treaty practice. However, it offers no original innovation of its own.

The scope of application of Chapter 14 is almost identical to that of Chapter 11. One notable difference concerns the key definition of "investment," circumscribing the economic operations protected by the USMCA. Instead of using a closed definition based on the notion of enterprise, it uses an open-ended definition based on that of assets, which means that it introduces a certain level of flexibility, but also of uncertainty (art. 14.1). Otherwise, it is also applicable both at the pre-investment and post-investment stages, with new specification that only concrete actions to make an investment are protected at the pre-investment stage (art. 14.1, fn. 3). This should limit exaggerated claims at this early phase of the life of an investment. Foreign investment in financial services is still largely excluded from the scope of Chapter 14, as well as those in cultural industries but only in Canada (arts 14.3 and 32.6). The same exceptions to the protection offered by Chapter 11 are applicable to Chapter 14, regarding national security, taxation measures or balance of payments (arts 32.2–4). General exceptions for health or environmental measures are, however, not applicable, in contrast with the Canadian treaty practice but in line with the NAFTA and the CPTPP (art. 32.1). The USMCA introduces a new exception for indigenous peoples rights, also applicable to Chapter 14 (art. 32.5). Those exceptions are important tools in protecting the right to regulate.

The legal protection offered by Chapter 14 to foreign investors and their investments may be categorized, like that of Chapter 11, between obligations subject to reservations or not. The usual MFN and NT clauses are provided, together with the performance requirement and key personnel clauses, typical of the North American approach (arts 14.4–5, 14.10–11). The MFN and NT clauses codify the interpretation developed in arbitral practice regarding the notion of "like circumstances," imposing to take into account legitimate public welfare objectives that may justify distinctions between investors. All these clauses are subject to the same complex set of reservations than in Chapter 11, grandfathering a series of specific federal measures and all subnational measures, as well as carving out sensitive sectors specified by each country (art. 14.12).

The rest of the substantive protection offered by Chapter 14 is not subject to any reservation. It includes the FET, expropriation and freedom of transfer of funds clauses (arts 14.6–9). In addition, Chapter 14 codifies post-NAFTA arbitral and treaty practice regarding the protection of the right to regulate with respect to those clauses. The notes of interpretation of Chapter 11 are codified in the FET clause, notably to curtail its scope to that of the minimum standard of treatment of customary international law. The controversial notion of indirect expropriation is defined with great detail in order to exclude from its scope non-discriminatory measures adopted to protect legitimate public welfare objectives (annex 14-B). The right to regulate is also reaffirmed in an extended clause, with the significant limit, similar to NAFTA, that measures adopted, for instance, to protect health or the environment must be consistent with Chapter 14. Finally, a new clause is provided to compel states to encourage their investors to observe international standards on corporate social responsibility (art. 14.17). This provision contributes to re-balance the protection offered to foreign investors by increasing their own responsibility to act as good corporate citizens.

Dislocation in Terms of Dispute Settlement

The contrasted position of all three countries on ISDS in the USMCA dislocated the unified North American approach to investment dispute settlement. ISDS continues to exist in US–Mexico relations, but it is now fragmented in two regimes, both different from the regime found in NAFTA. A general regime of ISDS reproduces closely that of NAFTA and is applicable to disputes in all fields covered by Chapter 14 (annex 14-D). It also codifies subsequent arbitral and treaty practice concerning transparency of the proceedings, such as the power of the tribunal to accept *amicus curiae* briefs. However, the scope of the general regime is significantly limited compared to Chapter 11. First, investors must, from now on, first submit their claims to domestic courts and wait 30 months before gaining access to arbitration. Second, it is only open to claims concerning a violation of the MFN and/or NT clause(s) at the post-investment stage, and to those involving the violation of the expropriation clause, but only in case of direct expropriation. This means that claims involving the most controversial provisions of Chapter 11 are now barred from that general ISDS regime, namely disputes claiming breach of the FET clause or indirect expropriation. A second regime of ISDS supplements the general one in US–Mexico relations, but only in a series of specific sectors of the economy where regulatory reforms were conducted, namely oil and gas, electricity, telecom, road and rail transport, canals and dams (annex 14-E). Under this sectoral ISDS regime, claims can involve the breach of all substantive protection provisions of Chapter 14, as opposed to the general regime, but it is only open to investments governed by a state contract.

This stands in stark contrast to investment disputes involving Canada under the USMCA, for which ISDS is completely eliminated. One should mention that investment disputes in Canada–Mexico relations can, nevertheless, be submitted to ISDS under the CPTPP, of which both countries are party. The USMCA foresees a transitory ISDS regime of three years for disputes concerning "legacy investments," which refer to investments that were made while the NAFTA was in force (annex 14-C). The Chapter 11 ISDS regime will remain applicable to those disputes. This transitory regime is applicable to investment disputes that are no longer covered by ISDS under the USMCA. After the lapse of this three-year period, ISDS will no longer be available for the settlement of investment disputes in US–Canada relations. This represents a significant departure from the NAFTA and the previous North American approach.

One must not equate the abolition of ISDS with the disappearance of investment disputes in US–Canada relations, or in US–Mexico relations for disputes no longer subject to ISDS. Investment flows will continue within North America and investment disputes are likely to arise from time to time. However, those disputes will need to be settled differently (Côté 2018, pp. 441–444). First, investors may be tempted to channel their investments through a subsidiary or a shell corporation, located in a third country with which the host state is bound under a treaty providing ISDS. For instance, a US investor could plan its investment in Canada through a subsidiary located in Mexico, in order to benefit from ISDS in the CPTPP. The abolition of ISDS could therefore encourage treaty shopping and raise the issue of potential abuse of right or call for the application of the denial of benefits clause (Voon et al. 2014; Feldman 2012).[12]

Second, the state-to-state dispute settlement mechanism of Chapter 31 of the USMCA will remain available for the resolution of disputes involving the breach of the substantive protection offered by Chapter 14. Of course, resort to this mechanism means that the home state of the investor will decide to politicize the dispute by bringing it before a Chapter 31 panel. This will also raise a series of rather new or overlooked legal issues, including whether the rule of exhaustion of local remedies is applicable, or if the home state may claim damages before such panels (Roberts 2014; Potestà 2013).

Third, even if ISDS is abolished in the USMCA, nothing prevents an investor and a host state to both agree *ex post facto* to ISDS, for instance, by consenting to submit their dispute to ICSID and to choose Chapter 14 as the applicable law. Of course, the great difference here is that the host state must consent specifically to arbitration on a case-by-case basis, as opposed to ISDS where this consent is given in advance under a treaty.[13]

Finally, domestic courts remain the most obvious forum for the settlement of investment disputes not covered by ISDS under the USMCA. This represents a return to the philosophy of customary international law regarding disputes over damages caused to private persons, where local remedies must be exhausted by the private person, before its state of nationality may exert diplomatic protection on the international plane.[14] In that case, the domestic law of the host state will be the law applicable to the dispute, not the treaty provisions. This raises the important issue of the conformity of the substantive protection afforded by domestic law with Chapter 14 of the USMCA. One study already expressed doubts about the conformity of Canadian law with Chapter 11 of the NAFTA (de Mestral and Morgan 2017).

Conclusion

What is the impact of the USMCA on the North American approach to investment law and policy? The answer to this question calls for some nuances. There is still a common approach to substantive protection of foreign investors and their investments, both within North America and in the external treaty practice of the United States, Canada, and Mexico to a lesser extent. The CPTPP represents the most important external iteration of this North American approach. However, there is no more common approach to ISDS within North America. For the moment, the previous approach to ISDS continues to prevail in the external bilateral treaty practice of the three countries, with the notable exception of the CETA, but for how long? Is the abolition of ISDS between the United States and Canada an indication of things to come? While it is possible that ISDS will remain a key feature of bilateral treaties with developing, capital-importing countries; recent treaties, like the RCEP or the EU–China Comprehensive Agreement on Investment, show that the USMCA is not unique in the abandonment of ISDS. Thus, the new piecemeal North American approach to ISDS could become the global approach. Nevertheless, the abolition of ISDS does not mean the disappearance of investment disputes. The recent decision of the Biden administration abrogating the permit for the construction of the Keystone XL pipeline indicates that re-politicization of the settlement of these disputes can be expected (White House 2021, sec. 6). Governments will not be able to avoid pressure to intervene in the problems of private investors with foreign countries, the very purpose for which ISDS was—yet imperfectly—created.

Notes

1. Chapter 8 of the CETA on investment has been provisionally applied with the notable exception of the investment court system.
2. The EU and Mexico reached an agreement in principle on April 21, 2018, on the trade parts of a new association agreement, including a chapter on investment and a separate one on investment dispute resolution. See online at https://trade.ec.europa.eu/doclib/press/index.cfm?id=1833.
3. The CPTPP incorporates with almost no amendment the text of the previous Trans-Pacific Partnership (TPP) signed in 2016, including its chapter 9 on investment, but which never came into force after the refusal

of the United States to ratify it. The CPTPP entered into force in late December 2018 between six states parties.

4. See *Canada—Administration of the Foreign Investment Review Act (Complaint by the United States)*, GATT Doc L/5504, 1984. The Foreign Investment Review Act (SC 1973-74, c 46) was replaced with the Investment Canada Act (RSC 1985, c 28, 1st Supp).
5. The cultural exemption came to be typical of the Canadian treaty practice, but not of that of the US.
6. North American treaty practice split on this particular issue, as Canada included general exceptions in its subsequent agreements, while the US never did.
7. The Convention on the Settlement of Investment Disputes between States and Nationals of Other States (signed March 18, 1965, entered into force October 14, 1966), establishing the International Centre for Settlement of Investment Disputes (ICSID) (ICSID Convention). The ICSID created an Additional Facility to offer arbitration rules to disputes not covered by the ICSID Convention. The United Nations Commission on International Trade Law (UNCITRAL) also adopted arbitration rules for the settlement of international commercial disputes.
8. See *Ethyl Corporation v Canada*, Award on Jurisdiction, 38 ILM 708 (NAFTA Chap 11, June 24, 1998).
9. All data are taken from the "Investment Dispute Settlement Navigator" on the *Investment Policy Hub* operated by the United Nations Conference on Trade and Development, https://investmentpolicy.unctad.org/.
10. See the Bipartisan Congressional Trade Priorities and Accountability Act of 2015, sec 102, 114th Congress. https://www.congress.gov/bill/114th-congress/senate-bill/995/text.
11. See *TransCanada Corporation v United States*, Order of the Secretary-General Taking Note of the Discontinuance of the Proceeding, ICSID Case No ARB/16/21 (NAFTA Chap 11, March 24, 2017).
12. The denial of benefits clause allows a host state to refuse the protection of an investment agreement to investments owned or controlled by third country investors.
13. This solution is contemplated explicitly in a series of exchange of letters between New Zealand and Brunei, Malaysia and Vietnam, made at the time of the signature of CPTPP on March 8, 2018.
14. See International Law Commission. Draft Articles on Diplomatic Protection, A/61/10 (2006), art. 14. https://legal.un.org/ilc/texts/instruments/english/commentaries/9_8_2006.pdf.

REFERENCES

Adès, Julie, and Alexandre Larouche-Maltais. 2019. *From NAFTA to CUSMA: The changes, The additions, and what remains*. Ottawa: The Conference Board of Canada. https://www.conferenceboard.ca/temp/9803cd70-9167-46aa-990e-7b587fc4675c/10323_From%20NAFTA%20to%20CUSMA_RPT.pdf.

Alschner, Wolfgang, and Dmitriy Skougarevskiy. 2016. The new gold standard? Empirically situating the trans-pacific partnership in the investment treaty universe. *The Journal of World Investment & Trade* 17 (3): 339–373.

Alvarez, Jose E. 2016. Is the trans-pacific partnership's investment chapter the new 'gold standard'? *Victoria University of Wellington Law Review* 47 (4): 503–544.

Côté, Charles-Emmanuel. 2012. Le Canada et l'investissement direct étranger: entre ouverture et inquiétude. In *L'investissement et la nouvelle économie mondiale: trajectoires nationales, réseaux mondiaux et normes internationales*, edited by Mathieu Arès and Eric Boulanger, 241–314. Bruxelles: Bruylant.

Côté, Charles-Emmanuel. 2017. An experienced, developed democracy: Canada and investor-state arbitration. In *Second thoughts: Investor state arbitration between developed democracies*, edited by Armand de Mestral, 89–130. Waterloo: Centre for International Governance Innovation.

Côté, Charles-Emmanuel. 2018. Investissement. *Annuaire canadien de droit international* 56: 424–452.

de Mestral, Armand. 1998. The North American Free Trade Agreement: A comparative analysis. *Collected Courses of the Hague Academy of International Law* 275: 219–416.

de Mestral, Armand, and Robin Morgan. 2017. Does Canadian law provide remedies equivalent to NAFTA Chapter 11 arbitration? In *Second thoughts: Investor state arbitration between developed democracies*, edited by Armand de Mestral, 155–186. Waterloo: Centre for International Governance Innovation.

Feldman, Mark. 2012. Setting limits on corporate nationality planning in investment treaty arbitration. *ICSID Review—Foreign Investment Law Journal* 27 (2): 281–302. https://doi.org/10.1093/icsidreview/sis026.

Feller, A.H. 1935. *The Mexican claims commission: 1923–1934*. New York: Macmillan.

Fraser, Niall M., and Francisco Garcia. 1994. Conflict analysis of the NAFTA negotiations. *Group Decision and Negotiation* 3 (4): 373–391.

Gantz, David A. 2020. *An introduction to the United States-Mexico-Canada agreement: Understanding the new NAFTA*. Cheltenham: Edward Elgar.

Lantis, Jeffrey S. 2008. *The life and death of international treaties: Double-edged diplomacy and the politics of ratification in comparative perspective*. Oxford: Oxford University Press.

Leckow, Ross B., and Ian A. Mallory. 1991. The relaxation of foreign investment restrictions in Canada. *ICSID Review—Foreign Investment Law Journal* 6 (1): 1–42.

Lester, Simon. 2018. Brady-Lighthizer ISDS Exchange. *International Economic Law and Policy Blog*, March 21. https://ielp.worldtradelaw.net/2018/03/brady-lighthizer-isds-exchange.html.

Marcoux, Jean-Michel. 2019. The renegotiation of NAFTA: The 'most advanced' free trade agreement? *European Yearbook of International Economic Law* 10: 257–284.

Paterson, Robert K. 1991. Canadian investment promotion and protection treaties. *Canadian Yearbook of International Law* 29: 373–390.

Perezcano, Hugo. 2019. Trade in North America: A Mexican perspective on the future of North America's economic relationship. In *The future of North America's economic relationship—From NAFTA to the new Canada-United States-Mexico agreement and beyond—Special report*, 7–14. Waterloo: Centre for International Governance Innovation.

Potestà, Michele. 2013. State-to-state dispute settlement pursuant to bilateral investment treaties: Is there potential? In *International courts and the development of international law: Essays in honour of Tullio Treves*, ed. Nerina Boschiero, Tullio Treves, Cesare Pitea, and Chiara Ragni, 753–768. The Hague: Asser Press.

Raby, Jean. 1990. The investment provisions of the Canada-United States free trade agreement: A Canadian perspective. *American Journal of International Law* 84 (2): 394–443.

Robert, Maryse. 2000. *Negotiating NAFTA: Explaining the outcome in culture, textiles, autos, and pharmaceuticals*. Toronto: University of Toronto Press.

Roberts, Anthea. 2014. State-to-state investment treaty arbitration: A hybrid theory of interdependent rights and shared interpretive authority. *Harvard International Law Journal* 55 (1): 1–70.

Thomas, J.C. 1999. Investor-state arbitration under NAFTA Chapter 11. *Canadian Yearbook of International Law* 37: 99–138.

Vandevelde, Kenneth J. 1988. The bilateral investment treaty program of the United States. *Cornell International Law Journal* 21 (2): 201–276.

Vandevelde, Kenneth J. 2017. *The first bilateral investment treaties: U.S. postwar friendship, commerce, and navigation treaties*. Oxford: Oxford University Press.

VanDuzer, J. Anthony. 1998. Investor-state dispute settlement under NAFTA Chapter 11: The shape of things to come? *Canadian Yearbook of International Law* 35: 263–90.

VanDuzer, J. Anthony. 2007. Enhancing the procedural legitimacy of investor-state arbitration through transparency and amicus curiae participation. *McGill Law Journal* 52 (4): 681–724.

Voon, Tania, Andrew Mitchell, and James Munro. 2014. Legal responses to corporate manoeuvring in international investment arbitration. *Journal of International Dispute Settlement* 5 (1): 41–68.

Official Documents

Canada. 2018. *Prime Minister Trudeau and Minister Freeland Speaking Notes for the United States-Mexico-Canada Agreement Press Conference,* January 10. https://pm.gc.ca/en/news/speeches/2018/10/01/prime-min ister-trudeau-and-minister-freeland-speaking-notes-united-states.

Canada. 2020. *Statement by the deputy prime minister on the entry-into-force of the new NAFTA,* June 30. https://pm.gc.ca/en/news/statements/2020/ 06/30/statement-deputy-prime-minister-entry-force-new-nafta.

Comprehensive and Progressive Agreement for Trans-Pacific Partnership (CPTPP), signed March 8, 2018, entered into force December 30, 2018. https://www.mfat.govt.nz/en/trade/free-trade-agreements/free-trade-agr eements-in-force/cptpp/comprehensive-and-progressive-agreement-for-trans-pacific-partnership-text-and-resources/.

Comprehensive Economic and Trade Agreement (CETA), signed October 30, 2016, entered provisionally into force September 21, 2017. https://www.int ernational.gc.ca/trade-commerce/trade-agreements-accords-commerciaux/ agr-acc/ceta-aecg/text-texte/toc-tdm.aspx?lang=eng.

Energy Charter Treaty, signed December 17, 1994, entered into force April 16, 1998.https://www.energycharter.org/fileadmin/DocumentsMedia/Legal/ ECT-Positive_Annex_W.pdf.

European Union—China Comprehensive Agreement on Investment, agreement in principle announced on December 30, 2020. https://trade.ec.europa.eu/ doclib/press/index.cfm?id=2237.

North American Free Trade Commission (NAFTC). 2001. *Notes of interpretation of certain Chapter 11 provisions.* https://www.international.gc.ca/ trade-agreements-accords-commerciaux/topics-domaines/disp-diff/NAFTA-Interpr.aspx?lang=eng.

North American Free Trade Agreement (NAFTA), signed December 17, 1992, entered into force January 1, 1994, suspended July 1, 2020. https://www.int ernational.gc.ca/trade-commerce/trade-agreements-accords-commerciaux/ agr-acc/nafta-alena/fta-ale/index.aspx?lang=eng.

Office of the United States Trade Representative (USTR). 2017. *Summary of objectives for the NAFTA renegotiation,* November. https://ustr.gov/sites/def ault/files/files/Press/Releases/Nov%20Objectives%20Update.pdf.

Regional Comprehensive Economic Partnership(RCEP), signed November 15, 2020. https://rcepsec.org/legal-text/.

Trans-Pacific Partnership (TPP), signed February 4, 2016. https://www.intern ational.gc.ca/trade-commerce/trade-agreements-accords-commerciaux/agr-acc/tpp-ptp/text-texte/toc-tdm.aspx?lang=eng.

United Nations Conference on Trade and Development (UNCTAD). 2020. *World Investment Report 2020: International production beyond the pandemic.* https://unctad.org/system/files/official-document/wir2020_en.pdf.

United States–Canada Free Trade Agreement (USCFTA), signed January 2, 1988, entered into force January 1, 1989, suspended January 1, 1994. https://www.international.gc.ca/trade-commerce/assets/pdfs/agreem ents-accords/cusfta-e.pdf.

United States–Mexico–Canada Agreement (USMCA), signed November 30, 2018, amended December 10, 2019, entered into force July 1, 2020. https://www.international.gc.ca/trade-commerce/trade-agreements-accords-commerciaux/agr-acc/cusma-aceum/text-texte/toc-tdm.aspx?lang=eng.

White House. 2021. *Executive order on protecting public health and the environ-ment and restoring science to tackle the climate crisis*, January 21. https://www.whitehouse.gov/briefing-room/presidential-actions/2021/01/20/exe cutive-order-protecting-public-health-and-environment-and-restoring-science-to-tackle-climate-crisis/.

CHAPTER 7

Digital Trade

Gilbert Gagné and Michèle Rioux

If it were simply to identify what changes the United States–Mexico–Canada Agreement (USMCA) brings to the North American Free Trade Agreement (NAFTA), this chapter would be much more concise. When it comes to electronic commerce (or digital trade to use the new terminology), it would be about explaining that everything is new! When NAFTA was concluded in 1992, there were a total of 10 websites on the World Wide Web. Digital trade then was not a concern for negotiators of trade agreements a year before the creation of MP3. *Yahoo! Search* became in 1994 the first web directory and the business development of Internet had really begun with the online websites eBay and Amazon in 1995. The objective of this chapter is thus to highlight the evolution

G. Gagné (✉)
Department of Politics & International Studies, Bishop's University, Sherbrooke, QC, Canada
e-mail: gagne@ubishops.ca

M. Rioux
Department of Political Science, Université du Québec à Montréal, Montreal, QC, Canada
e-mail: rioux.michele@uqam.ca

© The Author(s), under exclusive license to Springer Nature Switzerland AG 2022
G. Gagné and M. Rioux (eds.), *NAFTA 2.0*, Canada and International Affairs,
https://doi.org/10.1007/978-3-030-81694-0_7

of the provisions on digital trade in trade agreements, which resulted in USMCA Chapter 19 and the possible way forward from there.

A key question is where does this appetite to link digital trade to the rules governing the liberalization of trade come from? Clearly, in view of hegemonic ambitions and the dominance of its Internet firms, the United States has major political and economic motives to push for the absence of restrictions in trade in digital products or "digital freedom." To support this objective, the US government has developed a discourse favoring the free flow of information, freedom of expression, competition, the fight against protectionism, economic profitability, individual free choice and anti-elitism.

After describing the early US efforts to have a framework regulating electronic commerce within the World Trade Organization (WTO), a second section turns to the series of preferential trade agreements (PTAs) concluded by the United States as a path for securing rules and standards on e-commerce. A third section focuses specifically on the provisions relating to digital trade in the USMCA, while the fourth section considers the recent plurilateral initiative under WTO auspices to revive e-commerce discussions. Some concluding remarks follow.

THE WTO DEAD END (1998–2015)

The observation of the fabulous world growth of Internet has led to the US aim of developing a framework for regulating electronic commerce in trade agreements. The favored venue for such endeavor has been the WTO. Then, the WTO has taken up the subject of e-commerce and its General Council in 1998 launched the Work Program on Electronic Commerce as a response to the growing importance of e-commerce via the Internet in world trade. The 1998 Declaration provided for the establishment of a work program to consider all trade-related aspects of electronic commerce and the presentation of a report to the Third Ministerial Conference. The 1998 Declaration also included a moratorium, which specified that: "members will continue their current practice of not imposing customs duties on electronic transmission" (WTO, n.d.).

The work program continued after the third meeting of the Ministerial Conference held in Seattle in 1999. At the fourth meeting in Doha in 2001, ministers agreed to maintain the work program and to extend the moratorium on tariffs. They instructed the General Council to present a report on the progress made on this issue at the meeting in Cancun in 2003 (WTO, n.d.). It was to be the same every year until 2015, the work program simply being renewed, without much progress. Two main reasons may explain this apparent dead end: emerging issues associated with the distribution of films and music (from piracy to legal downloading and then online streaming); and the difficulty for developing states to measure their economic interests in the transformations caused by the development of the digital economy.

The work program also allowed for the consideration of challenges related to electronic commerce by the Council for Trade in Services, the Council for Trade in Goods, the Council for Trade-Related Aspects of Intellectual Property Rights and the Committee on Trade and Development. During these years, a number of issues notes were produced by the WTO secretariat and several member states submitted papers presenting their positions (WTO, n.d.).

There is as well the debate on the classification of digital products, either as goods or services, or another category altogether. The United States has favored an interpretation of digital products as "goods," to have them regulated under the General Agreement on Tariffs and Trade (GATT), rather than as "services," regulated under the General Agreement on Trade in Services (GATS), entailing more modest obligations.

However, until recently, the WTO's work program had languished, notably due to the wider debate on how to respond to developing country demands that began with the Doha Round. The United States quickly grasped that the multilateral path was not very promising in the short term and, by the beginning of the twenty-first century, was consolidating its efforts toward PTA negotiations.

The PTA Path of the United States

If the WTO route cannot be taken in setting e-commerce rules and standards, the US government must find other forums that will be more receptive. In the early 2000s, US trade negotiators were called upon to introduce a new standard for e-commerce into PTAs. The aim was to develop a chapter on electronic commerce in these agreements, which was to apply the principles of national treatment (NT), most-favored-nation (MFN) and market access to digital products (see Wunsch-Vincent 2003).

The enormous negotiating power of the US government means that no state could resist this will.[1] The first agreement including a chapter on electronic commerce was concluded with Jordan in 2000. The chapter is very short, the US format for such a chapter not yet defined at the time of this negotiation. Each party shall seek to refrain from: (a) imposing customs duties on electronic transmissions; (b) imposing unnecessary barriers on electronic transmissions, including digitized products; and (c) impeding the supply by electronic means of services subject to trade commitments under the agreement (US–Jordan PTA, art. 7.1). The scope of the chapter is limited, but the provision of services by electronic means was subject for the first time to the NT and MFN principles.

The e-commerce chapters of the US PTAs with Singapore, Chile and Australia were negotiated concurrently. Their structure is rather similar and the agreement with Australia became the model for subsequent agreements. Its chapter on electronic commerce includes: (a) that measures affecting the supply of electronically delivered or performed services are subject to the relevant obligations contained in the chapters on services, investment and financial services, subject to any exceptions under these chapters (US–Australia PTA, art. 16.2); (b) a commitment not to impose tariffs on digital products (art. 16.3); (c) non-discriminatory treatment of digital products (art. 16.4); (d) a definition of "digital products"[2]; and (e) provisions on electronic authentication, digital certificates, consumer protection, paperless commerce (arts 16.5–16.7).

Similarly to the agreements with Singapore and Chile, those with Central America and the Dominican Republic, Morocco, Bahrain and Panama include the first four elements of the e-commerce chapter of the US–Australia PTA. The US PTAs with Oman, Peru and Colombia, on the other hand, also include the fifth element.

The agreement with Korea reproduces the provisions of the agreement with Australia, but innovates in certain respects. It contains a statement of principles on accessing and using the Internet for electronic commerce.

---

[1] The United States has so far 14 PTAs in force that contain a chapter on electronic commerce: Jordan (signed in 2000), Singapore (2003), Chile (2003), Australia (2004), Central America and the Dominican Republic (2004), Morocco (2004), Bahrain (2004), Oman (2006), Peru (2006), Colombia (2006), Panama (2007), Korea (2007), USMCA (2018), Japan (2020).

[2] "Digital products means the digitally encoded form of computer programs, text, video, images, sound recordings, and other products, regardless of whether they are fixed on a carrier medium or transmitted electronically" (art. 16.8.4).

These principles aim to ensure that consumers have access to the services of their choice and use the services, devices, digital products and applications of their choice (US–Korea PTA, art. 15.7). Also, the parties are expected to endeavor to refrain from imposing or maintaining unnecessary barriers to the electronic flow of information across borders (art. 15.8).

The chapter on electronic commerce, therefore, has evolved along the US PTAs being concluded over the years (see: Azmeh et al. 2020; Burri and Polanco 2020; Froese 2019). A recent trade agreement the United States has concluded is the one with Japan. This is a very limited agreement that only affects certain food and industrial products. What is interesting is that a specific agreement on digital trade has also been concluded (US–Japan Digital Trade Agreement). This shows how much of a priority this is for the US government. In form, the agreement is close to the one concluded under the USMCA. Yet, it goes further, notably with provisions on cryptography (Gantz 2020, pp. 170–71).

THE USMCA

A sign of the times, the text of the USMCA provides for the transition from what was called "electronic commerce" during the 2000s to the more contemporary name of "digital trade." With the agreement on digital trade with Japan, the USMCA is the one that goes furthest in regulating digital trade. By comparison, two other major PTAs include a chapter on electronic commerce. The one in the Comprehensive Economic and Trade Agreement, between Canada and the European Union (EU), only provides for cooperation in this area, without binding commitments for the parties. The one in the Trans-Pacific Partnership (TPP) Agreement, negotiated at US initiative, is much more far-reaching. In fact, the e-commerce chapters in the TPP and USMCA follow on the US approach developed in PTA negotiations since the early 2000s for the regulation of electronic commerce, while adding new elements. Much of the text in both chapters is identical. The TPP does not go as far as the USMCA in the range of topics being addressed, but it is clearly its inspiration.

In both agreements, there are new provisions on the protection of personal data, cross-border transfer of information by electronic means, location of computer installations, cyber security, prohibition on requiring the transfer of source codes to a party's territory to gain access to its market (TPP, ch. 14). The USMCA adds to this list open government data and the limitation of the legal liability of interactive computer services for the content they offer (USMCA, ch. 19).

In sum, USMCA provides that personal data and information may be transferred across borders and that limits on data storage and processing are kept to a minimum (art. 19.11). It limits the ability of governments to require companies to disclose source codes and proprietary algorithms (art. 19.16). It promotes open access to public information (art. 19.18). It limits the liability of Internet platforms for the third-party content that these platforms host or process, outside the domain of intellectual property enforcement (art. 19.17).

These above subjects are just appearing in trade agreements. The scope of digital chapters, in turn, is becoming increasingly broad, at the same time as it touches on issues that are not limited to trade and fall more within states' domestic policies. In this respect, the USMCA does not prevent parties from adopting their own regulations on digital trade, as long as these are applied in a manner consistent with the agreement.

The TPP and USMCA digital chapters appear to be the current foundation on which the United States wishes to rest in order to extend the rules contained therein to a possible WTO agreement. The PTA approach has revealed its limits in the United States when one takes into account the reluctance of a large part of its population and elected officials to liberalize trade. A multilateral agreement focusing on digital trade remains the preferred strategy for the United States. Yet, this is still troublesome, as tensions on this subject have somehow persisted among WTO members.

The WTO Reinvigorated?

In parallel with the PTA approach, the United States has also invested the territory of plurilateralism, attempting to regroup several states behind its objective of institutionalizing on the world stage a number of rules on digital trade that meet the needs of several large American companies. Note two initiatives in recent years: the Anti-Counterfeiting Trade Agreement (ACTA) and the Trade in Services Agreement (TISA). Although never officially shelved, both initiatives encountered such difficulties in the negotiation or adoption process that neither succeeded.

Some provisions of ACTA had found their way into the TPP, particularly in the area of intellectual property, but the United States has been unable to benefit from them following President Trump's withdrawal of the United States from the agreement. Those in the US administration who see it as a priority to "multilateralize" e-commerce rules are inclined to do so in the WTO, which was always the first-choice forum.

Relaunched in December 2017 at the Eleventh WTO Ministerial Conference in Buenos Aires, discussions on a possible e-commerce deal seem for many members a way to revitalize the organization and reconfirm its relevance (WTO 2017). On January 25, 2019, on the sidelines of the Davos Forum, 76 states issued a joint declaration reiterating their willingness to start negotiations on the regulation of electronic commerce within the framework of the WTO (WTO 2019a). The United States, China, the EU and Canada are among the promoters of these negotiations, while India and almost all African countries are opposed. This declaration echoes the tiered strategy adopted by the United States in the early 2000s, which aimed to disseminate its norms and principles in this area through PTAs first, and then to aim for their transfer at the WTO level. The latter step will not be so easy to climb, however, important players in the WTO remaining bitter about the results of the Doha Round (see Ciuriak 2019).

The Davos Declaration was followed in June 2019 by the Osaka Declaration, which reiterated the willingness of signatory states to see to the establishment of international rules at the WTO on aspects of electronic commerce that are linked to international trade (WTO 2019b). Negotiations are continuing and the WTO reported in December 2020 that texts have been drafted on the following issues: spam and source code, open government data, e-signatures and authentication, and consumer protection. Discussions take place in groups made up of the 86 WTO members participating in these negotiations, as of late 2020 (WTO 2020). Note that the WTO now has 164 members.

Shy until recently on the subject, the EU announced its guidelines on electronic commerce in April 2019 (EU 2019). The European proposal covers several aspects of electronic commerce aimed at ensuring functional data flows for businesses, improving market access and regulatory predictability, while remaining committed to consumer protection and privacy.

Concluding Remarks

The United States has been well ahead in pursuing its interests and devising a strategy relating to trade in digital products. The US first attempted to develop a framework for regulating electronic commerce within the WTO. Dissatisfied with the lack of progress, the American government then negotiated a series of PTAs as a means of securing e-commerce rules and standards. The renegotiation of the NAFTA represents a key recent outcome of this strategy, while the USMCA encompassed, as of late 2018, the most advanced chapter and provisions on digital trade. The importance of electronic commerce remains a major incentive for states to agree on global provisions to regulate it. Yet, the recently resumed WTO e-commerce negotiations might prove no less challenging.

REFERENCES

Azmeh, Shamel, Christopher Foster, and Jaime Echavarri. 2020. The International Trade Regime and the Quest for Free Digital Trade. *International Studies Review* 22 (3): 671–692.

Burri, Mira, and Rodrigo Polanco. 2020. Digital Trade Provisions in Preferential Trade Agreements: Introducing a New Dataset. *Journal of International Economic Law* 23 (1): 187–220.

Ciuriak, Dan. 2019. *World Trade Organization 2.0: Reforming Multilateral Trade Rules for the Digital Age*. Centre for International Governance Innovation, Policy Brief No. 152, July. https://live.cigionline.org/sites/default/files/documents/PB%20no.152_5.pdf.

Comprehensive Economic and Trade Agreement (CETA), signed October 30, 2016, entered (provisionally) into force September 21, 2017. http://international.gc.ca/trade-commerce/trade-agreements-accords-commerciaux/agr-acc/ceta-aecg/text-texte/toc-tdm.aspx?lang=eng. Accessed January 8, 2021.

European Union (EU). 2019. *Joint Statement on Electronic Commerce*. April 26. https://trade.ec.europa.eu/doclib/docs/2019/may/tradoc_157880.pdf.

Froese, Marc D. 2019. Digital Trade and Dispute Settlement in RTAs: An Evolving Standard? *Journal of World Trade* 53 (5): 783–809.

Gantz, David A. 2020. *An Introduction to the United States-Mexico-Canada Agreement: Understanding the New NAFTA*. Cheltenham, UK/Northampton, MA: Edward Elgar.

General Agreement on Tariffs and Trade (GATT), signed October 20, 1947, entered into force January 1, 1948. https://www.wto.org/english/docs_e/legal_e/gatt47_e.pdf.

General Agreement on Trade in Services (GATS), signed April 15, 1994, entered into force January 1, 1995. https://www.wto.org/english/docs_e/legal_e/26-gats.pdf.

Trans-Pacific Partnership (TPP) Agreement, signed February 4, 2016. https://ustr.gov/trade-agreements/free-trade-agreements/trans-pacific-partnership/tpp-full-text.

United States-Australia Free Trade Agreement (US-Australia PTA), signed May 18, 2004, entered into force January 1, 2005. https://ustr.gov/trade-agreements/free-trade-agreements/australian-fta/final-text.

United States-Jordan Free Trade Agreement (US-Jordan PTA), signed October 24, 2000, entered into force December 17, 2001. https://ustr.gov/trade-agreements/free-trade-agreements/jordan-fta/final-text.

United States-Korea Free Trade Agreement (US-Korea PTA), signed June 30, 2007, entered into force March 15, 2012. https://ustr.gov/trade-agreements/free-trade-agreements/korus-fta/final-text.

United States-Japan Digital Trade Agreement, signed October 7, 2019. https://ustr.gov/sites/default/files/files/agreements/japan/Agreement_between_the_United_States_and_Japan_concerning_Digital_Trade.pdf.

United States-Mexico-Canada Agreement (USMCA), signed November 30, 2018; Protocol of Amendment signed December 10, 2019, in force July 1, 2020. https://www.international.gc.ca/trade-commerce/trade-agreements-accords-commerciaux/agr-acc/cusma-aceum/text-texte/toc-tdm.aspx?lang=eng.

WTO. 2017. *Joint Statement on Electronic Commerce*. WT/MIN(17)/60, December 13. https://docs.wto.org/dol2fe/Pages/SS/directdoc.aspx?filename=q:/WT/MIN17/60.pdf&Open=True.

WTO. 2019a. *Joint Statement on Electronic Commerce*. WT/L/1056, January 25. https://trade.ec.europa.eu/doclib/docs/2019/january/tradoc_157643.pdf.

WTO. 2019b. *Azevêdo Joins Prime Minister Abe and Other Leaders to Launch "Osaka Track" on the Digital Economy*. June 28. https://www.wto.org/english/news_e/news19_e/osaka_declration_on_digital_economy_e.pdf.

WTO. 2020. *E-commerce Co-convenors Release Update on the Negotiations, Welcome Encouraging Progress*. December 14. https://www.wto.org/english/news_e/news20_e/ecom_14dec20_e.pdf.

WTO. n.d. *Electronic Commerce: Briefing Note. Work Continues on Issues Needing Clarification*. https://www.wto.org/english/tratop_e/ecom_e/ecom_briefnote_e.htm.

Wunsch-Vincent, Sacha. 2003. The Digital Trade Agenda of the U.S.: Parallel Tracks of Bilateral, Regional and Multilateral Liberalization. *Aussenwirtschaft* 58: 7–46.

CHAPTER 8

Intellectual Property

Nathaniel Lipkus and Madison Black

Canada's Historical Approach to Intellectual Property in Trade Agreements

For the past 30 years, since entry into the original North American Free Trade Agreement (NAFTA), Canada has had a reputation on the world stage for striking a balance between the rights of intellectual property (IP) owners and users. Unlike less—developed countries, Canada has historically had strong research capability and an open economy that has been relatively attractive for foreign direct investment. However, unlike dominant economies such as the United States and the European Union (EU), Canada has generally not captured the value of the IP that Canadians create and has hence not been a net IP exporter to foreign trading partners.

Canada's IP policy, reflecting its status as a net IP importer aspiring to become a net exporter, strikes a careful balance between IP protection and access. This balance is manifest in Canadian copyright laws,

N. Lipkus (✉) · M. Black
Osler, Hoskin & Harcourt LLP, Toronto, ON, Canada
e-mail: NLipkus@osler.com

© The Author(s), under exclusive license to Springer Nature   109
Switzerland AG 2022
G. Gagné and M. Rioux (eds.), *NAFTA 2.0*,
Canada and International Affairs,
https://doi.org/10.1007/978-3-030-81694-0_8

which recognize rights of copyright users as stand-alone rights that are not merely exceptions to the rights of copyright owners.[1] The balance also appears in policy statements underpinning Canada's pharmaceutical patent linkage laws, recognizing the constant need to balance the objectives of potent enforcement of pharmaceutical patents and affordable access to medicines.[2]

From the outside, the Canadian IP approach is seen as respectful of both IP owners and the broader public, and Canada has consequently played an outsized role in setting international IP norms. The Canadian government has typically advanced its balanced IP approach at the negotiating table for bilateral and multilateral trade agreements. Where Canada has sided with countries seeking to expand IP protection, the expansion has been perceived as more reasonable. Where Canada has sided with countries seeking to preserve exceptions or limitations on intellectual property rights (IPRs), its position has presented a formidable barrier to IPR expansion.

CANADA'S INTELLECTUAL PROPERTY COMMITMENTS PRECEDING THE USMCA

IP was not historically part of free trade agreements (FTAs). IP does not enhance free trade but rather restricts it in favor of other policy objectives, such as providing adequate rewards for the creation of new works, inventions and designs, and protecting consumers who might otherwise be deceived or confused by the unlawful or misleading use of trademarks. Until NAFTA in 1994, no FTA featured an IP chapter (Maskus and Ridley 2016, p. 4).

Following the crystallization of a coherent American IP policy, IP formed part of the agenda during the Uruguay Round of trade talks at the World Trade Organization (WTO). The United States was pushing for IP protection on par with its own domestic standards, which at the time were far more expansive than Canada's and most of the rest of the world. At the WTO, the United States faced significant pushback, principally from India and Brazil and other less developed countries (Watal and Taubman 2015, pp. 299–301).

With a multilateral bargain in the works, Canada, the United States and Mexico took to negotiating their own trilateral IP chapter in the context of NAFTA. The NAFTA IP chapter (ch. 17) was modeled on a draft chapter of the anticipated Agreement on Trade-Related Aspects of

Intellectual Property Rights (TRIPS) (Levy and Weiser 1993, p. 676). Canada's agreement to certain minimum IP standards across all major types of IP, and refusal to agree to others, led to the first IP FTA chapter of its kind. The achievement set a strong foundation for a deal at the multilateral level. Indeed, the balance struck in TRIPS closely resembles the balance struck in NAFTA.

Following TRIPS, the United States and the EU pivoted toward entry into bilateral FTAs with smaller countries, often imposing "TRIPS-plus" IP provisions reflecting measures that they were not able to achieve at the TRIPS negotiating table (Grosse Ruse-Khan 2011, p. 328; Akhtar et al. 2020, pp. 27, 31, 38). These measures often included enhanced pharmaceutical IP protection, removal of exceptions to patentability and extended and expanded copyright protection.

The EU advanced such a position when negotiating the Comprehensive Economic and Trade Agreement (CETA) with Canada in the early 2010s, culminating in an agreement in 2014 (Webster 2014, p. E565). Although Canada resisted many of the EU's IP demands, Canada did agree to enhance pharmaceutical IP protection and introduce significantly expanded protection for Geographical Indications (GIs). Canada also agreed to further harmonize its IP system with the international community by complying with widely adopted international copyright, trademark, industrial design and patent treaties (CETA, arts 20.7, 20.13, 20.26).

Canada took further steps to expand IP protection during negotiations of the Trans-Pacific Partnership (TPP) Agreement. The United States had attempted to include extensive TRIPS-plus provisions that would have gone quite far to harmonize the TPP states parties with US IP law. Canada and the other parties eventually did agree to several IP-enhancing measures, including extended copyright and patent protection, market protection for biological medicines and stronger trade secret measures. As negotiations toward the United States–Mexico–Canada Agreement (USMCA) began, the United States' withdrawal from TPP led to suspension of many of these measures in the Comprehensive and Progressive Agreement for Trans-Pacific Partnership (CPTPP) (Global Affairs Canada 2018a; b).

Intellectual Property Protection in the USMCA

Although the United States has repeatedly accused Canada of providing inadequate IP protection (USTR 2016, 2017, 2018, 2019), Canada had undergone such a transformation of its IP laws as result of CETA and TPP commitments that perceived inadequacies had been nearly fully addressed by the time negotiation of the USMCA began. Canada's efforts to suspend IP commitments in the TPP also gave Canada and Mexico some negotiating room within the USMCA.

In the end, the commitments in the USMCA reflect a bargain very similar to the bargain struck in TPP before the US had withdrawn, with the notable exceptions that Canada agreed to enhance protection for biologic medicines (ten instead of eight years) and to provide patent term adjustments for delays at the Patent Office. The former obligation was ultimately removed as part of a bargain between US House Democrats and the White House (Wiseman et al. 2019).

The structure of the USMCA's IP chapter, Chapter 20, is typical of IP chapters within trade agreements. After setting out the parties' general commitments, the chapter is subdivided into sections devoted to enumerated forms of IP—trademarks, GIs, patents and pharmaceuticals, industrial designs, copyrights and trade secrets—followed by a section on IP enforcement.

Although typical in form, the chapter goes further than other developed country trade agreements in setting minimum standards for IP protection, and Canada's reputation for taking a balanced approach to IP will cause the USMCA IP chapter to set new norms for IP protection as future trade agreements are negotiated.

General Provisions

Cooperation

Section B (arts 20.12 to 20.16) of Chapter 20 establishes a framework for cooperation between the parties for matters concerning IP. This institutional framework provides a mechanism to ensure the United States, Mexico and Canada maintain communication and exchange of information regarding domestic IP policy and law, beyond the specific obligations and commitments contained in the USMCA. The cooperative framework requires each party to establish a Committee on Intellectual Property Rights (IPR Committee), composed of government representatives, that shall meet within a year of the USMCA coming into force, and on an as-needed basis thereafter (USMCA, art. 20.14). The IPR Committee is responsible for dealing with a wide range of issues for which inter-country coordination is important, but detailed negotiation was not practical or possible, including most notably:

i. approaches for reducing infringement and effective strategies for removing underlying incentives for infringement;
ii. strengthening border enforcement of IPRs;
iii. exchanging information on the value of trade secrets;
iv. enhancing procedural fairness with respect to choice of venue in patent litigation;
v. coordinating the recognition and protection of GIs.

These enumerated topics are those of particular current interest on which the law and domestic policy are expected to evolve over the medium term, and coordination on these topics is likely to drive the parties' domestic policies on these topics. Beyond the matters overseen by the IPR Committee, the provisions specifically require the parties to cooperate with respect to patent law and policy, namely through facilitating and sharing information and harmonization of processes to reduce the complexity and cost of obtaining patent protection (USMCA, art. 20.15).

Investor-State Dispute Settlement

A notable omission from the USCMA, as compared to NAFTA, is a mechanism for investor-state dispute settlement (ISDS) involving Canada and another party.

Formerly, under Chapter 11 of NAFTA, Canadian investors were able to submit a claim to arbitration against the United States or Mexican governments for failure to comply with international investment obligations, and foreign investors were able to assert the same against the Canadian government, subject to specific exceptions. Eli Lilly famously, though unsuccessfully, sued the Canadian government in 2013 under this mechanism in relation to the Canadian courts' application of the utility requirement in patent law.[3] Chapter 14 of the USMCA replaces Chapter 11 of NAFTA, and while a modified ISDS mechanism is still available for the United States and Mexico, Canada did not consent to the provisions and, as such, is not subject to the framework.[4]

Canada's decision to withhold consent means matters of IP law between Canada and the United States are no longer subject to review by arbitral tribunals under the ISDS framework. This leaves investors to seek recourse in cases of disputes either to the USMCA's general state-to-state dispute settlement mechanism or to the other party's domestic courts. However, Canada is still subject to an ISDS framework with Mexico as part of the CPTPP, thereby leaving open the possibility that investment issues concerning IP law could be addressed through such a framework.

TRADEMARKS

Section C (arts 20.17 to 20.27) of Chapter 20 outlines the parties' commitments with respect to trademark protection. However, the USMCA does not create significant new obligations for Canada's trademark regime. The requirements outlined in Section C were already included in Canada's recently modernized Trademarks Act as part of the ratification of international trademark treaties to which Canada committed in CETA, including the Madrid Protocol[5] and the Singapore Treaty,[6] and in the CPTPP.

The USMCA trademark provisions are intended to facilitate trademark protection by harmonizing the trademark regimes within the United States, Canada and Mexico, and reducing the operational and administrative burdens associated with securing trademark protection. For example, the provisions seek to confirm a broad scope of trademark protection by extending beyond visual marks to include sound and scent marks (art. 20.17), and by permitting collective and certification marks (art. 20.18).

GEOGRAPHICAL INDICATIONS

Although GIs were not a particularly controversial topic in early IP chapters in trade agreements, this form of IP has become more controversial of late, and Canada has been in the middle of the controversy.

Historically, Canada had limited protection for GIs, covering wine and spirits only, and recognizing GI protection via its "official mark" pathway, which provides special protection for marks owned by public authorities (Trademarks Act, s 9). However, as the policy of the EU and its members is to expand protection for GIs, CETA saw Canada provide special protection for GIs for various foods in addition to wine and spirits and create a mechanism for registration of GIs in Canada (CETA, art. 20.17, annex 20-C).

In contrast with the EU, the United States has been vocally opposed to the protection of GIs, and expansive GI protection was one issue preventing meaningful progress of the Transatlantic Trade and Investment Partnership, a proposed trade agreement between the EU and the United States (Johnson 2017, p. 15; Puccio 2016, p. 14; European Commission 2016, p. 17). During TPP negotiations, the United States committed participants to restrictions on GI protection to ensure that GIs would not unduly interfere with legitimate trademark rights (TPP, arts 18.30–18.36). These measures were not suspended when the United States withdrew from the TPP.

Like in the TPP, the GI provisions in the USMCA provide safeguards against overly protective GIs. The GI provisions, however, are structured so as not to be inconsistent with the GI commitments made by Canada in CETA.

Section E (arts 20.29 to 20.35) of Chapter 20 of the USMCA addresses GI-related matters. Article 20.30 sets out obligations regarding the processing of applications for GI protection. Key features of Article 20.30 are clauses (g) through (k), which provide mechanisms for opposing and cancelling GIs and require that written reasons be provided when such decisions are made. Article 20.31 then provides grounds on which a GI must be made vulnerable to objection or cancellation, including where the GI is confusing with a pre-existing trademark or reflects a term customary in common language as the common name for the relevant good in the territory. Article 20.32 goes so far as to provide guidelines for determining whether a term is the term customary in the common language for the good.

Article 20.35 concerns the safeguards to be applied when a party recognizes a GI pursuant to an international agreement. This provision immunizes previously agreed GIs and GIs for wine and spirits from several of the GI restrictions in Section E. However, for future GIs recognized by trade agreements, Article 20.35 will require that such recognition be subject to procedures that may result in successful opposition to GIs. In this respect, Canada may now be hamstrung in recognizing GIs in future trade agreements in the manner in which they are recognized under CETA.

PATENTS AND PHARMACEUTICALS

The intersection between IP and trade policy around the world has been largely driven by patents and other IP forms directed to pharmaceutical and biotechnological products. Much of the TRIPS negotiation related to the extension of patent and trade secret protection for pharmaceuticals (Watal and Taubman 2015, pp. 68, 80, 111). The HIV/AIDS crisis in the late 1990s and early 2000s centered around inadequate flexibility in TRIPS to allow for countries with domestic manufacturing capacity to enable supply of essential HIV/AIDS medicines to developing countries without violating TRIPS (Cohen-Kohler et al. 2008, p. 233).

Since Canada abolished its compulsory licensing regime at the time of the original NAFTA, Canada has incrementally enhanced its pharmaceutical IP protection to meet and then exceed international norms. With the USMCA, Canada's trade commitments in the field of patents and pharmaceuticals are among the most significant in the world. Canada has now acceded to essentially all of the United States' demands for pharmaceutical IP protection that had followed TRIPS.

Section F (arts 20.36 to 20.51) of Chapter 20 addresses patents and undisclosed test or other data relating to agricultural, biotechnological and pharmaceutical products. For the most part, this section codifies commitments that already reflect Canadian law, with some noteworthy observations.

Article 20.36 of the USMCA sets out the minimum requirements for patentable subject matter. A sentence under the analogous, though suspended, provision of the TPP (art. 18.37) allowing parties to restrict patent claims to new processes using a known product has been removed. Under the USMCA, a party may not limit claims for new processes of using a known product to those that do not claim the use of the product as such. This commitment should not change Canadian law, but it does reflect an agreement among USMCA parties that restrictions on patentability of pharmaceuticals seen in other countries, most notably in India, ought not to be permitted.

Provisions for adjusting terms of patent protection for Patent Office delays have also been incorporated into the USMCA. A similar provision was included in the TPP (art. 18.46) but was suspended when the United States withdrew from that agreement. Article 20.44 provides for adjustment of a patent's term to compensate for delays in issuance of a patent beyond five years from the date of filing or three years after an examination request, whichever is later. Practically, this change will provide greater protection to patentees forced to wait longer for patent issuance, but may also make determination of a patent's expiry date more difficult. Canada will have 4.5 years to implement this change, which has the potential to significantly affect Canadian patent practice.

The provision linked most directly to healthcare costs at the time of the USMCA's negotiation was the guaranteed period of market protection for new biologic medicines. Currently, Canada provides eight years of guaranteed protection. The originally unveiled USMCA required a period of market protection for biologics lasting at least ten years from a product's date of first marketing approval, and this concession was widely viewed as Canada's most significant within the IP chapter. However, after the Democratic Party took control of the US House of Representatives in the 2018 midterm elections, this provision was removed as part of a bargain between the White House and House Democrats to move forward with the USMCA (Wiseman et al. 2019).

INDUSTRIAL DESIGNS

Section G (arts 20.52 to 20.55) of Chapter 20 outlines the parties' agreement regarding the protection of industrial designs (protected as design patents in the United States). As is the case with the trademark provisions, the USMCA does not create any new obligations for Canada's industrial design law. The requirements outlined in Section G of the USMCA were already included in recent changes to the Industrial Design Act,[7] after Canada acceded to the Hague Agreement[8] in 2018.

Summarily, the USCMA requires each party to ensure that industrial design protection is available to a standard consistent with the requirements outlined in TRIPS (art. 20.52). The parties' industrial design regime must utilize an electronic system to apply for industrial design protection and must make protected industrial designs available for viewing to the public (art. 20.54). The provisions also require at least 15 years of industrial design protection (art. 20.55) and provide for a grace period where any information publicly disclosed by the applicant within 12 months of its industrial design application will not be used to determine whether the industrial design is new, original or non-obvious and, thus, eligible for protection.

COPYRIGHT

Section H (arts 20.56 to 20.68) of Chapter 20 details the scope and standards for protection of copyright and related rights in the United States, Canada and Mexico, many of which were considered during the TPP negotiations. Canada's copyright regime seeks to balance the rights of creators and users, and, arguably, the copyright provisions in the USCMA allow for such balance. Yet, implementation of some USMCA provisions into Canadian law required modifying the Copyright Act to provide increased protection to creators. The most notable provisions are discussed below.

The most notable change to Canadian copyright law following ratification of the USMCA is an increase in the term of copyright protection. Article 20.62 provides for a term of copyright protection of not less than 70 years after an author's death, an increase from Canada's previous 50-year term. Article 20.62 also provides for two additional bases for calculating a term of protection, if not based on the life of a natural person: (i) not less than 75 years from the end of the calendar year of the first authorized publication of the work, performance or phonogram; or (ii) failing such authorized publication within 25 years from the creation of the work, performance or phonogram, not less than 70 years from the end of the calendar year of the creation of the work, performance or phonogram.

Article 20.61 requires each party to provide performers and producers of phonograms the exclusive right to authorize or prohibit the broadcasting or any communication to the public of their performances or phonograms and the making available to the public of those performances or phonograms in such a way that members of the public may access them from a place and time individually chosen by them. However, parties have the ability to tailor the legal rights held by creators in broadcasts through analog transmissions and other non-interactive means, provided any limitations adopted by the party do not prejudice the right of the creator to obtain equitable remuneration.

Articles 20.66 and 20.67 require each party to establish adequate and effective legal remedies and penalties to guard against the circumvention of a creator's effective technological measure (i.e. digital mechanism that control access to a protected work) or rights management information (i.e. any information that is attached to or embodied in a work to permit identification of the creator), respectively.

Section H includes several other commitments that should not materially affect current Canadian law, including, for example: the general obligation to establish a copyright regime providing for the creators' rights of reproduction, communication and distribution of their works, performances or phonograms (arts 20.57–20.59.); no hierarchy of authorization between authors, performers or producers (art. 20.60); compliance with Article 18 of the Berne Convention[9] and TRIPS Article 14.6 regarding works in the public domain (art. 20.63); only limited exceptions and limitations to the exclusive rights granted to creators that do not unreasonably prejudice their interests (art. 20.64); the ability for any economic rights in copyrights or related rights to be contractually transferred (art. 20.65); and the ability for collective management societies to administer royalties (art. 20.68).

TRADE SECRETS

Section I (arts 20.69 to 20.77) of Chapter 20 deals with trade secret protection. Unlike for other types of IP, there is not currently a unified international approach for trade secret protection. Trade secrets can be protected under criminal law, contract or tort law, or by way of dedicated statute at the federal or provincial/state level. At the time of the first NAFTA, none of the parties had a dedicated trade secret statute at the federal level, and trade secret commitments under NAFTA were comparatively light.

The situation has evolved, in light of recent US concerns that certain foreign governments and companies are misappropriating US-originating trade secrets with impunity. However, unlike the United States, which now provides for trade secret protection through dedicated legislation at the federal[10] and state[11] level, Canada currently does not have federal or provincial legislation dedicated solely to the protection of trade secrets. Instead, protection of trade secrets in Canada occurs through the common law,[12] the Security of Information Act and the Criminal Code, depending on the circumstances. However, many of the protective measures found in the United States regarding trade secret protection made their way into the TPP (art. 18.78) and most recently into the USMCA, signaling a trend toward establishing a more cohesive and uniform approach to trade secret policy.

In general, the USMCA calls for more specific requirements for the protection of trade secrets, thereby enhancing the notion of trade secrets as a proprietary asset, particularly through civil and criminal enforcement. Article 20.70 of the USMCA requires each party to establish civil judicial procedures for trade secret protection, with no limit on the duration of protection, so long as the information still constitutes a trade secret as defined in Article 20.72.[13] Further, Articles 20.74 and 20.77 enhance trade secret protection in the course of civil proceedings by providing mechanisms for litigants to prevent public disclosure in the course of litigation, and preventing government officials from disclosing trade secrets outside the scope of their official duties. Given trade secret protection in Canada has been a product of common law, these provisions likely do not require any specific changes to legislation at this time, though specific issues may expose themselves in the course of future litigation, potentially necessitating legislative reform.

Article 20.71 of the USMCA requires criminal procedures and penalties for the unauthorized and willful misappropriation of a trade secret, and such procedures and penalties may be limited to acts which are for the purposes of commercial advantage or financial gain; related to a product or service in national or international commerce; or intended to injure the owner of the trade secret. A similar requirement is also found under the TPP (art. 18.78). While Canada's Security of Information Act (sec. 19) already criminalized economic espionage and satisfied the TPP requirements, the Criminal Code(sec. 391) was recently amended to criminalize the misappropriation or unauthorized communication of a trade secret by anyone, thereby criminalizing trade secret disclosure beyond the scope of foreign economic espionage. The trade secret provisions in the Criminal Code are *mens rea* offences—the perpetrator must have actual knowledge of the information as a trade secret and must knowingly have obtained that information by deceit, falsehood or fraudulent means—and provide a specific carve-out for trade secrets obtained by independent development or through reverse engineering.

In addition to enhancing protection of trade secrets through the imposition of civil and criminal procedures and penalties, the USMCA acknowledges the commercial value and utility of trade secrets as licensable information. Article 20.76 ensures that commercialization of trade secrets can be leveraged by preventing parties from discouraging or impeding the voluntary licensing of a trade secret through the imposition of excessive or discriminatory conditions.

ENFORCEMENT

Section J (arts 20.78 to 20.88) of Chapter 20 deals with parties' commitments concerning enforcement of IPRs. As noted above, Canada has been widely criticized by the United States for not adequately enforcing IPRs, causing Canada be placed on the United States Trade Representative's "Priority Watch List" in its annual Special 301 Report on IPRs as recently as 2018 (USTR 2018). The United States cited poor border enforcement, specifically the lack of customs authority to inspect or detain counterfeit or pirated goods transshipping through Canada, and deficient copyright protection, as key issues. Following negotiation of the USMCA, Canada was moved to the lesser Watch List in 2019, where it remained in 2020 (USTR 2019, 2020).

The USMCA provisions regarding border measures acknowledge the importance of cooperation between the parties with a view to eliminating international trade in counterfeit and pirated goods. Perhaps most importantly, from the United States' perspective, the provisions specifically require border control agents to intercept counterfeit goods traveling through Canada on their way to other markets.

Article 20.83 requires each party to provide for an application system, whereby a right holder can initiate procedures for a party's authorities to suspend and detain suspected counterfeit or pirated goods. The provisions mandate specific features of the application system, including evidentiary requirements and the provision of a security or a bond to protect against abuse of the system. As referenced above, the provisions specifically require each party to initiate border measures *ex officio* against suspected counterfeit or pirated goods under customs' control that are imported, destined for export, in transit and passing through a free trade zone or bonded warehouse and allow the parties to exchange information regarding such counterfeit or pirated goods.

Prior to ratification, a system of this nature was already in effect in Canada by way of the Request for Assistance applications under the Copyright Act (subsecs 44.01–44.12) and Trademarks Act (subsecs 51.03–51.12). However, customs officers were expressly prevented from intercepting counterfeit goods entering Canada during transit only (Copyright Act, subsection 44.01.2.b; Trademarks Act, subsection 51.03.2.d). In implementing the USCMA, the Copyright Act and Trademarks Act were recently amended to provide Canada's customs officers with the ability to prevent counterfeit or pirated goods being transshipped through

Canada's borders to foreign manufacturers into other markets, like in the United States (CUSMA Implementation Act, subsections 31, 109.3).

While Canada gave way to the US request for stricter border control measures during USMCA negotiations, it did not concede with respect to another contentious issue: liability of Internet service providers (ISPs) for matters of copyright infringement. Article 20.88 of the USMCA sets up a system of legal remedies for right holders and safe harbors for ISPs by establishing a framework whereby ISPs have the ability to preclude liability for copyright infringements that they do not control, initiate or direct. The framework is referred to as a "Notice and Takedown" framework, whereby ISPs are not liable for copyright infringement if they receive notice of such infringement and expeditiously remove or disable access to the infringing content on their networks. However, Annex 20-B (Annex to Section J) indicates that the Notice and Takedown obligations under Paragraphs 3, 4 and 6 of Article 20.88 do not apply to a party, provided it continues to keep certain other limitations and exceptions in place: Canada's "Notice and Notice" regime qualifies as such an exception. The Notice and Notice regime, established under the Copyright Act (subsecs 41.25–41.26), requires ISPs who receive notice from copyright owners regarding infringing content to forward those notices on to Internet subscribers, alerting them that their Internet accounts are linked to copyright infringing activities.

Other notable changes with regard to enforcement include stronger policy language concerning the imposition of statutory damages for IP infringement, and criminalization of activities that interfere with satellite signals. Specifically, Article 20.81 sets out the requirement for damages to compensate for the injury to the right holder suffered as result of the infringement, with the ability for a copyright or trademark right holder to elect pre-established damages or additional damages (which may include punitive or exemplary damages), both of which should be determined so as to have a deterrent effect on future behavior. Article 20.85 requires each party to make the interception of satellite signals, or the manufacturing and distributing of equipment to facilitate such interception, a criminal offence, an issue that was already addressed in Canada pursuant to the Radiocommunications Act.[14]

Going Forward

Generally speaking, although lengthy, the IP chapter within the USMCA does not contain too many obligations requiring changes to Canadian IP law. Rather, Chapter 20 codifies the current state of USMCA parties' mutual understanding regarding minimum IP protection and harmonization. Canada has agreed to a few notable expansions of IP protection, including to copyright term and patent term adjustments, with delays in implementation of these measures permitted.

Overall, the USMCA sets a new baseline level of protection for IP chapters in trade agreements for countries having elevated protection and also sets an anchor to protect against the broad GI protection that the EU is actively seeking as part of its trade policy. It is not unlikely that the United States, if it seeks to join the CPTPP, will try to introduce aspects of the USMCA into the CPTPP to broaden the impact of the USMCA IP deal. Like the IP chapter in NAFTA, Chapter s 20 of the USMCA may set new norms for international IP protection that persist for decades to come.

Notes

1. See *CCH Canadian Ltd v Law Society of Upper Canada*, 2001 SCC 13, 1 SCR 339; *Theberge v Galerie D'Art du Petit Champlain Inc*, 2002 SCC 34, 2 SCR 336.
2. See Regulations Amending the Patented Medicines (Notice of Compliance) Regulations, 2017.
3. See *Eli Lilly and Company v. Canada* (2017), International Centre for Settlement of Investment Disputes. http://icsidfiles.worldbank.org/icsid/ICSIDBLOBS/OnlineAwards/C3544/DC10133_En.pdf.
4. Canada did consent to Annex 14-C, which allows for submission of a claim to arbitration concerning a legacy investment (defined as an investment that occurred between NAFTA 1994's in-force date and termination date) in accordance with Chapter 11 of NAFTA for three years following the USCMA's coming into force date, along with the conclusion of existing claims. See USMCA (ch. 14, annex 14-C).
5. Protocol Relating to the Madrid Agreement Concerning the International Registration of Marks, done June 27, 1989.
6. Singapore Treaty on the Law of Trademarks, done March 28, 2006.
7. Industrial Design Act, RSC 1985, c I-9.
8. Geneva Act of the Hague Agreement Concerning the International Registration of Industrial Designs, done July 2, 1999.

9. Berne Convention for the Protection of Literary and Artistic Works, done September 9, 1886, revised July 24, 1971.
10. Defend Trade Secrets Act, 18 USC § 1836.
11. Uniform Trade Secrets Act (1985).
12. See *Cadbury Schweppes Inc. v. FBI Foods Ltd,* (1999) 1 SCR 142, 167 DLR (4th) 577 (SCC); *Merck Frosst Canada Ltd. v. Canada (Health),* 2012 SCC 3, 1 SCR 23.
13. Article 20.72 defines "trade secret" as information that: (a) is secret in the sense that it is not, as a body or in the precise configuration and assembly of its components, generally known among or readily accessible to persons within the circles that normally deal with the kind of information in question; (b) has actual or potential commercial value because it is secret; and (c) has been subject to reasonable steps under the circumstances, by the person lawfully in control of the information, to keep it secret.
14. Radiocommunications Act, RSC 1985, c R-2 (subsecs 9–10).

References

Akhtar, Shayerah Ilias, Liana Wong, and Ian F. Fergusson. 2020. *Intellectual Property Rights and International Trade.* Congressional Research Service, RL3429. https://fas.org/sgp/crs/row/RL34292.pdf.

Cohen-Kohler, Jillian Clare, Lisa Forman, and Nathaniel Lipkus. 2008. Addressing Legal and Political Barriers to Global Pharmaceutical Access: Options for Remedying the Impact of the Agreement on Trade-Related Aspects of Intellectual Property Rights (TRIPS) and the Imposition of TRIPS-plus Standards. *Health Economics, Policy and Law* 3 (3): 229–256.

Grosse Ruse-Khan, Henning. 2011. The International Law Relation Between TRIPS and Subsequent TRIPS-Plus Free Trade Agreements: Towards Safeguarding TRIPS Flexibilities? *Journal of Intellectual Property Law* 18 (2): 325–65.

Johnson, Renée. 2017. *Geographical Indications (GIs) in U.S. Food and Agricultural Trade.* Congressional Research Service, R44556. https://fas.org/sgp/crs/misc/R44556.pdf.

Levy, Charles S., and Stuart M. Weiser. 1993. The NAFTA: A Watershed for Protection of Intellectual Property. *International Lawyer* 27 (3): 671–689.

Maskus, Keith E, and William Ridley. 2016. *Intellectual Property-Related Preferential Trade Agreements and the Composition of Trade.* Robert Schuman Centre for Advanced Studies, Research Paper No. 2016/35. https://www.oecd.org/site/stipatents/IPSDM17_1.1_Maskus_paper.pdf.

Puccio, Laura. 2016. *EU-US Negotiations on TTIP: A Survey of Current Issues.* European Parliamentary Research Service, PE 586.606. https://www.eur

oparl.europa.eu/RegData/etudes/IDAN/2016/586606/EPRS_IDA(201
6)586606_EN.pdf.

Watal, Jayashree, and Antony Taubman. 2015. *The Making of the TRIPS Agreement. Personal Insights from the Uruguay Round Negotiations*. Geneva: World Trade Organization. https://www.wto.org/english/res_e/booksp_e/trips_agree_e/history_of_trips_nego_e.pdf.

Webster, Paul Christopher. 2014. CETA: A Win for Canada or European Pharma? *Canadian Medical Association Journal* 186 (15): E565–66. https://www.ncbi.nlm.nih.gov/pmc/articles/PMC4203620/.

Wiseman, Paul, Linda A. Johnson, and Kevin Freking. 2019. North America Trade Pact Deals Rare Setback to Big Pharma. *The Associated Press*, December 19. https://apnews.com/article/fb54abbce60e1fe44926becb84e86edf.

OFFICIAL DOCUMENTS

Agreement on Trade-Related Aspects of Intellectual Property Rights (TRIPS), signed April 15, 1994, entered into force January 1, 1995. https://www.wto.org/english/docs_e/legal_e/31bis_trips_e.pdf.

Canada-United States-Mexico Agreement (CUSMA) Implementation Act, SC 2020, c 1.

Comprehensive and Progressive Agreement for Trans-Pacific Partnership (CPTPP), signed March 8, 2018, entered into force December 30, 2018. https://www.mfat.govt.nz/en/trade/free-trade-agreements/free-trade-agreements-in-force/cptpp/comprehensive-and-progressive-agreement-for-trans-pacific-partnership-text-and-resources/.

Comprehensive Economic and Trade Agreement (CETA), signed October 30, 2016, entered provisionally into force September 21, 2017. http://international.gc.ca/trade-commerce/trade-agreements-accords-commerciaux/agr-acc/ceta-aecg/text-texte/toc-tdm.aspx?lang=eng.

Copyright Act, RSC 1985, c C-42.

Criminal Code, RSC 1985, c C-46.

European Commission. 2016. *Report of the 13th Round of Negotiations for the Transatlantic Trade and Investment Partnership*. http://trade.ec.europa.eu/doclib/docs/2016/may/tradoc_154581.pdf.

Global Affairs Canada. 2018a. *Economic Impact of Canada's Participation in the Comprehensive and Progressive Agreement for Trans-Pacific Partnership*, February 16. https://www.international.gc.ca/trade-commerce/trade-agreements-accords-commerciaux/agr-acc/cptpp-ptpgp/impact-repercussions.aspx?lang=eng.

Global Affairs Canada. 2018b. *What does the CPTPP Mean for Intellectual Property?* November 23. https://www.international.gc.ca/trade-commerce/

trade-agreements-accords-commerciaux/agr-acc/cptpp-ptpgp/sectors-sec teurs/ip-pi.aspx?lang=eng.

North American Free Trade Agreement (NAFTA), signed December 17, 1992, entered into force January 1, 1994, suspended July 1, 2020. https://www.int ernational.gc.ca/trade-commerce/trade-agreements-accords-commerciaux/ agr-acc/nafta-alena/fta-ale/index.aspx?lang=eng.

Office of the United States Trade Representative (USTR). 2016. *USTR Releases Special 301 Report on Protection of American Intellectual Property Rights Across the World*, April 27. https://ustr.gov/about-us/policy-offices/press-office/press-releases/2016/april/ustr-releases-special-301-report.

Office of the United States Trade Representative (USTR). 2017. *USTR Releases 2017 Special 301 Report on Intellectual Property Rights*, April 28. https://ustr.gov/about-us/policy-offices/press-office/press-releases/2017/april/ ustr-releases-2017-special-301-report.

Office of the United States Trade Representative (USTR). 2018. *USTR Releases 2018 Special 301 Report on Intellectual Property Rights*, April 27. https:// ustr.gov/about-us/policy-offices/press-office/press-releases/2018/april/ ustr-releases-2018-special-301-report.

Office of the United States Trade Representative (USTR). 2019. *USTR Releases Annual Special 301 Report on Intellectual Property Protection and Review of Notorious Markets for Piracy and Counterfeiting*, April 25. https://ustr.gov/about-us/policy-offices/press-office/ press-releases/2019/april/ustr-releases-annual-special-301.

Office of the United States Trade Representative (USTR). 2020. *USTR Releases Annual Special 301 Report on Intellectual Property Protection and Review of Notorious Markets for Counterfeiting and Piracy*, April 29. https://ustr. gov/about-us/policy-offices/press-office/press-releases/2020/april/ustr-rel eases-annual-special-301-report-intellectual-property-protection-and-review-notorious.

Security of Information Act, RSC 1985, c O-5.

Trademarks Act, RSC 1985, c T-13.

Trans-Pacific Partnership (TPP), signed February 4, 2016. https://www.intern ational.gc.ca/trade-commerce/trade-agreements-accords-commerciaux/agr-acc/tpp-ptp/text-texte/toc-tdm.aspx?lang=eng.

United States – Mexico – Canada Agreement (USMCA), signed November 30, 2018, amended December 10, 2019, entered into force July 1, 2020. https://www.international.gc.ca/trade-commerce/trade-agreements-accords-commerciaux/agr-acc/cusma-aceum/text-texte/toc-tdm.aspx?lang=eng.

CHAPTER 9

From the NAFTA to the USMCA: Competition, Monopolies and State-Owned Enterprises

Michèle Rioux

The European Union (EU) developed a very ambitious supranational law dealing with state and private conducts. This is a unique and quite elaborate scheme of cooperation and integration at the regional level. In North America, by contrast, the regional integration model is decentralized and based on national laws (Fora 2014). The United States–Mexico–Canada Agreement (USMCA) does not fundamentally change this model, but it certainly integrates several new cooperation initiatives that emerged in the field of competition with the entry into force and the renegotiation of the North American Free Trade Agreement (NAFTA) (Bradford and Büthe 2015). North America adopted a decentralization model rather

M. Rioux (✉)
Department of Political Science, Université du Québec à Montréal, Montreal, QC, Canada
e-mail: rioux.michele@uqam.ca

© The Author(s), under exclusive license to Springer Nature Switzerland AG 2022
G. Gagné and M. Rioux (eds.), *NAFTA 2.0*, Canada and International Affairs,
https://doi.org/10.1007/978-3-030-81694-0_9

127

than aiming at the creation of a supranational body. As Davidow points out:

> Assuming that one had very strong ambitions regarding competition rules within a free trade zone, there appear to be three major goals one might want to achieve: 1) standardization of the national antitrust laws of the member states within the zone; 2) institutionalization of mechanisms to ensure cooperation in the enforcement of the national laws to trans-border violations; 3) creation of a supranational body to arbitrate disputes or to enforce an international antitrust law which embodies the same principles as are contained in the national laws of the member states. (Davidow 1987, p. 26)

In this chapter, I analyze the provisions of Chapter 21 of the USMCA regarding competition policy and of Chapter 22 on state-owned enterprises (SOEs) and designated monopolies, while comparing them with Chapter 15 of the NAFTA dealing with competition policy, monopolies and state enterprises. I first look at NAFTA (section 1) before discussing the innovations of the USMCA (section 2). Then, after highlighting key aspects of NAFTA and the USMCA, I conclude on the importance of competition chapters in trade agreements, their strategic dimension and their limits in relation to regional and global competition regulation (section 3).

Chapter 15 of the NAFTA

Before NAFTA, the United States–Canada Free Trade Agreement (USCFTA) opened grounds for widespread and significant economic restructuring aimed at making North America the leader of innovation and competitiveness in the world economy. Facing pressures from the United States to deregulate the Canadian economy and many instances of US extraterritorial antitrust measures or trade conflicts, Canada wished to secure its access to the US market and suggested that the agreement should allow for the use of competition laws and principles to deal with anti-dumping and other competition issues. The United States had signed a free trade agreement (FTA)with Israel that did not follow that route and, as it happened, Chapter 15 of the NAFTA did not exempt Canada from the anti-dumping or countervailing duty laws. Not only was the United States reluctant, but one must put this in the context of stormy antitrust relations and different competition law approaches, even though Canada and the United States both adopted antitrust laws at the end of the nineteenth century.[1] Despite significant integration between the two economies, national competition laws strongly differ in terms of their institutions and approaches. Besides, the United States had adopted a strong stance on foreign trade.

Nevertheless, the convergence of economic policies resulted from a close relationship between US President Ronald Reagan and Canadian Prime Minister Brian Mulroney who both supported *laisser-faire, laisser-passer* as a proactive approach to increase competition. Brian Mulroney embarked on privatization and deregulation of several industrial sectors. The USCFTA and later NAFTA were about deregulation and using trade to allow for greater competitiveness in North America.

Two words dominated in economic policy debates: innovation and competition. Policy guidelines prioritized innovation and competition in almost every national and international policy regulatory sites. This was conducive to a retreat of the state in the economic sphere. Yet, according to Davidow (1987, p. 32), "[h]armonization of U.S. and Canadian antitrust approaches would not be a simple matter." For instance, extraterritoriality is specified in the United States, whereas in Canada it is not, since it reflects the British tradition of using territoriality as a basis for jurisdiction. The United States restricted this extraterritorial reach in 1982 with the use of the effects doctrine on domestic and export markets but it is much more significant than in Canada. The differences did not prevent cooperation but justified a regional decentralized approach based on cooperation of national authorities.

> Given that there are major obstacles to beginning the negotiations and to achieving an agreement, it appears doubtful that competition law harmonization will be achieved at this time or in conjunction with these [USCFTA] negotiations. ... Creation of the [free trade] zone, in turn, could then ultimately lead to further U.S.-Canadian coordination in the antitrust area. (Davidow 1987, pp. 36–37)

The situation got complicated as, early in the process of creating the USCFTA, Mexico was undergoing a process of economic changes in the hope of reaching a similar deal with the United States. When negotiation started, Canada joined in.

Mexico's economic industrial structures and economic policies were not easily harmonized with the United States and Canada. Mexico prepared in advance for NAFTA and, with regard to competition issues, was willing to make changes to its laws and policies to promote and enforce fair trade and free competition to gain better conditions for access to the US market.

> Though Mexico offered attractive natural advantages, such as a highly trainable, wage competitive workforce and a close proximity to the U.S. border, Mexico's inward-looking and protectionist policies increased the risk of doing business in Mexico. Monopolies, collusion, and corruption were the rule rather than the exception- a fact that further deterred foreign businesses from trading and investing in Mexico. Now, under NAFTA, U.S. and Canadian businesses that may potentially invest in Mexico should consider what protections the Agreement affords to avoid some of these problems. These businesses should first examine the dispute resolution mechanism available for competition or antitrust disputes. ... While NAFTA provides a formal dispute resolution mechanism for conflicts regarding monopolies and state enterprises, it specifically exempts all other competition conflicts. (Murtaugh Collins 1994, pp. 161–162)

NAFTA (art. 1501.1) engaged the three countries to "adopt or maintain measures to proscribe anticompetitive business conduct." The required nature or form of such measures was not specified but included any law, regulation, procedure, requirement or practice.[2] Paradoxically, competition issues are exempted from dispute settlement under the NAFTA (art. 1501.3). Article 1501.2 states the importance of coordination and cooperation for effective enforcement of competition laws in the FTA zone.

This was especially precarious since, unlike Canada and the United States, Mexico did not have an antitrust tradition because it had sought to protect the national economy from US domination and American firms' monopolistic power. The effectiveness of consultations and cooperation efforts depended on the three trade partners to work on a common approach (Murtaugh Collins 1994, p. 164). Within this context, just months prior to the entry into force of the NAFTA, Mexico created a Federal Competition Commission.

> [T]he Commission has set the following two broad objectives to guide Mexico's change in strategy: (1) "to set the foundations of a modern market economy that can generate sustained growth in the medium term" and (2) "to redefine the State's role in the economy so that it may assist more effectively those that are most in need". (Murtaugh Collins 1994, p. 174)

This brings us to the issue of monopolies and state enterprises, that is, enterprises owned or controlled by governments. Parties can designate monopolies as well as establish and maintain SOEs, but they must ensure they act in a manner that is not inconsistent with the obligations under NAFTA through regulatory control, administrative supervision or the application of other measures (arts 1502 and 1503). Additional provisions target monopolies, notably they must act solely in accordance with commercial considerations in their purchase or sale of the monopoly good or service in the relevant market, and not use their monopoly position to engage, either directly or indirectly, in anticompetitive practices in a non-monopolized market in their territory that adversely affect an investment of an investor of another party (art. 1502.3).

NAFTA aimed to promote fair competition, but this was a means to competitiveness gains at the global level rather than a goal in itself. Each country remained sovereign with regard to defining its competition policy and exempted competition disputes from dispute settlement except for conflicts regarding monopolies and state enterprises. The United States saw competition policy issues related to NAFTA as a market access instrument. For Canada and Mexico, the interest was more related to find ways to face unilateral measures against alleged dumping issues or extraterritorial enforcement of US antitrust laws. Their interest was as well to reorient economic policies toward neoliberal policy approaches since the latter were apparently to bring a revival of North America as a competitive economic space able to face rivals from the EU and Asia.

Many were skeptic but, in the 1990s, North America, and more specifically the United States, became the leader in a trade and digital revolution that transformed trade and investment. North America as a regional economic space managed to regain competitive edge with very competitive and innovative technology industries. This led to new digital trade roads, contrasting with two decades of sluggish economic activities in the 1970s and 1980s, when North America was looking to revitalize its economic insertion to the world economy. Harmonization in terms of competition policy has mostly meant alignment on the US model of trade and investment regulation.

This process participated in a more general strategy of norm diffusion deployed by the United States. After the agenda on competition issues was abandoned at the World Trade Organization (WTO), the International Competition Network (ICN) was created in the early 2000s. This contributed to enhanced cooperation at the regional scale. Between 1994 and the USMCA, a significant number of cooperation agreements were signed by the three North American partners and cooperation of national competition authorities was systematically organized and followed upon. Cooperation on competition policy has also taken place within the Organization for Economic Cooperation and Development (OECD), especially on issues such as coverage of competition laws, exceptions and exemptions from such laws and the core competition policy principles that may be included in a multilateral agreement.

CHAPTERS 21 AND 22 OF THE USMCA

The USMCA aims at the same goal as NAFTA, that is, ensuring the regulation of anticompetitive business conducts (Sokol 2009). The USMCA provisions seek to make sure that parties apply their respective national competition laws to commercial activities in their territories and, to this end, maintain national enforcement authorities. Yet, Chapters 21 and 22 build on 25 years of regional and international cooperation efforts that have led to more ambitious trade agreements, cooperation agreements and initiatives with regard to competition issues. As a result, the USMCA contains more ambitious competition enforcement and cooperation provisions. According to Brown and Ackhurst (2018), the extent to which the parties will take advantage of these enhanced mechanisms for cooperation remains to be seen since it is actually business as usual for competition law in the region.

Thus, the USMCA is more precise and ambitious and integrates many of the provisions developed in cooperation agreements on competition issues since NAFTA was signed. Under Chapter 21, the parties shall take appropriate action with respect to anticompetitive conduct on their own territory and elsewhere when a conduct has an appropriate nexus to their jurisdiction. They may provide for certain exemptions from the application of competition laws provided these are transparent and based on public policy objectives (art. 21.1).

Parties' competition authorities must abide by robust procedural fairness commitments (art. 21.2). These include: transparency, reasonable time frame, representation by legal counsel, confidentiality of strategic information, legal and factual basis of violations, ensuring decisions are communicated in writing, the opportunity to engage with national competition authorities, judicial review by a court or independent tribunal, and the criteria used for calculating a fine must be publicly known.

NAFTA recognized the importance of cooperation between competition authorities for enforcement. Article 21.3 of the USMCA provides that the parties shall cooperate notably in the area of consumer welfare, information sharing, common law enforcement concerns and activities such as training programs.[3] This may open the door to more cooperation on competition law enforcement in relation to merger reviews and cartels (Brown and Ackhurst 2018). The USMCA includes new provisions on consumer protection to create efficient, competitive markets and enhance consumer welfare. These require each party to adopt or maintain consumer protection laws that proscribe fraudulent and deceptive commercial activities. The provisions also call for cooperation and coordination that include the exchange of consumer complaints and other enforcement information (art. 21.4).

While the USMCA sets out more detailed requirements for enforcement than NAFTA did, the provisions will not have a practical impact on competition enforcement in North America. Such cooperative practices are commonplace and already exist through bilateral antitrust cooperation agreements (e.g. the Canada–Mexico Cooperation Agreement on Competition Law Enforcement) and more informal means. Also, in spite of all these new developments, like in the case of NAFTA, the USMCA provides that no party shall have recourse to dispute settlement under Chapter 14 (investment) or Chapter 31 (dispute settlement).

As for Chapter 22, the objective is to create a level playing field between private enterprises and SOEs and their private competitors. It preserves the Canadian and Mexican governments' ability to support SOEs that provide public services while addressing practices that favor SOEs engaged in commercial activities, ensuring that their activities are based on commercial considerations. Parties must make sure those entities act in a manner that is not inconsistent with their obligations under the USMCA. Similar to the Working Group on Trade and Competition under NAFTA, a Committee on State-Owned Enterprises and Designated Monopolies, composed of government representatives of each party, is created (art. 22.12). Within six months of the USMCA's entry into force, further negotiations shall begin so as to extend the application of the disciplines in this chapter (art. 22.14).

The USMCA builds on the WTO's exceptions for SOEs. Chapter 22 stipulates that SOEs act as commercial enterprises, except for providing a public service, buying and selling goods and services in a non-discriminatory manner. This resonates with a recent trade agreement, notably the Comprehensive and Progressive Agreement for Trans-Pacific Partnership, under which countries are required to disclose certain information regarding their SOEs (transparency) designed to encourage good corporate governance. The USMCA exempts SOEs with revenue below a certain dollar threshold, provides for country-specific exclusions and defines SOEs more clearly (when a state party owns more than 50% of the share capital, controls more than 50% of the voting rights, controls the enterprise through any other ownership interest or appoints a majority of members of the board of directors).

Chapter 22 could impact on SOEs in Mexico and Canada, as well as on the way North America responds to competition issues related to the COVID-19 pandemic. This resonates with Mexico's membership in the CPTPP and the investor-state dispute settlement provisions in strategic sectors (energy, telecom and infrastructure) under the USMCA. Let us recall that important reforms to competition law took place in Mexico in 2006, 2011 and in 2014 when the Mexican Antitrust Act was adopted (see Carreño Núñez de Álvarez and Alcantra 2019). Mexico's 2014 constitutional reform opened the country's electricity and energy markets to non-state investors, foreign and domestic. Undoubtedly, the Mexican competition environment has evolved in the context of the NAFTA and the WTO.[4]

Finally, under Annex 22-B, "if a panel has been established pursuant to Chapter 31 (Dispute Settlement) to examine a complaint arising under Article 22.4 (Non-Discriminatory Treatment and Commercial Considerations) or Article 22.6 (Non-Commercial Assistance), the disputing Parties may exchange written questions and responses, as set forth in paragraphs 2, 3, and 4, to obtain information relevant to the complaint that is not otherwise readily available." This contrasts with the fact that Chapter 21 is exempted from dispute settlement.

ISSUES, CHALLENGES AND CONCLUSION

NAFTA included competition law and enforcement commitments and required parties to maintain competition laws and cooperate in their enforcement. These obligations were not subject to dispute settlement, except for those regarding the notification and non-discriminatory treatment of monopolies and state enterprises. Chapter 15 provided for a

Working Group on Trade and Competition and trade officials from the three countries to report and make recommendations regarding the interaction of trade and competition policies in the region.

The USMCA builds on NAFTA and many institutional and normative innovations in other trade agreements, at the OECD, the ICN[5] and other governance sites. If NAFTA's effect on competition law and enforcement in North America was limited, the USMCA's impact will depend on the three partners to intensify their cooperation. Sokol (2007, p. 235) considers that "... in spite of the non-binding nature of competition policy chapters in Latin American [trade agreements], these chapters may still have value."

According to Sokol (2007), trade agreements may identify, shape and implement norms of competition policy. The current challenge is more complicated as the UMSCA partners will have to respond to competition issues arising from new global value chains that bring into interaction different economic models, the Big Tech monopolistic power and its impact (Browdie et al. 2020), as well as the pandemic situation shaping essential and non-essential sectors in different ways in the world economy (Imundo 2020). Strategic interests are always in the background of trade agreements and this is the case of the USMCA. Competition is a strategic and complex policy field, nationally and globally. It is based on notions that are challenged by fluctuations and structural changes. Competition policy is also a controversial domain as theories and approaches defining a market economy in terms of acceptable and unacceptable conducts of actors, private and public, are debated in terms of strategic, distributive and democratic terms.

NOTES

1. "To trace the history of U.S.-Canadian antitrust relations is to embark upon a roller coaster ride. Rigorous extraterritorial enforcement of U.S. antitrust policy against Canada has been followed by reactive Canadian blocking legislation" (Davidow 1987, p. 27). Davidow provides a documented historical account of these tensions.
2. In the case of Mexico, the Federal Law of Economic Competition; in the case of Canada, the Competition Act; and in the US case, the Sherman Act, Clayton Act and Federal Trade Commission Act. NAFTA required enforcement through "appropriate action" without specifying what this constituted.

3. The parties acknowledge the importance of cooperation and coordination internationally and the work of organizations, notably the Competition Committee of the OECD, and the ICN.
4. Within the WTO a dispute involving the Mexican telecommunications sector was resolved in favor of the United States. This marked the first WTO antitrust case (*Mexico—Measures Affecting Telecommunications Services*, 2004). Obligations in this sector are at the intersection of trade, competition and industrial policies, allowing to address combined public and private restraints to trade and competition (Fox 2006).
5. See the website of the ICN for more information, https://www.internati onalcompetitionnetwork.org/document-library/.

References

Bradford, Anu, and Tim Büthe. 2015. Competition Policy and Free Trade: Antitrust Provisions in PTAs. In *Trade Cooperation: The Purpose, Design and Effects of Preferential Trade Agreements*, ed. Andreas Dür and Manfred Elsig, 246–274. Cambridge: Cambridge University Press.

Browdie, Megan, Jacqueline Grise, Howard Morse, and Elizabeth Giordano. 2020. United States: Technology Mergers. *Global Competition Review*, October 19. https://globalcompetitionreview.com/review/the-antitrust-rev iew-of-the-americas/2021/article/united-states-technology-mergers.

Brown, Erin, and Kevin Ackhurst. 2018. *NAFTA, the USMCA, and Competition Law in North America*. Norton Rose Fulbright, October. https://www.nor tonrosefulbright.com/en-us/knowledge/publications/bc429788/nafta-the-usmca-and-competition-law-in-north-america.

Carreño Núñez de Álvarez, Fernando, and Paloma Alcantra. 2019. Mexico: Overview. *Global Competition Review*, September 20. https://globalcompet itionreview.com/review/the-antitrust-review-of-the-americas/2020/article/ mexico-overview.

Comprehensive and Progressive Agreement for Trans-Pacific Partnership (CPTPP), signed March 8, 2018, entered into force December 30, 2018. https://www.mfat.govt.nz/en/trade/free-trade-agreements/free-trade-agr eements-in-force/cptpp/comprehensive-and-progressive-agreement-for-trans-pacific-partnership-text-and-resources/.

Davidow, Joel. 1987. The United States/Canadian Antitrust Relationship in the Context of a Free Trade Zone. *Canada-United States Law Journal* 12 (8): 25–37. https://scholarlycommons.law.case.edu/cuslj/vol12/iss/8.

Fora, Andreea-Florina. 2014. Regional Trade Agreements and Competition Policy. Case Study: Eu, Asean And Nafta. University of Oradea. *Annals of Faculty of Economics* 1 (1): 86–94. https://ideas.repec.org/a/ora/journl/ v1y2014i1p86-94.html.

Fox, Eleanor M. 2006. The WTO's First Antitrust Case – *Mexican Telecom*: A Sleeping Victory for Trade and Competition. *Journal of International Economic Law* 9 (2): 271–292. https://doi.org/10.1093/jiel/jgl012.

Imundo, Aimee. 2020. United States: Department of Justice. *Global Competition Review*, October 20. https://globalcompetitionreview.com/review/the-antitrust-review-of-the-americas/2021.

Murtaugh Collins, Kathleen. 1994. Harmonizing the Antitrust Laws of NAFTA Signatories. *Loyola of Los Angeles International and Comparative Law Review* 17: 157–96. http://digitalcommons.lmu.edu/ilr/vol17/iss1/5.

North American Free Trade Agreement (NAFTA), signed December 17, 1992, entered into force January 1, 1994. https://www.nafta-sec-alena.org/Home/Legal-Texts/North-American-Free-Trade-Agreement.

Sokol, D. Daniel. 2007. Order Without (Enforceable) Law: Why Countries Enter into Non-Enforceable Competition Policy Chapters in Free Trade Agreements. *Chicago-Kent Law Review* 83 (1): 231–92. https://studentorgs.kentlaw.iit.edu/cklawreview/wp-content/uploads/sites/3/vol83no1/Sokol.pdf.

Sokol, D. Daniel. 2009. Competition Policy and Comparative Corporate Governance of State-Owned Enterprises. *Brigham Young University Law Review* 6: 1713–1812. https://ssrn.com/abstract=1548631.

United States – Canada Free Trade Agreement (USCFTA), signed January 2, 1988, entered into force January 1, 1989. http://www.international.gc.ca/trade-agreements-accords-commerciaux/assets/pdfs/cusfta-e.pdf.

United States-Mexico-Canada Agreement (USMCA), signed November 30, 2018, entered into force July 1, 2020. https://ustr.gov/trade-agreements/free-trade-agreements/united-states-mexico-canada-agreement/agreement-between.

CHAPTER 10

The USMCA: A "New Model" for Labor Governance in North America?

*Sandra Polaski, Kimberly A. Nolan García,
and Michèle Rioux*

The North American Free Trade Agreement (NAFTA) put the North American region on a new path of labor governance by including labor provisions in a preferential trade agreement (PTA). This path led to a second generation of PTAs, albeit with major modifications, dealing with labor issues. The renegotiation of NAFTA has marked yet another step in this institutional trajectory by updating the labor provisions to reflect

S. Polaski (✉)
Global Economic Governance Initiative, Boston University, Boston, MA, USA

K. A. Nolan García
Facultad Latinoamericana de Ciencias Sociales (FLACSO), Mexico City, Mexico

M. Rioux
Department of Political Science, Centre for the Study of Integration and Globalization, Université du Québec à Montréal, Montreal, QC, Canada
e-mail: rioux.michele@uqam.ca

© The Author(s), under exclusive license to Springer Nature   139
Switzerland AG 2022
G. Gagné and M. Rioux (eds.), *NAFTA 2.0*,
Canada and International Affairs,
https://doi.org/10.1007/978-3-030-81694-0_10

changing political and economic realities. The United States–Mexico–Canada Agreement (USMCA) includes new language, mechanisms and processes updating the North American Agreement on Labor Cooperation (NAALC) as it incorporates features of the intermediate generation of labor chapters and reaches beyond.

In this chapter, we survey the process from the NAALC to the USMCA. A first section describes the NAALC and its balance sheet on enforcement. A second section summarizes the major changes to labor chapters negotiated by the US and Canada after NAFTA. A third section addresses the political tensions within and across the three countries that motivated changes in the USMCA, as well as setting limits for their reach. A fourth section compares three generations of labor cooperation linked to trade agreements in North America and concludes on the novelty of the USMCA in terms of labor governance, while pointing to some unsettled grounds in relation to labor issues in North America.

NAFTA and the NAALC

NAFTA broke new ground by linking labor rights to trade law. Unlike the integration approach of the European Union aiming to construct a social floor, NAFTA did not involve social integration or convergence of labor and living standards. It was intended to integrate production across North America to make the continent's firms more competitive in a global economy (Deblock and Rioux 1993). This fueled debates over its impacts on employment, triggering opposition by trade unions and civil society in the three countries, anticipating that competitiveness gains would be made at the expense of workers' rights and environmental standards (Cameron and Tomlin 2000; Hafner-Burton 2009; Kay 2011; Mayer 1998; Stillerman 2003). In response, the NAALC was appended to NAFTA as the three countries agreed to a side agreement.

NAALC created a framework for addressing labor rights violations that might arise as result of trade. It reminded governments of their obligations in applying their national labor laws, and their commitments to promote 11 labor principles (freedom of association; the right to collective bargaining; the right to strike; the prohibition of forced labor; the prohibition of child labor; minimum employment standards such as minimum wages and overtime pay; elimination of employment discrimination on the basis of race, religion, age, sex or other grounds as determined by each country's domestic laws; equal remuneration between men and women; the prevention of occupational diseases and accidents at work; compensation in the event of an accident at work or occupational disease and the protection of the labor rights of migrant workers). It created a Labor Cooperation Commission, made up of a Council of Labor Ministers and a Secretariat (suspended in 2010).[1] National Administrative Offices (NAOs) were created in each country to report to the ministries of Labor, to serve as "coordination points" for the enforcement of the agreement and to receive complaints from the public. From 1994 to 2019, 46 public submissions were filed concerning 38 cases of labor rights violations.[2] More than 60% of public submissions filed (28 cases) were filed against Mexico, while a third of public submissions, 15 out of 46, concerned labor rights violations in the United States, and three were filed against Canada.[3] Nearly every complaint filed against Mexico (23 cases) listed violations of the right to freedom of association or the right to bargain collectively as the main labor violations, even when health and safety, discrimination or other issues were included in the file. Public submissions filed against the US centered largely on the labor rights of migrant workers (10 cases), while often referencing violations of other rights, such as freedom of association, safety and health, minimum standards of employment and discrimination. The complaints against Canada focused on violations of the right to freedom of association.

Once public submissions were filed with an NAO, governments decided whether or not to formally review the case and they did so most of the time. The review process ended with a report compiled by the NAO, and recommendations for action that could include consultations between Labor ministers. For certain types of labor rights, an "Evaluation Committee of Experts" could be convened and if parties remained unsatisfied, matters could be sent to an arbitral panel for cases concerning child labor, minimum wage and technical labor standards and occupational safety and health. In practice, all NAALC submissions ended in ministerial consultations, even for cases that qualified for higher order resolution procedures. In a few instances, NAALC submissions led to policy changes and practices, particularly in Mexico, but these were mostly limited in scope and reach (Compa 1997; Finbow 2006; Hertel 2003; Oehri 2017; Singh and Adams 2001; Williams 2003). There is some evidence, though sparse, that pressure on Mexico and publicity around cases led to plant-level changes in labor rights protections (Graubart 2009; Singh and Adams 2001; Stillerman 2003). The fact that an early surge in public submissions tapered off by 1998, to only a few cases a year, suggests that labor unions and civil society became disillusioned with the process and its limited capacity to correct labor rights violations.

The design of the NAALC oversight and enforcement mechanism is frequently identified as a source of limitations in this regard (Buchanan and Chaparro 2008). One important critique was that addressing government behavior had little effect on labor rights violations at the workplace level. In NAALC's design, there were no provisions for the resolution of labor rights violations at the plant level, such as rehiring workers fired for union activity. Furthermore, there were explicit commitments to prevent any intrusion by other states into the labor enforcement of other countries, in recognition of the deep concern by Mexico and Canada over sovereignty with regard to potential US measures (Weiss 2003).[4]

Critics lamented that cases ended in ministerial consultations, rather than fines and trade sanctions, as unions and other stakeholders had hoped. While a majority of cases related to violations of the right to freedom of association and the right to collective bargaining, which were not eligible for expert review and arbitral remedy under the NAALC's tiered system, even in cases that did qualify for such reviews, the governments opted for cooperative activities, educational forums and the sharing of best practices.

The preference of governments for cooperation rather than penalties for labor rights violations underscores a major critique of the NAALC, which is that the outcome depended on the will of states to enforce NAALC. Civil society was welcome to submit complaints, but the management of the case process was in the hands of governments, which introduced a strong political dimension into the enforcement mechanism. NAO offices decided whether public submissions would be taken up for review, which depended on objective criteria around the case and on strategic considerations for governments to pursue cases or not. In some instances, governments decided to stop participating in the NAALC (Nolan García 2011b).[5] A number of experts argued that the governments were reluctant to risk trade conflicts over issues such as labor rights violations (Perez-Lopez and Griego 1995; Englehart 1998; Polaski et al. 2019; Polaski 2022).

In the early years, the public submission process was used extensively by unions and civil society, including by an emerging transnational civil society (see: Compa 2001; Finbow 2006; Graubart 2008; Kay 2011; Nolan García 2011a). As an instrument to address labor rights within NAFTA, it proved to be disappointing. NAFTA failed to generate substantial new employment and, in some sectors, led to declining wages and net job losses (Polaski et al. 2020; Hakobyan and McLaren 2016).[6] NAALC showed obvious limitations and US and Canadian unions, pro-labor political parties and progressive civil society groups advocated for profound changes to the approach to labor rights in subsequent US and Canadian PTA negotiations.

A Second-Generation Model

Due to the dissatisfaction with the NAALC, changes were introduced in the US and Canada that led to a second generation of labor clauses.[7] Among the most important changes, labor provisions were now included in a specific chapter of trade pacts, rather than a side agreement on labor cooperation. This was more than symbolic, as it meant that labor disputes became subject to the same dispute resolution mechanisms as conflicts over issues such as tariff rules or intellectual property rights. For the US, the 2000 US–Jordan PTA negotiated by the Clinton administration was the first to include labor provisions in the body of the agreement and provided for monetary and trade sanctions similar to those of the other chapters of the agreement.[8]

A bipartisan agreement between the US executive and Congress in 2007 laid out higher requirements for labor obligations and enforcement in future US PTAs (USTR 2007).The US–Colombia PTA introduced a new set of issues and a new approach into the second-generation model, addressing pervasive violence against workers who tried to defend their rights in Colombia (Villarreal 2014) and requiring reforms as a condition for submitting the agreement to ratification in the US. The US and Colombia negotiated a Labor Action Plan that required legislative and administrative reforms, including stronger penalties against those responsible for anti-union practices and strengthened protection of at-risk trade union leaders by law enforcement. The Obama administration also insisted on labor law reforms by Panama as a condition for ratifying the PTA, specifically to amend the country's labor code to cover special economic zones that were exempt from its application until then.

In Canada, the NAALC model was replaced with a model developed with Peru in 2008 (Rioux and Deblock 2015). Canada abandoned the "side-agreement" and introduced a chapter on labor into the agreement itself with an appendix similar to the parallel agreements accompanying previous PTAs. National laws could now be challenged, to some extent, by trading partners if they fail to incorporate International Labor Organization (ILO) standards or if their enforcement is systematically deficient. Canada signed agreements with Colombia, Panama, Jordan, Honduras, South Korea and Ukraine in line with a second-generation template. Canada since 2005 has also been instrumental in the emergence of an international dialogue on trade and labor cooperation issues, and it has been documented that there was a path toward convergence with the US on these issues that occurred around 2007 (Rioux and Deblock 2015). Later, in the Comprehensive Economic and Trade Agreement, Canada accepted the EU model on ILO Conventions and regarding the enforcement mechanism that excluded sanctions.

The second-generation model was further developed in the Trans-Pacific Partnership (TPP) negotiated by the US, Canada, Mexico and nine other countries in 2015. These negotiations were the largest and most important since NAFTA, involving 12 countries in the Americas, Asia and Oceania, including a number of countries with contestable labor practices. The US insisted on including separate agreements, called labor consistency plans, with three of the countries involved, Brunei, Vietnam and Malaysia, and reached agreements with each of them in November 2015. The US and Mexico carried out a separate, behind-the-scenes negotiation over reforms to Mexico's Constitution and its laws on freedom of association and collective bargaining (Bensusán and Middlebrook 2020). Academics and labor advocates in Mexico and the US argued that Mexico's corporatist system of unionism had become unrepresentative and, in some cases, corrupt (see De la Garza Toledo 2003; Bouzas Ortíz and Hernández Cervantes 2007; Bensusán and Middlebrook 2012; Bensusán and Alcade 2013).

The negotiations were kept secret due to Mexican sensitivities about sovereignty and US respect for those concerns (Bensusán and Middlebrook 2020). Mexico submitted reforms to the Constitution and the federal labor law to Mexico's Senate in 2016. The constitutional reforms were adopted and sent to the states, where approval by a majority of the 32 states' Congresses was required. President Trump pulled the US out of the TPP in January 2017 but, in Mexico, by February 2017 a majority of states had approved and the constitutional amendments took effect. Mexico thus faced a constitutional change without a new trade agreement with the US. Mexico's labor law reforms were then suspended until the renegotiation of NAFTA, but countries that negotiated the TPP, including Mexico and Canada, ratified the agreement without the US under a new name, the Comprehensive and Progressive Agreement for

Trans-Pacific Partnership (CPTPP). The CPTPP consolidated the second-generation model and added elements that would be integrated and further developed in the USMCA.

USMCA: A THIRD-GENERATION MODEL?

The renegotiation of NAFTA was politically fraught, arising from the denunciation of that agreement by Trump, and a backdrop of widespread public disapproval of this PTA in the US. However, the business sector in all three countries strongly supported North American economic integration for reasons explored in this volume. With regard to labor provisions, criticisms of NAFTA and the TPP were resonating in the US and, perhaps most significantly, the skepticism over trade's impact on workers by a large bloc in the US Congress meant that any agreement would face a difficult ratification process. The US negotiating team was part of the largely anti-union Trump administration, however it was led by Robert Lighthizer, who understood that any new agreement would be difficult to ratify without strong labor provisions and was open to dialogue with US unions.

In Mexico, the labor law reform process that had stalled after the US withdrawal from the TPP resumed in a contested fashion. Legislative proposals were introduced by competing political parties and the unions affiliated with them. A bill introduced by the *Partido Revolucionario Institucional* (PRI) would have effectively rolled back the constitutional reforms, while one introduced by the *Partido de la Revolución Democrática (PRD)* and the independent Mexican union federation *Unión Nacional de Trabajadores* (UNT) would have carried them forward (Brooks 2018). A third bill, submitted by the *Partido de Acción Nacional (PAN)*, captured business sector interests. Meanwhile, the UNT and the American Federation of Labor and Congress of Industrial Organizations (AFL–CIO) filed a public submission under the existing NAALC submission process claiming that the PRI counter-reform bill would violate the NAALC (US Department of Labor 2018). The Mexican negotiating team was largely the same as in the TPP, but this changed with an election in July 2018 when the progressive candidate, Andrés Manuel López Obrador won a sweeping victory and his coalition also won a majority in both the Senate and Chamber of Deputies. López Obrador appointed an experienced trade negotiator, Jesús Seade, and the US and Mexico engaged in bilateral talks that moved swiftly. Canada joined the talks and the USMCA was signed on November 30, 2018, the day before López Obrador became president.

When the Democrats won a majority in the US House of Representatives, giving them control over ratification once they took office in January 2019, they took the position that the enforcement mechanisms in the USMCA were not adequate, particularly with respect to labor obligations. A tense negotiation played out between the US executive and congressional leaders and, in December 2019, an agreement was reached to add a Protocol of Amendment that would establish new enforcement procedures. The Protocol was then negotiated between the US and Mexico, before Canada agreed to an identical protocol with Mexico. Both the labor chapter and the Protocol introduce changes to the parties' obligations and to mechanisms for enforcement that go beyond the first and second generations of PTAs with labor provisions. Changes fall into three categories: those for all three parties, specific to Mexico, and those that entail bilateral enforcement mechanisms.

Among the changes that affect all parties, a notable expansion of obligations is found in a new paragraph that recognizes that workers must be free to exercise their labor rights in a climate free of violence, threats and intimidation and requires that "no Party shall fail to address violence or threats of violence against workers, directly related to exercising or attempting to exercise [these] rights" (USMCA, art. 23.7). The problem of violence against workers exercising their rights was addressed in the side agreement to the US–Colombia PTA but it was not incorporated into the trade agreement; thus, the USMCA represents the first explicit protection against violence in a PTA that binds all parties, and that is subject to enforcement mechanisms. Other important expansions of obligations relate to the obligation to "adopt and maintain statutes and regulations, and practices thereunder, governing acceptable conditions of work with respect to minimum wages, hours of work, and occupational safety and health," which was in the TPP, but was defined in the USMCA to include wage-related benefit payments, such as retirement and healthcare (USMCA, art. 23.1, fn. 1). Another important expansion is found in a footnote on the right to freedom of association, that states: "the right to strike is linked to the right to freedom of association, which cannot be realized without protecting the right to strike." (art. 23.3, fn. 6). The prohibition on forced or compulsory labor within the countries was expanded to an outward-facing responsibility to prevent imports produced with forced labor from non-party countries (art. 23.6).

A paragraph provides protection to migrant workers, by recognizing their vulnerability with respect to labor protections and requiring that "each Party shall ensure that migrant workers are protected under its labor laws, whether they are nationals or non-nationals of the Party" (art. 23.8). If NAALC included protection for migrant workers, the USMCA makes this a binding and enforceable obligation.

The USMCA also includes statements of shared commitments. The parties "recognize the goal of trading only in goods produced in compliance" with the labor chapter (art. 23.2.3). While a commitment is less than an obligation, it is significant because it communicates the purpose of the parties, for example, to dispute settlement panels in future disputes. Similarly, a new paragraph adds to the existing obligation of parties to eliminate "discrimination in respect of employment and occupation," by supporting the "goal of promoting equality of women in the workplace," including through policies "that [a party] considers appropriate" dealing with sexual harassment, pregnancy, sexual orientation, gender identity and caregiving responsibilities, as well as providing job-protected leave for birth or adoption of a child and care of family members and protection against wage discrimination (art. 23.9).

The USMCA also narrows the second-generation model limitations on enforceability. It relaxes the requirement that violations of the labor obligations must occur "in a manner affecting trade or investment between the Parties," the standard that led to the US loss in a case against Guatemala (Polaski 2017; Compa et al. 2018).[9] In the USMCA, "a manner affecting trade or investment" is understood broadly as anything that "involves: (i) a person or industry that produces a good or supplies a service traded between the Parties or has an investment in the territory of the Party that has failed to comply with this obligation; or (ii) a person or industry that produces a good or supplies a service that competes in the territory of a Party with a good or a service of another Party." (ch. 23, fns 4, 8, 11, 13). It further closes the loophole exploited in the Guatemala case by instructing dispute settlement panels to "presume that a failure is in a manner affecting trade or investment between the Parties, unless the responding Party demonstrates otherwise," thus reversing the burden of proof (ch. 23, fns 5, 9, 12, 14). It restricts the scope of the limitation found in earlier labor chapters that a violation must involve a "sustained or recurring course of action or inaction." It does so by adding a footnote "for greater certainty" that defines a sustained or recurring course of action or inaction as "sustained" if "consistent or ongoing," and as "recurring" if it "occurs periodically or repeatedly and when the occurrences are related or the same in nature" (art. 23.5, fn. 10).

Labor provisions specific to Mexico are found in Annex 23-A, *Worker Representation in Collective Bargaining in Mexico*, attached to the labor chapter as an integral part of the agreement. It requires Mexico to adopt and maintain specific measures "necessary for the effective recognition of the right to collective bargaining" (annex 23-A.1). It adds the respectful observation that "the Mexican government incoming in December 2018 has confirmed that each of these provisions is within the scope of the mandate provided to the government by the people of Mexico in the elections." These are now included as explicit obligations, similar to the pattern established by the US in negotiations with Colombia, Vietnam, Malaysia and Brunei, that required labor reforms.[10] These range from substantive protections for freedom of association and the right to collective bargaining to reforms promoting union democracy, including the right to a secret, direct and personal vote in union elections and worker approval for collective bargaining agreements prior to their registration and publication at new, decentralized labor administrative centers. Reforms place the enforcement of these rights in the hands of impartial conciliation centers and new labor courts. The changes intend to dismantle the long-existing corporatist system, under which decisions on individual and collective labor rights were handled by tripartite conciliation and arbitration boards that were considered to be ineffective or corrupt.

A new enforcement mechanism regarding violations of workers' rights at the level of the firm or facility has been created under the Protocol (USMCA, ch. 31, annex 31-A). It complements the dispute settlement mechanism that offers recourse for a failure by a government to enforce the labor obligations of the agreement. The *United States–Mexico Facility-Specific Rapid Response Labor Mechanism* creates an entirely novel procedure for filing and investigating claims related to violations of freedom of association and the right to collective bargaining by a firm, called "denial of rights." The approach acknowledges that while governments are responsible for enforcing labor laws, in the private sector it is the employer who directly denies the rights. The mechanism includes a complex, multi-stage process to determine whether denial of rights has occurred and includes multiple opportunities for resolution of disputes through government-to-government exchanges. If a firm is found to have denied workers' rights and failed to remedy the denial, it can face penalties that include suspension of preferential tariff treatment or the imposition of penalties on goods or services from the facility. In case of repeated violations, the firm can be denied market access to the complaining trading partner country.[11] This mechanism has several potential advantages: (1) it can allow for a precise targeting of firms rather than broad targeting of an entire country, therefore reducing the political tensions that a charge against a government could entail; (2) given that the offending firm faces direct economic consequences for violations, the interests of the firm are better aligned with the rights of workers and the government interests and (3) it can avoid collateral damage to compliant firms and create a deterrent effect that encourages voluntary compliance with labor laws.

Conclusion: The USMCA as a Third-Generation Model of Trade-Labor Linkage?

The NAALC was innovative but ultimately disappointing. Subsequent negotiations of labor provisions allowed for a second generation of US and Canadian PTAs to gradually develop with stronger obligations and enforcement. The USMCA includes many provisions of the second-generation model, while forging a path toward a third generation of labor chapters (Table 10.1).

The USMCA consolidates the approach of an enforceable labor chapter in a PTA, confirming that labor disputes should be subject to the same dispute resolution mechanisms as other trade issues. While the USMCA continues to promote cooperation between countries to end disputes through government-to-government dialogue and dispute settlement, it also includes a mechanism to resolve labor rights violations at the firm level. This strengthens enforcement precisely where the NAALC was weakest: an inability to address violations of the right to association and the right to collective bargaining, the need for a mechanism to address violations as they occurred at the level of the firm and the specific patterns of labor rights violations in Mexico.[12] The requirement that disputes must affect trade is also greatly narrowed and the burden of proving a trade relationship is reversed to the defending party. Obligations are as well expanded to new domains.

Since the USMCA took effect in 2020, it is too early to assess its impacts. An initial interim report by an independent expert board created by the US Congress to monitor Mexico's labor reform and compliance

Table 10.1 Generations of PTAs addressing labor issues

First generation (NAALC)	Second generation	Toward a third generation
Status of agreements Side agreements	Chapter in the PTA	Chapter in the PTA
Obligations Refer to 11 principles that "the parties are committed to promoting" in domestic law	Refer to ILO 1998 Declaration (national laws must respect ILO core principles and provide for conditions of work with respect to minimum wages, hours of work, and occupational safety and health)	Include previous obligations and add protection of workers against violence for union activities, right to strike, requirement that labor laws protect migrant workers, requirement that parties prevent imports made with forced labor and commitments on gender rights
Enforceability No requirement that violations be trade related	Requires that violations occur "in a manner affecting trade" and be sustained	Narrows the requirement for trade linkage and extent of violations of standards
Non-derogation from labor laws to promote trade or investment Not included	Non-derogation clause	Non-derogation clause
Changes to labor laws or enforcement No action plans	Emerging action plans	Strengthened and mandatory pre-ratification action plan including constitutional, labor law and enforcement reforms in the case of Mexico
Enforcement possibilities Limited: state-to-state, politicized and ineffective	Stronger enforcement commensurate with other trade obligations; only state-to-state mechanisms	New enforcement procedures at firm and facility level; more robust state-to-state arbitration rules; complaint mechanisms simpler and more accessible to the public

with its labor obligations under the USMCA noted both progress and serious concerns (IMLEB 2020). Yet, the USMCA potentially takes a step toward more meaningful transnational regulation of workers' rights in North America. The expanded scope of obligations and the rigor and originality of some of the new provisions suggest that it has the potential to remedy labor rights violations through trade mechanisms. It could then help translate trade growth into upward convergence of living standards. In North America, this is particularly relevant for Mexico, where wages have failed to converge toward US and Canadian levels.

As Asia plays an expanded role in global supply chains, North American governments and corporate sectors are revisiting the desirability of regional production networks, while the COVID-19 pandemic has led to demands for domestic industrial policies to revive battered national economies. Such trends in policies could face constraints under some of the deregulatory terms of the USMCA, but the consolidation of a third generation of trade-labor regulation has the potential to put North America on a road to economic and social upgrading in the region's interests.

NOTES

1. The Secretariat provided support to the Ministerial Council, conducted research and assisted states parties in cooperative activities (92 cooperation activities between 1994 and 2002 on safety and health, elimination of discrimination in employment, freedom of association, productivity, quality and protection of migrant workers).
2. See Nolan García (2013) updated by the author. Eight public submissions were filed at more than one NAOs; note that submissions had to be submitted to a NAO in a country other than where violations took place, to avoid governments reviewing and reporting on their own conduct.
3. The industrial relations in Canada place labor law mostly within the jurisdiction of the provinces and less at federal level, and the NAALC focused on federal government actions.
4. Article 42 of the NAALC states: "Nothing in this Agreement shall be construed to empower a Party's authorities to undertake labor law enforcement activities in the territory of another Party.".
5. The US NAO chose not to advance any cases during the Bush administration (2001–2009), and Mexico stopped cooperating fully with the US after the 2001 Puebla case.

6. In both Canada and the US certain regions and industries were left with losses over the years. In the US grievances became a political weapon in the 2016 presidential election leading to the election of Donald Trump.

7. See Table 10.1 in section "Conclusion: The USMCA as a Third-Generation Model of Trade-Labor Linkage?" of the chapter.

8. Subsequent PTAs limited the use of arbitration and created an enforcement mechanism for the labor chapter that was less stringent than in previous agreements. The same ambivalence was seen in Canada, with the signing of some PTAs with strong enforcement mechanisms, while others relied solely on cooperation. Around 2008, both countries embraced the stronger approach of ambitious PTA labor chapters fully enforceable.

9. After submission of a complaint against Guatemala's practices, the US engaged with the country to improve Guatemala's enforcement of labor laws through action plans that failed to produce results. The US requested review by an arbitral panel to apply trade sanctions for non-compliance under the terms of their PTA. Although the panel found that Guatemala was in violation, it ruled that the US had not demonstrated the effect of such violations on trade and dismissed the case.

10. Regarding Colombia, the action plan was not attached to the PTA but was a condition for submitting the PTA to ratification. See Obama White House Archives (2011).

11. The procedure relies on panels of independent labor experts to investigate claims and recommend remedies (USMCA, art. 31-A.10).

12. Submissions to the ILO Committee of Experts on the Application of Conventions and Recommendations resulted in determinations that such problems were a matter of serious concern in Mexico. Observation, Freedom of Association and Protection of the Right to Organize Convention, 1948 (No. 87), Mexico. https://www.ilo.org/dyn/normlex/en/f? p=1000:13100:0::NO:13100:P13100_COMMENT_ID:3343978.

References

Bensusán, Graciela, and Arturo Alcalde. 2013. *El sistema de justicia laboral en México: situación actual y perspectivas*. Friedrich-Ebert-Stiftung México, No. 1/2013, June. http://library.fes.de/pdf-files/bueros/mexiko/10311.pdf.

Bensusán, Graciela, and Kevin J. Middlebrook. 2012. *Organized Labour and Politics in Mexico: Changes, Continuities and Contradictions*. London: Institute for the Study of the Americas.

Bensusán, Graciela, and Kevin J. Middlebrook. 2020. Cambio político desde afuera hacia adentro: Influencia comercial estadounidense y reforma de los derechos laborales en México. *Foro Internacional* 60 (3): 985–1039. https://doi.org/10.24201/fi.v60i3.2670.

Bouzas Ortiz, José Alfonso, and Aleida Hernández Cervantes. 2007. *Contratación Colectiva de Protección en México: Informe a la Organización Regional Interamericana de Trabajadores*. http://frecuencialaboral.com/contratosdep roteccion.html.

Brooks, Tequila. 2018. *Mexican Congressional Session Closes without Passing Legislation Implementing Labor Justice Reform*. American Bar Association, June.

Buchanan, Ruth, and Rusby Mariela Chaparro. 2008. International Institutions and Transnational Advocacy: The Case of the North American Agreement on Labor Cooperation. *UCLA Journal of International Law and Foreign Affairs* 13 (1): 129–160.

Cameron, Maxwell A., and Brian W. Tomlin. 2000. *The Making of NAFTA: How the Deal Was Done*. Ithaca, NY: Cornell University Press.

Compa, Lance. 1997. NAFTA's Labor Side Accord: A Three-Year Accounting. *Law and Business Review of the Americas* 3 (3): 6–23.

Compa, Lance. 2001. NAFTA's Labor Side Agreement and International Labor Solidarity. *Antipode* 33 (3): 451–467.

Compa, Lance, Jeffrey Vogt, and Eric Gottwald. 2018. *Wrong Turn for Workers' Rights: The US-Guatemala CAFTA Labor Arbitration Ruling – And What To Do About It*. International Labor Rights Forum, April 12. https://laborr ights.org/publications/wrong-turn-workers%E2%80%99-rights-us-guatemala-cafta-labor-arbitration-ruling-%E2%80%93-and-what-do.

Deblock, Christian, and Michèle Rioux. 1993. NAFTA: The Trump Card of the United States? *Studies in Political Economy* 41 (1): 7–44.

De la Garza Toledo, Enrique. 2003. La crisis de los modelos sindicales en México y sus opciones. In *La situación del trabajo en México*, ed. Enrique de la Garza Toledo and Carlos Salas, 349–377. Mexico City: Plaza y Valdés.

Englehart, Frederick. 1998. Withered Giants: Mexican and U.S. Organized Labor and the North American Agreement on Labor Cooperation. *Case Western Reserve Journal of International Law* 29: 321–386.

Finbow, Robert. 2006. *The Limits of Regionalism: NAFTA's Labour Accord*. Aldershot: Ashgate.

Graubart, Jonathan. 2008. *Legalizing Transnational Activism: The Struggle to Gain Social Change from NAFTA's Citizen Petitions*. University Park: University of Pennsylvania Press.

Graubart, Jonathan. 2009. The Legalization of Transnational Political Opportunity Structures: Mobilization of NAFTA's Labor Citizen Petitions for Domestic Political Gain. In *Contentious Politics in North America*, ed. Laura MacDonald and Jeffrey Ayres. New York: Palgrave.

Hafner-Burton, Emilie M. 2009. *Forced to Be Good: Why Trade Agreements Boost Human Rights*. Ithaca: Cornell University Press.

Hakobyan, Shushanik, and John McLaren. 2016. Looking for Local Labor Market Effects of NAFTA. *Review of Economics and Statistics* 98 (4): 728–741. https://doi.org/10.1162/REST_a_00587.

Hertel, Shareen. 2003. Una contienda acotada: La defensa transnacional de los derechos laborales de las mujeres en las maquiladoras de México. *Región y Sociedad* 26 (16): 153–191.

Independent Mexico Labor Expert Board (IMLEB). 2020. *Interim Report*, December 15. https://aflcio.org/sites/default/files/2020-12/IMLEB%20Interim%20Report%20%26%20Separate%20Statement%20of%20Members%20Marculewicz%20%26%20Miscimarra.pdf.

Kay, Tamara. 2011. *NAFTA and the Politics of Labor Transnationalism*. Cambridge: Cambridge University Press.

Mayer, Frederick. 1998. *Interpreting NAFTA: The Science and Art of Political Analysis*. New York: Columbia University Press.

García, Nolan, and A. Kimberly. 2011. The Evolution of United States – Mexico Labor Cooperation (1994–2009): Achievements and Challenges. *Politics and Policy* 39 (1): 91–117.

García, Nolan, and A. Kimberly. 2011. Transnational Advocates and Labor Rights Enforcement in the North American Free Trade Agreement. *Latin American Politics and Society* 53 (2): 29–60.

Nolan García, Kimberly A. 2013. *NAALC Labor Rights Dispute Resolution Dataset, 1994–2013*.Laboratorio Nacional de Políticas Públicas. http://datos.cide.edu/handle/10089/17312.

North American Agreement on Labor Cooperation (NAALC), signed September 14, 1993, entered into force January 1, 1994. https://www.canada.ca/en/employment-social-development/services/labour-relations/international/agreements/naalc.html#p3.

North American Free Trade Agreement (NAFTA), signed December 17, 1992, entered into force January 1, 1994. https://www.nafta-sec-alena.org/Home/Legal-Texts/North-American-Free-Trade-Agreement.

Obama White House Archives. 2011. *Leveling the Playing Field: Labor Protections and the U.S.-Colombia Trade Promotion Agreement*. https://obamawhitehouse.archives.gov/sites/default/files/09302011_labor_protections_and_the_colombia_trade_agreement.pdf. Accessed December 29, 2020.

Oehri, Myriam. 2017. Civil Society Activism under US Free Trade Agreements: The Effects of Actorness on Decent Work. *Politics and Governance* 5 (4): 40–48.http://dx.doi.org/10.17645/pag.v5i4.1085.

Office of the United States Trade Representative (USTR). 2007. *Trade Facts:Bipartisan Trade Deal*. https://ustr.gov/sites/default/files/uploads/factsheets/2007/asset_upload_file127_11319.pdf.

Perez-Lopez, Jorge F., and Eric Griego. 1995. The Labor Dimension of the NAFTA: Reflections on the First Year. *Arizona Journal of International & Comparative Law* 12 (2): 473–522.

Polaski, Sandra. 2017. *Twenty Years of Progress at Risk: Labor and Environmental Protections in Trade Agreements.* Boston University Global Development Policy Center, Global Economic Governance Initiative, Policy Brief 004, October. https://www.bu.edu/gdp/files/2017/10/Polaski.10-2017.Final_.pdf. Accessed December 29, 2020.

Polaski, Sandra. 2022, March. The Strategy and Politics of Linking Trade and Labor Standards: An Overview of Issues and Approaches. In *Handbook on Globalisation and Labour Standards*, ed. Kimberly Ann Elliott. Cheltenham, UK/Northampton, MA: Edward Elgar. https://www.researchgate.net/publication/340384810_The_strategy_and_politics_of_linking_trade_and_labor_standards_An_overview_of_issues_and_approaches. Accessed March 24, 2021.

Polaski, Sandra, Jeronim Capaldo, and Kevin P. Gallagher. 2019. *Small Gains & Big Risks: Evaluating the Proposed United States-Mexico-Canada Agreement.* Boston University Global Development Policy Center, Global Economic Governance Initiative, Policy Brief 007, June. http://www.bu.edu/gdp/files/2019/06/PolicyBrief7NAFTAPolaskiCalpadoGallagher2019.pdf. Accessed December 29, 2020.

Polaski, Sandra, Sarah Anderson, John Cavanagh, Kevin Gallagher, Manuel Pérez-Rocha and Rebecca Ray. 2020. *How Trade Policy Failed U.S. Workers – And How to Fix It.* Institute for Policy Studies, Boston University Global Development Policy Center, and Groundwork Collaborative. http://www.bu.edu/gdp/files/2020/09/GWC2054_Taxation_Paper_FIN.pdf. Accessed December 29, 2020.

Protocol of Amendment to the United States-Mexico-Canada Agreement (USMCA), signed December 10, 2019. https://ustr.gov/sites/default/files/files/agreements/FTA/USMCA/Protocol-of-Amendments-to-the-United-States-Mexico-Canada-Agreement.pdf.

Rioux, Michèle, and Christian Deblock. 2015. Humanizing Trade: A North American Perspective in the Making. In *Global Governance Facing Structural Changes*, ed. Michèle Rioux and Kim Fontaine-Skronski, 101–126. New York: Palgrave Macmillan.

Singh, Parbudyal, and Roy J. Adams. 2001. Neither a Gem nor a Scam: The Progress of the North American Agreement on Labor Cooperation. *Labor Studies Journal* 26 (1): 1–15.

Stillerman, Joel. 2003. Transnational Activist Networks and the Emergence of Labor Internationalism in the NAFTA Countries. *Social Science History* 27 (4): 577–601.

United States – Mexico – Canada Agreement (USMCA), signed November 30, 2018, amended December 10, 2019, entered into force July 1, 2020. https://www.international.gc.ca/trade-commerce/trade-agreements-accords-commerciaux/agr-acc/cusma-aceum/text-texte/toc-tdm.aspx?lang=eng.

US Department of Labor. 2018. *Bureau of International Labor Affairs; Office of Trade and Labor Affairs; North American Agreement on Labor Cooperation; Notice of Extension of the Period for Acceptance for Submission #2018-01 (Mexico)*. https://public-inspection.federalregister.gov/2018-05866.pdf?152 1549936.

Villarreal, M. Angeles. 2014. *The U.S.-Colombia Free Trade Agreement: Background and Issues*. Congressional Research Service, RL34470. https://fas.org/sgp/crs/row/RL34470.pdf. Accessed December 29, 2020.

Villarreal, M. Angeles, and Ian F. Fergusson. 2017. TheNorth American Free Trade Agreement (NAFTA). *Congressional Research Service*, R42965. https://fas.org/sgp/crs/row/R42965.pdf. Accessed December 29, 2020.

Weiss, Marley S. 2003. Two Steps Forward, One Step Back - Or Vice Versa: Labor Rights Under Free Trade Agreements from NAFTA, Through Jordan, via Chile, to Latin America, and Beyond. *University of San Francisco Law Review* 37: 689–755.

Williams, Heather L. 2003. Labor Tragedy and Legal Farce: The Han Young Struggle in Tijuana, Mexico. *Social Science History* 27 (4): 525–550.

CHAPTER 11

NAFTA and the Environment: Decades of Measured Progress

Noémie Laurens, Zachary Dove, Jean-Frédéric Morin, and Sikina Jinnah

Introduction

The conclusion of the North American Free Trade Agreement (NAFTA) in 1992 marked a decisive turning point in how preferential trade agreements (PTAs) address environmental protection. Along with its environmental side agreement, formally called the North American Agreement

A previous version of this chapter was originally published as "NAFTA 2.0: The Greenest Trade Agreement Ever?" *World Trade Review* 18 (4): 659–677. This chapter updates the original publication based on the Protocol of Amendment to the USMCA agreed on December 10, 2019.

N. Laurens (✉) · J.-F. Morin
Department of Political Science, Université Laval, Quebec City, QC, Canada
e-mail: noémie.laurens.1@ulaval.ca

Z. Dove
Politics Department, University of California, Santa Cruz, CA, USA

G. Gagné and M. Rioux (eds.), *NAFTA 2.0*,
Canada and International Affairs,
https://doi.org/10.1007/978-3-030-81694-0_11

on Environmental Cooperation (NAAEC), NAFTA created 46 new environmental provisions that were never included in any PTA beforehand (Morin et al. 2017). Many of these provisions, including, for instance, on the inappropriateness to relax environmental measures to encourage investment, or on the enforcement of domestic environmental laws, became templates for dozens of later PTAs (see Jinnah and Morin 2020).

Interestingly, despite the Trump administration's numerous rollbacks on US environmental policy,[1] the United States–Mexico–Canada Agreement (USMCA) includes far more environmental provisions than its predecessor. The United States Trade Representative (USTR) even asserts that NAFTA parties "have agreed to the most advanced, most comprehensive, highest-standard chapter on the Environment of any trade agreement" (USTR 2018) and regards the USMCA in general as "a new paradigm for future agreements" (USTR 2019, p. 11).

This chapter extends existing analyses of the USMCA's environmental provisions (e.g., Tienhaara 2019; Vaughan 2018) by investigating how these provisions compare with those included in NAFTA[2] and with the renegotiating objectives of the three parties. It argues that the provisions that the USMCA eliminated from NAFTA are equally, if not more, interesting from an environmental governance perspective than those it added. Nevertheless, the agreement mainly replicates environmental provisions that were already included in previous PTAs, especially in the Trans-Pacific Partnership (TPP), and still falls short in some areas, most notably a lack of climate provisions.

The chapter is organized as follows. Using the Trade and Environment Database (Morin et al. 2018), the first section presents the three NAFTA parties' renegotiation objectives as they relate to the environment and discusses how each country approaches environmental governance within its trade agreements. The second section provides a detailed comparison of the environmental provisions within NAFTA and the USMCA to explain how the agreements differ. The third section examines two contested NAFTA measures that were jettisoned from the USMCA. Finally, the conclusion briefly summarizes our findings and highlights some of the USMCA's missed opportunities.

S. Jinnah
Environmental Studies Department, University of California, Santa Cruz, CA, USA

COMPARATIVE NEGOTIATING
OBJECTIVES ON THE ENVIRONMENT

States define environmental negotiating objectives for their trade agreements in various ways. In the US case, these negotiating objectives are highly specific, reflecting concrete legal requirements that the President must include specific environmental provisions within a trade agreement in order to avoid Congressional amendment or filibuster. In particular, the President is bound by the Bipartisan Congressional Trade Priorities and Accountability Act of 2015 (TPA 2015), which is the current basis for Trade Promotion Authority, colloquially referred to as "fast-track authority," under which NAFTA was renegotiated. Trade Promotion Authority requires, for example, that the US includes, within its negotiating objectives, environmental provisions related to eliminating fisheries subsidies; addressing illegal, unreported, and unregulated fishing; and requiring trading partners to implement their obligations under seven listed multilateral environmental agreements (MEAs). It is not surprising, therefore, that the USMCA's environmental provisions are largely consistent with previous US PTAs, which were also negotiated under "fast-track authority."[3]

Reflective of the well-documented practice of replicating or "boilerplating" of environmental provisions in trade agreements over time (Allee and Elsig 2019; Jinnah and Lindsay 2016; Jo and Namgung 2012; Morin et al. 2017), some of the US negotiating objectives for the USMCA echo provisions included in NAFTA's environmental side agreement (USTR 2017). These include provisions preventing NAFTA parties from derogating from enforcing their environmental regulations in order to attract investment; establishing means for stakeholder participation; and ensuring there are adequate procedures for enforcing environmental laws (see Charnovitz 1994). While US environmental provisions were previously only related to the environment in general, the United States has recently adopted the use of sectoral provisions as well, which address specific environmental issue areas, such as fisheries, forests, and endangered species (Morin and Rochette 2017). Additionally, it is now standard practice in US agreements to subject the environmental provisions to the agreement's dispute settlement mechanism (Jinnah 2011).[4]

In contrast to the United States, where negotiation objectives are defined by TPA-2015, Canada has a parliamentary system that provides the executive branch with full control over trade negotiations. As such, we must rely on public speeches to identify Canada's negotiating objectives. As outlined in a 2017 speech by the Foreign Affairs Minister, the Trudeau government championed a "progressive" trade agenda that would address indigenous rights, gender equality, strong labor standards, enhanced environmental provisions, and the right of the government to regulate in the public interest. Importantly, with regard to the environment, Canada's objective was to integrate "enhanced environmental provisions to ensure no NAFTA country weakens environmental protection to attract investment, for example, and that fully supports efforts to address climate change" (Global Affairs Canada 2017).

Canada's approach to including environmental provisions in its trade agreements is similar to that of the US. All but two of Canada's post-NAFTA trade agreements include significant numbers of environmental provisions, although these agreements include slightly fewer provisions on specific issue areas (see Fig. 11.1). Prior to 2016, Canada, like the US, took a more general approach to environmental provisions. However, recent Canadian agreements have also included large numbers of sectoral provisions that address specific issue areas, such as monitoring of genetically modified organisms and protection of migratory species. Moreover, Canada has only very recently (since 2016) begun to subject its environmental provisions to the agreement's dispute settlement mechanism, which would allow for use of sanctions in the case of non-compliance.[5]

Finally, the best public articulation of Mexico's renegotiation priorities for NAFTA is found in an August 2017 article by the Ministry of

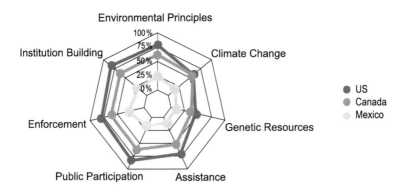

Fig. 11.1 Percentage of USMCA parties' PTAs that include specific environmental provisions

Economy. Mexico's priorities were grouped into four themes: strengthen the competitiveness of North America; move toward inclusive and responsible trade; take advantage of twenty-first century opportunities; and promote the certainty of trade and investment (Secretaría de Economía 2017). Specific references to the environment were sparse, but Mexico aimed to strengthen cooperation and dialogue on trade and environment issues. An additional priority was to take advantage of opportunities for private investment in its recently liberalized oil, gas, petrochemicals, and electricity sectors (Oxford Business Group, n.d.).

In contrast to the US and Canada, Mexico has been far less consistent with including environmental provisions in its trade agreements. NAFTA, the USMCA, and the Comprehensive and Progressive Agreement for Trans-Pacific Partnership (CPTPP)[6] stand out as the only agreements Mexico is party to that include significant numbers of environmental provisions. Otherwise, while most of Mexico's agreements concluded after NAFTA include provisions related to environmental exceptions, few additional environmental provisions are included. Outside of NAFTA, the USMCA, and CPTPP, provisions on specific environmental issues are scarce in Mexico's PTAs (see Fig. 11.1). Additionally, Mexico lacks an overall approach to compliance; apart from the USMCA, CPTPP, and NAFTA, Mexico's agreements generally do not have compliance mechanisms for environmental provisions, except for a few agreements negotiated in the 1990s that provide for an intergovernmental committee.

Comparing NAFTA and the USMCA's Environmental Provisions

NAFTA's and the USMCA's environmental provisions are similar in many respects. The USMCA maintains 75% of the environmental provisions originally included in NAFTA (see Table 11.1). This is not surprising given that, as mentioned above, most US negotiating objectives for the USMCA mirror provisions already included in NAFTA. In addition to comparable provisions on regulatory sovereignty, enforcement of domestic environmental laws, and public participation, the USMCA and NAFTA share the same approach to environmental cooperation. For example, they both encourage trade in environmental goods, the exchange of scientific information related to the environment, joint studies, and the harmonization of environmental measures. They also include similar environmental exceptions to trade in goods, services,

Table 11.1 List of NAFTA's environmental provisions

NAFTA's environmental provisions	Also included in the USMCA and/or the ECA	Originally only included in the NAAEC and now included in the USMCA's main text
Preamble refers to the environment	■	
Prevention principle	■	■
Sovereignty over resources	■	
Sovereignty in determining level of environmental protection according to state priorities	■	
Sovereignty in the enforcement of environmental measures	■	■
No extraterritorial enforcement activities	■	■
No right of action under a party's domestic law	■	
Recognition of a development gap or of different capabilities	■	
Inappropriate to encourage investment by relaxing environmental measures	■	■
Maintain existing level of environmental protection	■	■
States should provide for high levels of environmental protection	■	
States should enhance, strengthen, or improve levels of environmental protection	■	
Definition of environmental laws	■	■
Scientific knowledge when conducting environmental risk assessment		■
Public participation in the adoption of environmental measures	■	

NAFTA's environmental provisions	Also included in the USMCA and/or the ECA	Originally only included in the NAAEC and now included in the USMCA's main text
Publication of environmental laws, regulations, and administrative rulings	■	■
Commitment to monitor the state of the environment		■
Requirement to conduct environmental assessment	■	
Commitment to strengthen state's own capacities in environmental research and science		
Coherence between the environment and economic activities or development	■	■
Coherence between the environment and domestic trade and/or investment policies	■	
Commitment to enforce domestic environmental measures	■	
Specific governmental action for enforcement of environmental measures	■	■
Private access to remedies, procedural guarantees, and appropriate sanctions	■	■
Commitment to consider alleged violation brought by a citizen	■	■
Factual report on enforcement of domestic environmental measures	■	■
Education or public awareness on environmental matters	■	
Promotion of voluntary measures	■	■

(continued)

Table 11.1 (continued)

NAFTA's environmental provisions	Also included in the USMCA and/or the ECA	Originally only included in the NAAEC and now included in the USMCA's main text
Economic instruments		■
Joint scientific research	■	■
Specific means to conduct scientific cooperation on environmental matters	■	■
Joint environmental assessment and study or monitoring of environmental concerns	■	■
Specific means to exchange information on environmental matters	■	■
Provision of information when taking measures to protect the environment	■	
Communication between customs authorities on offenses related to environmental protection	■	
Harmonization of environmental measures	■	
Harmonization of non-environmental measures not to be used as an obstacle to environmental protection		
Prohibit the export to the other party of environmentally harmful goods whose use or import is prohibited within that party's territory		
General exceptions for trade in goods: life (or health) of animal and/or plant	■	
General exceptions for trade in goods: conservation of natural resources	■	

NAFTA's environmental provisions	Also included in the USMCA and/or the ECA	Originally only included in the NAAEC and now included in the USMCA's main text
Right to prepare, elaborate, adopt, or apply TBT measures related to the environment	■	
Right to derogate from the regular adoption procedure of a TBT measure in case of emergency	■	
General exception for investment	■	
Specific exception for establishment	■	
Specific exception for performance requirements		
Exclusion of environmentally harmful inventions from patentability	■	
General exception for procurement	■	
General exceptions for trade in services: life (or health) of animal and/or plant	■	
Other environmental restrictions related to a specific sector of services	■	
SPS measures and the environment	■	
Technical assistance, training, or capacity-building provided to another party	■	■
Emergency assistance in case of natural disaster		
Other norms on disasters	■	■
Seas and oceans	■	■
Management of transboundary waterways	■	■

(continued)

Table 11.1 (continued)

NAFTA's environmental provisions	Also included in the USMCA and/or the ECA	Originally only included in the NAAEC and now included in the USMCA's main text
Endangered species and their illegal trade	■	■
Invasive or alien species	■	■
Protected areas, parks, and natural reserves	■	■
Air pollution	■	■
Environmental standards on vehicles	■	
Hazardous waste	■	
Pesticides, fertilizers, toxic, or hazardous products and chemicals		
Contact point on environmental matters	■	
Commitment to communicate the decisions or recommendations of joint environmental institutions	■	■
Public participation in the implementation of the agreement	■	■
Creation of an intergovernmental committee	■	
Establishment of an international secretariat to administer environmental norms of the treaty		
Environmental experts for state-state dispute over failure to enforce environmental measures or other environmental provisions of the agreement	■	■

NAFTA's environmental provisions	Also included in the USMCA and/or the ECA	Originally only included in the NAAEC and now included in the USMCA's main text
Environmental report in state-state dispute over failure to enforce environmental measures or other environmental provisions of the agreement	■	■
Environmental report in state-state dispute over trade provisions of the agreement		
Environmental report in investor-state dispute		
Non-jurisdictional mechanism for failure to enforce domestic environmental law		
Monetary enforcement assessments for failure to enforce domestic environmental law		
Suspension of benefits in case of failure to enforce domestic environmental law or to pay		
Non-jurisdictional DSM for environmental provisions	■	■
General DSM applying to environmental provisions	■	
General suspension of benefits applying to environmental provisions	■	
Exclusion of multilateral environmental agreements' DSM		
Implementation of 1972 Stockholm Declaration		
Implementation of 1992 Rio Declaration		

(continued)

Table 11.1 (continued)

NAFTA's environmental provisions	Also included in the USMCA and/or the ECA	Originally only included in the NAAEC and now included in the USMCA's main text
Implementation of other agreements related to the environment	■	
Prevalence of CITES	■	
Prevalence of Montreal Protocol	■	
Prevalence of Basel Convention	■	
Prevalence of other agreements related to the environment	■	
Other references to other institutions related to the environment		
International standards or risk assessments carried out by international organizations should be used or taken into account when designing environmental measures		
Party should use methods of risk assessment developed by international organizations		

intellectual property, sanitary and phytosanitary measures, and technical barriers to trade.

Furthermore, the USMCA (art. 24.25.3) maintains the Commission for Environmental Cooperation (CEC) created by the NAAEC, which is intended to foster cooperation among the NAFTA partners to address environmental issues on the North American continent.[7] Therefore, the CEC Secretariat will continue to be responsible for submissions on enforcement matters—allowing citizens and non-governmental organizations to allege that a USMCA party is failing to effectively enforce its domestic environmental laws—and for preparing a factual record if the submission warrants so. This procedure has been widely criticized by scholars, notably due to its slowness (Knox 2014). While the CEC Joint Public Advisory Committee recommended in 2001 a maximum timeline of two years between the filing of a submission and the publication of a factual record, the procedure actually took an average of five years for the years 2003 to 2008, and more than seven years in 2012 (Knox 2014, pp. 89–90). It is therefore noteworthy that the USMCA provides shorter time requirements than were included in the NAAEC, which could speed up the submission on enforcement matters procedure.[8] In addition, the CEC's activities will be complemented by the action of the "Environment Committee for Monitoring and Enforcement" established under the US USMCA Implementation Act. This committee will be tasked to monitor the implementation of the USMCA's environmental obligations and to carry out assessments of Canada and Mexico's environmental laws and policies.[9]

Despite the similarity between NAFTA's and the USMCA's environmental provisions, more than two and a half decades have passed since the adoption of the former. In that time, the way trade agreements address environmental issues has evolved significantly, and the USMCA reflects many of these developments. These developments are both structural and substantive. Structurally, for example, 33 environmental provisions that were only included in NAFTA's environmental side agreement (the NAAEC) now appear in the main text of the USMCA,[10] including, but not limited to, environmental dispute settlement, public participation, submissions on enforcement matters, and specific environmental issues such as endangered species and air pollution (see Table 11.1). Therefore, one way in which the USMCA is stronger than NAFTA is by including environmental provisions within the main trade agreement, and subjecting them to the agreement's dispute settlement mechanism, as is now standard practice in recent US trade agreements. Importantly, this means that environmental provisions are now fully enforceable through the use of trade sanctions, rather than just through the use of highly circumscribed penalties.

Substantively, Chapter 24 of the USMCA contains issue-specific provisions on water, coastal areas, plastic pollution, wetlands, contaminated lands, fisheries, forests, genetic resources, ozone layer depletion, and genetically modified organisms that were not included in NAFTA (see Fig. 11.2). In total, the USMCA addresses 30 environmental issues that were not mentioned in NAFTA. While the inclusion of issue-specific environmental provisions was until recently primarily a characteristic of European trade deals, NAFTA parties increasingly add issue-specific provisions to more general environmental provisions in their PTAs. This gradual shift is particularly noticeable since the signature of the US–Peru PTA in 2006 (Morin and Rochette 2017). Moreover, while the NAAEC only dealt with interactions between environmental policies and economic development, the USMCA addresses interactions between the environment and energy policies, social issues, indigenous communities,

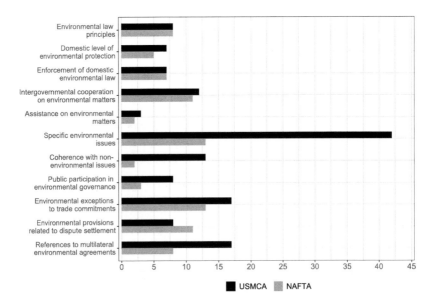

Fig. 11.2   Number of environmental provisions in NAFTA and the USMCA

and human health (see Fig. 11.2). The USMCA also adds provisions that were introduced in post-NAFTA PTAs, including on public participation in environmental impact assessments, public sessions of joint institutions, indirect expropriation of investments, and subsidies harmful to the environment.

The USMCA is also stronger than its predecessor in terms of obligations related to MEAs. Specifically, the Protocol of Amendment to the USMCA, agreed on December 10, 2019, restores NAFTA's Article 104 on the prevalence of MEA commitments in case of inconsistency with USMCA provisions. This protocol extends NAFTA's list of covered MEAs to include the International Convention for the Prevention of Pollution from Ships, the Ramsar Convention on Wetlands, the Convention on the Conservation of Antarctic Marine Living Resources, the International Convention for the Regulation of Whaling, and the Inter-American Tropical Tuna Convention. Article 24.8.4 of the USMCA further encourages the parties to fulfill their obligations under the seven covered MEAs, and Articles 1.3 and 24.8.5 enable adding additional MEAs in the future. These late additions to the USMCA's original text formed part of Democrats' demands for the agreement to be ratified in Congress[11] and echo the list of MEAs that must be mentioned in US PTAs, as set in the Bipartisan Agreement on Trade Policy signed on 10 May 2007, often referred to as the "May 10th agreement."

Finally, Fig. 11.2 shows that, as an exception, NAFTA includes more provisions related to dispute settlement than USMCA. This has to do with the fact that the NAAEC included a specific dispute settlement mechanism providing for consultations (art. 22), an arbitral panel (art. 24), a monetary enforcement assessment (art. 34.4), and a suspension of benefits (art. 36) should a party fail to enforce its domestic environmental laws. The USMCA, for its part, only addresses disputes in case of non-compliance with the environmental provisions of the agreement.

In sum, the USMCA reaffirms NAFTA's approach to environmental protection, and enhances it by bringing the environmental provisions into the main agreement and by adding environmental provisions that have either been introduced in PTAs after NAFTA's signature, or that reflect current practices in US PTAs. More specifically, the USMCA largely copies the TPP's environmental provisions. As referenced above, the best explanation for the similarity between the TPP and the USMCA is the "boilerplating" of environmental provisions from one trade agreement to the next. This practice contributes to coherence and consistency across PTAs, but it considerably limits the novel contribution of recent PTAs to environmental governance, and the USMCA makes no exception to this trend.

The Jettisoning of Two Contested Measures from the USMCA

The USMCA's contribution to environmental governance is perhaps more important as result of two NAFTA provisions that were removed from the agreement. Specifically, one of NAFTA's innovations consisted of strikingly detailed and comprehensive protections for investors (Chapter 11), including an investor–state dispute settlement (ISDS) system to enforce those protections. These provisions have been widely criticized by environmentalists, public interest groups, scholars, and politicians alike for giving foreign investors the power to sue governments for regulations that are designed to protect people or the environment (see McCarthy 2004; Nolan 2016).

There have been over 30 such cases under NAFTA as of 2018, which challenged policies in host countries related to environmental protection or resource management. Historically, these cases have been interpreted quite narrowly with ISDS tribunals ruling in favor of private investors (Sinclair 2018). For example, in one recent dispute, the US concrete company Bilcon initiated arbitration against Canada after a proposed quarry and marine terminal in the Canadian province of Nova Scotia, which would have been constructed and operated by Bilcon, was rejected after a lengthy environmental assessment. The environmental assessment found that the project would have had a significant and adverse impact on the "community core values" of the town of Digby Neck, the site of the proposed project. The project was rejected by the Nova Scotian and Canadian governments on these grounds. Bilcon argued that the environmental impact process unfairly and unreasonably considered "community core values," and that Nova Scotia officials had encouraged Bilcon to pursue the project, thereby providing Bilcon with a legitimate expectation that the project would have been approved. A majority of the tribunal found that by considering "community core values" in the environmental assessment process, Canada violated the national treatment standard (art. 1102) and minimum standard of treatment obligation (art. 1105) under NAFTA.[12] The arbiter appointed by Canada, Professor Donald McRae, provided a dissenting opinion wherein he cautioned that the tribunal's decision constituted an intrusion into domestic jurisdiction and that the decision risked creating a chill on environmental review processes.[13] Though Bilcon initially claimed over US$400 million in damages, the tribunal awarded Bilcon only US$7 million plus interest because Bilcon could not prove that the project "in all probability" would have been approved had the environmental review process been conducted fairly.[14] In other environment-related disputes, regulations that prevent the export of toxic polychlorinated biphenyl (PCB) wastes, phase out coal-fired electricity generation, prevent the conversion of land to extractive industrial use, and ban the disposal of radioactive wastes at sea have been challenged under NAFTA's ISDS procedures. Some argue that ISDS leads to a very real risk of regulatory chill, whereby regulators refrain from creating or enhancing environmental regulations to avoid being subject to costly litigation (see Sinclair 2018; Tienhaara 2018).

Important changes to ISDS under the USMCA signal a sharp divergence from both NAFTA and prior US and Canadian trade policy. Indeed, the removal of ISDS from the USMCA after a three-year period gives to this agreement a far more progressive stance on environmental issues than NAFTA, even if done unintentionally. However, it should be noted that it will still be possible, under certain circumstances discussed more thoroughly in Chapter 6 of this book on investment, for US and Mexican investors to bring claims against host governments for cases of direct expropriation or for violation of national treatment or most-favored-nation obligations. Moreover, the USMCA still allows for indefinite access to ISDS for US and Mexican investors on a wider range of claims for "covered government contracts" (annex 14-E 6.a) in certain sectors, including oil and natural gas. Therefore, in a win for multinational energy companies, such as Chevron and ExxonMobil, the USMCA will allow these companies to use ISDS to protect their investments in Mexico's newly liberalized oil and gas sector, which is particularly important for these companies after the election of President Obrador in Mexico, who has displayed opposition to the sector's liberalization. Nevertheless, the elimination of Canadian involvement in the USMCA's ISDS and the restricted availability of ISDS between Mexico and the US will have important implications for how US–Mexico–Canada trade and investment relations will shape environmental governance in North America, since many of the investor disputes previously brought against Canada and the other parties will no longer be possible under the USMCA.[15]

The second controversial element of NAFTA that was left out of the USMCA is the energy proportionality rule (art. 605), which requires that

Canada exports to the US at least the same proportion of its energy output as it did during the previous three years. This includes 74% of the oil and 52% of the natural gas that Canada produces (Laxer 2018). The withdrawal of this rule will make it easier for Canada to meet its mitigation commitments under the Paris Agreement. This is because the extraction of oil and gas accounts for more of Canada's greenhouse-gas (GHG) emissions than does its consumption. This means Canada's ability to reduce its GHG emissions through, for example, a carbon tax is restrained if it must continue to produce high volumes of oil and gas for export. If Canada were to reduce its oil and gas extraction with the proportionality rule still in place, it would be required to export more of what it produces, and rely on greater levels of oil imports to meet its domestic needs (Laxer 2018; see also Hughes 2010; Laxer and Dillon 2008). Therefore, in order to simultaneously meet Canadian domestic needs for oil and gas, and meet its commitments under the Paris Agreement, it must wind down its oil and gas exports (Laxer 2018; Ackerman et al. 2018). With the jettison of the proportionality rule in the new agreement, Canada will be able to rely on its own oil and gas for domestic use until replacements are viable.

Conclusion

The USMCA is notable in that it contains the largest number of environmental provisions of any PTA negotiated to date. Further, the agreement reflects a strengthening of environmental governance over NAFTA's approach by, in line with other recent US PTAs, bringing environmental provisions into the main agreement, and subjecting them to the same dispute settlement mechanism. This outcome is largely consistent with the negotiating objectives of the United States, Canada, and Mexico, which, as regards the environment, focused on upgrading the agreement to reflect recent practices in PTAs. In addition, the agreement could potentially enhance environmental governance in North America by its jettisoning of the ISDS mechanism and the energy proportionality rule. Therefore, NAFTA's renegotiation led to clear improvements in terms of environmental content.

Despite its high number of environmental provisions, however, the USMCA could do more to improve environmental governance in the context of North American trade relations. For instance, the agreement does not acknowledge the precautionary principle, providing that "where there are threats of serious or irreversible damage, lack of full scientific certainty shall not be used as a reason for postponing cost-effective measures to prevent environmental degradation" (Rio Declaration, principle 15). This principle usually appears in European PTAs and was first included in a Canadian trade deal with the signature of the Comprehensive Economic and Trade Agreement (CETA) in 2016. Yet, aside from some tangential provisions related to technical barriers to trade in NAFTA, which have also diffused to some Mexican PTAs,[16] the US tends to avoid including the precautionary principle in any of its PTAs. Indeed, one of its NAFTA renegotiation objectives was to ensure that regulating practices were "evidence-based."

Finally, as stressed by many analysts,[17] the USMCA does not explicitly mention climate change, global warming, or greenhouse gases. This can largely be explained by the US's TPA-2015, which prohibits the US from including obligations to reduce carbon emissions in its PTAs as a condition of fast-track authority (see Jinnah and Morin 2020, p. 170). This marks a setback for the Trudeau government's progressive trade agenda, especially since the CETA includes provisions on climate change (arts. 24.9 and 24.12.2). More generally, in light of the urgency of reducing greenhouse gases emissions and the potential for trade agreements and obligations to either stifle or support this task (see Das et al. 2018), this is an important missed opportunity.

NOTES

1. For a list of measures related to the environment taken by the Trump administration, see, for instance, Greshko et al. (2017).
2. For a general discussion of trade and environment issues, see Esty (2001); for a discussion on how NAFTA addresses the environment and the impacts on Mexico, see Gallagher (2004).
3. For a description of environmental provisions in US trade agreements, see Jinnah and Morgera (2013).
4. The US has linked some environmental provisions, such as those related to failure to enforce environmental laws, to dispute settlement since 2004 in a limited capacity. However, the 2007 Bipartisan Agreement on Trade Policy has since required that *all* US PTA environmental obligations "will be enforced on the same basis as the commercial provisions of our agreements – same remedies, procedures, and sanctions" (USTR 2007, p. 2). It should be noted that in practice, the use of such remedies, procedures, and sanctions to enforce environmental obligations is rare. At least part

of the reason for this may be that environmental NGOs appear to favor "constructive engagement" over trade sanctions to encourage progress on environmental commitments, at least in the case of Peru (Peinhardt et al. 2019).

5. Example, TPP, art. 20.23.1; CETA, art. 24.15.2; CUFTA, art. 12.21.8.
6. The CPTPP is the successor to the TPP following the US withdrawal in January 2017.
7. The Environmental Cooperation Agreement (ECA) further restates the functions of the CEC's Council, Secretariat, and Joint Public Advisory Committee.
8. For instance, the Secretariat must henceforth submit a draft factual record to the Council within 120 days of the Council's instruction to prepare a factual record (USMCA, art. 24.28.5). Moreover, the delay for a party to provide comments on the draft factual report, as well as the delay to publish the final report following its submission to the Council, are reduced from 45 to 30 days (USMCA, art. 24.28.5).
9. Executive Order on the Establishment of the Environment Committee for Monitoring and Enforcement under the USMCA Implementation Act, February 29, 2020.
10. As in the case of NAFTA, an ECA was signed alongside the USMCA's main text. Concluding environmental side agreements in addition to the PTA's Environment Chapter is common practice among the US and Canada (see, e.g., Canada–Panama 2010; Canada–Honduras 2013; US–Chile 2003; US–Singapore 2003; US–Peru 2006; US–Panama 2007). However, unlike its predecessors, the USMCA includes far more detailed and numerous environmental provisions in its Environment Chapter than in its ECA.
11. For a more detailed account of adds-on to the USMCA's original text, see United States (2019).
12. *Clayton/Bilcon v. Canada*, Award on Jurisdiction and Liability, March17, 2015. UNCITRAL Permanent Court of Arbitration (PCA) Case No. 2009–04.
13. *Clayton/Bilcon v. Canada*, Dissenting Opinion of Professor Donald McRae, March10, 2015. UNCITRAL Permanent Court of Arbitration (PCA) Case No. 2009–04.
14. *Clayton/Bilcon v. Canada*, Award on Damages, January 10, 2019. UNCITRAL Permanent Court of Arbitration (PCA) Case No. 2009–04.
15. However, the USMCA's Chapter 28 on "Good Regulatory Practices" provides alternative avenues for firms to influence regulation by allowing them to comment on regulations under development and to suggest improvements on existing regulations (Tienhaara 2019).
16. The NAFTA's provision, subsequently included in four Mexican PTAs (Mexico–Bolivia1994; Group of Three 1994; Mexico–Chile 1998; and

Mexico–Northern Triangle 2000), reads as follows: "Where a Party conducting an assessment of risk determines that available scientific evidence or other information is insufficient to complete the assessment, it may adopt a provisional technical regulation on the basis of available relevant information. The Party shall, within a reasonable period after information sufficient to complete the assessment of risk is presented to it, complete its assessment, review and, where appropriate, revise the provisional technical regulationin the light of that assessment" (art. 907.3).

17. See, e.g., Lilliston (2018), Mertins-Kirkwood (2018), Weber (2018), and Tienhaara (2019).

REFERENCES

Ackerman, Frank, Alejandro Álvarez Béjar, Gordon Laxer, and Ben Beachy. 2018. *NAFTA 2.0: For People or Polluters? A Climate Denier's Trade Deal versus a Clean Energy Economy*. Ottawa: The Council of Canadians.

Allee, Todd, and Manfred Elsig. 2019. Are the Contents of International Treaties Copied and Pasted? Evidence from Preferential Trade Agreements. *International Studies Quarterly* 63 (3): 603–613.

Charnovitz, Steve. 1994. The NAFTA Environmental Side Agreement: Implications for Environmental Cooperation, Trade Policy, and American Treaty-making. *Temple International and Comparative Law Journal* 8 (2): 257–314.

Das, Kasturi, Haro van Asselt, Susan Droege, and Michael Mehling. 2018. *Making the International Trade System Work for Climate Change: Assessing the Options*. Climate Strategies, July. https://tinyurl.com/ycrs7yxz. Accessed on September 29, 2021.

Esty, Daniel C. 2001. Bridging the Trade-Environment Divide. *Journal of Economic Perspectives* 15 (3): 113–130.

Gallagher, Kevin. 2004. *Free Trade and the Environment: Mexico, NAFTA, and Beyond*. Palo Alto: Stanford University Press.

Greshko, Michael, Laura Parker, Brian C. Howard, Daniel Stone, Alejandra Borunda, and Sarah Gibbens. 2017. A Running List of How President Trump Is Changing Environmental Policy. *National Geographic*. https://tinyurl.com/yck2u8g5. Accessed on September 29, 2021.

Hughes, Larry. 2010. Eastern Canadian Crude Oil Supply and Its Implications for Regional Energy Security. *Energy Policy* 38 (6): 2692–2699.

Jinnah, Sikina. 2011. Strategic Linkages: The Evolving Role of Trade Agreements in Global Environmental Governance. *The Journal of Environment & Development* 20 (2): 191–215.

Jinnah, Sikina, and Abby Lindsay. 2016. Diffusion Through Issue Linkage: Environmental Norms in US Trade Agreements. *Global Environmental Politics* 16 (3): 41–61.

Jinnah, Sikina, and Elisa Morgera. 2013. Environmental Provisions in US and EU Trade Agreements: A Comparative Analysis. *Review of European Comparative and International Environmental Law* 22 (3): 224–339.

Jinnah, Sikina, and Jean-Frédéric Morin. 2020. *Greening through Trade: How American Trade Policy Is Linked to Environmental Protection Abroad.* Cambridge: MIT Press.

Jo, Hyeran, and Hyun Namgung. 2012. Dispute Settlement Mechanisms in Preferential Trade Agreements: Democracy, Boilerplates, and the Multilateral Trade Regime. *Journal of Conflict Resolution* 56 (6): 1041–1068.

Knox, John H. 2014. Fixing the CEC Submissions Procedure: Are the 2012 Revisions up to the Task? *Golden Gate University Environmental Law Journal* 7 (1): 81–107.

Laxer, Gordon. 2018. *Escaping Mandatory Oil Exports: Why Canada Needs to Dump NAFTA's Energy Proportionality Rule.* Ottawa: The Council of Canadians.

Laxer, Gordon, and John Dillon. 2008. *Over a Barrel: Exiting from NAFTA's Proportionality Clause.* Edmonton: Parkland Institute.

Lilliston, Ben. 2018. *"New NAFTA" Continues Damaging Climate Legacy.* Institute for Agriculture & Trade Policy, October. https://tinyurl.com/y58 e4qm2. Accessed on September 29, 2021.

McCarthy, James. 2004. Privatizing Conditions of Production: Trade Agreements as Neoliberal Environmental Governance. *Geoforum* 35 (3): 327–341.

Mertins-Kirkwood, Hadrian. 2018. Updated NAFTA Deal a Profound Failure for Climate Action. *Behind the Numbers Blog*, October 12. https://tinyurl. com/y4wev3vu. Accessed on September 29, 2021.

Morin, Jean-Frédéric, and Myriam Rochette. 2017. Transatlantic Convergence of Preferential Trade Agreements Environmental Clauses. *Business and Politics* 19 (4): 621–658.

Morin, Jean-Frédéric, Andreas Dür, and Lisa Lechner. 2018. Mapping the Trade and Environment Nexus: Insights from a New Data Set. *Global Environmental Politics* 18 (1): 122–139.

Morin, Jean-Frédéric, Joost Pauwelyn, and James Hollway. 2017. The Trade Regime as a Complex Adaptive System: Exploration and Exploitation of Environmental Norms in Trade Agreements. *Journal of International Economic Law* 20 (2): 365–390.

Nolan, Michael. 2016. Challenges to the Credibility of the Investor-State Arbitration System. *American University Business Law Review* 5 (3): 429–446.

Oxford Business Group. n.d. *Reforms, Liberalization open Mexico's Energy Sector to Private Investment and Emphasize Clean, Sustainable Energy.* http://tinyurl.com/y2dh4rek. Accessed on September 29, 2021.

Peinhardt, Clint, Alisha A. Kim, and Viveca Pavon-Harr. 2019. Deforestation and the United States-Peru Trade Promotion Agreement. *Global Environmental Politics* 19 (1): 53–76.

Sinclair, Scott. 2018. *Canada's Track Record Under NAFTA Chapter 11: North American Investor–State Disputes to January 2018.* Ottawa: Canadian Centre for Policy Alternatives. https://tinyurl.com/y7xxeyfm. Accessed on September 29, 2021.

Tienhaara, Kyla. 2018. Regulatory Chill in a Warming World: The Threat to Climate Policy Posed by Investor-State Dispute Settlement. *Transnational Environmental Law* 7 (2): 229–250.

Tienhaara, Kyla. 2019. NAFTA 2.0: What Are the Implications for Environmental Governance? *Earth System Governance* 1: 100004.

Vaughan, Scott. 2018. USMCA Versus NAFTA on the Environment. *International Institute for Sustainable Development Blog*, October 3. https://tinyurl.com/y6pr5vcv. Accessed on September 29, 2021.

Weber, Bob. 2018. New Trade Deal Doesn't Address Climate Change: Environmentalists. *CTV News*, October 1. https://tinyurl.com/ya67u9jq. Accessed on September 29, 2021.

OFFICIAL DOCUMENTS

Bipartisan Congressional Trade Priorities and Accountability Act of 2015, S. 995, 114th Congress. https://tinyurl.com/vbsyrv7x. Accessed September 29, 2021.

Canada-Ukraine Free Trade Agreement (CUFTA), signed July 11, 2016, entered into force August 1, 2017. https://tinyurl.com/zsk893b4. Accessed September 29, 2021.

Comprehensive and Progressive Agreement for Trans-Pacific Partnership (CPTPP), signed March 8, 2018, entered into force December 30, 2018. https://tinyurl.com/2yyecefy. Accessed September 29, 2021.

Comprehensive Economic and Trade Agreement (CETA), signed October 30, 2016, entered provisionally into force September 21, 2017. https://tinyurl.com/eakp3j2c. Accessed on September 29, 2021.

Global Affairs Canada. 2017. *Address by Foreign Affairs Minister on the Modernization of the North American Free Trade Agreement (NAFTA).* August 14. http://tinyurl.com/ybuuptvj. Accessed on September 29, 2021.

North American Agreement on Environmental Cooperation (NAAEC), signed September 14, 1993, entered into force January 1, 1994. https://tinyurl.com/j8awnfm8. Accessed on September 29, 2021.

North American Free Trade Agreement (NAFTA), signed December 17, 1992, entered into force January 1, 1994. https://tinyurl.com/2cayvy8a. Accessed on September 29, 2021.

Office of the United States Trade Representative (USTR). 2007. *Bipartisan Agreement on Trade Policy.* https://tinyurl.com/q9qlo9m. Accessed on September 29, 2021.

Office of the United States Trade Representative (USTR). 2017. *Summary of Objectives for the NAFTA Renegotiation,* July 17. http://tinyurl.com/ycg rwnnq. Accessed on September 29, 2021.

Office of the United States Trade Representative (USTR). 2018. *United States–Mexico–Canada Trade Fact Sheet: Modernizing NAFTA into a 21st Century Trade Agreement.* http://tinyurl.com/y5xppvlm. Accessed on September 29, 2021.

Office of the United States Trade Representative (USTR). 2019. *2019 Trade Policy Agenda and 2018 Annual Report.* https://tinyurl.com/jayrptv5. Accessed on September 29, 2021.

Protocol of Amendment to the United States-Mexico-Canada Agreement, signed December 10, 2019. https://tinyurl.com/3n8jsy4p. Accessed on September 29, 2021.

Rio Declaration on Environment and Development (Rio Declaration). https://tinyurl.com/3sta6ra6. Accessed on September 29, 2021.

Secretaría de Economía. 2017. *Prioridades de México en las negociaciones para la modernización del Tratado de Libre Comercio de América del Norte.* http://tinyurl.com/y5t5buwh. Accessed on September 29, 2021.

Trans-Pacific Partnership (TPP), signed February 4, 2016. https://tinyurl.com/2huw9x2x. Accessed on September 29, 2021.

United States. House of Representatives, Committee on Ways and Means. 2019. *Improvements to the USMCA.* https://tinyurl.com/t7qmabd. Accessed on September 29, 2021.

United States-Mexico-Canada Agreement (USMCA), signed November 30, 2018, entered into force July 1, 2020. https://tinyurl.com/rtaucx5v. Accessed on September 29, 2021.

CHAPTER 12

Canada and International Regulatory Cooperation: A Comparison of USMCA, CETA and CPTPP

Christian Deblock

Regulatory cooperation (RC) now covers most areas of public regulation. Its main objective is to improve the latter's efficiency, consistency, predictability and accountability. The debate does not only involve the public sector; it also covers norms and standards, and increasingly corporate governance. A second, newer aspect of the debate concerns its international dimension.[1] The variety of national regulations, their differences and even their conflicts, constitute an important obstacle to trade and direct investment. Moreover, they may have a significant impact on the competitiveness of companies as well as that of nations.[2] With globalization and interconnection, the debate has taken on a new twist, as far as trade along value chains, commercial services or electronic commerce

C. Deblock (✉)
Department of Political Science, Université du Québec à Montréal, Montréal, QC, Canada
e-mail: deblock.christian@uqam.ca

© The Author(s), under exclusive license to Springer Nature
Switzerland AG 2022
G. Gagné and M. Rioux (eds.), *NAFTA 2.0*,
Canada and International Affairs,
https://doi.org/10.1007/978-3-030-81694-0_12

are concerned (Ahmed 2019). Finally, digital technologies appear and develop faster than regulations and institutions.

As we can see, there is no shortage of arguments to justify regulatory efficiency and international cooperation (Von Lampe et al. 2016).[3] However, despite some notable progress, the number of countries that have a coordinated approach or that use impact analysis remains limited. The situation is even worse on the international scene where efforts to improve regulatory transparency and develop recognized international standards are struggling to progress (OECD 2018). The Organization for Economic Cooperation and Development (OECD) is more than ever at the center of the debate, both on regulatory practices and on international regulatory cooperation (IRC). The same is true of the World Trade Organization (WTO), for a long time already at the forefront of the trade debate with the Agreement on the Application of Sanitary and Phytosanitary (SPS) Measures or, now, with the Agreement on Trade Facilitation. But, here again, progress is slow. No doubt for methodological reasons—the enhanced dialogue at the OECD and the consensus at the WTO—but also because the debate on regulations remains ultimately a political debate. More recently, from the 2010s, another path has been taken, that of preferential trade agreements (PTAs).

Several factors, including globalization and interconnection, are pushing states to go in this direction and include in the main body of agreements specific provisions on RC. In fact, this inclusion is one of the main features of third-generation agreements. Three of them deserve attention in this chapter: the Comprehensive Economic and Trade Agreement (CETA) between Canada and the European Union (EU), the Comprehensive and Progressive Agreement for Trans-Pacific Partnership (CPTPP) and the latest, the United States–Mexico–Canada Agreement (USMCA). Not only because they are pioneering agreements, but above all because each of these PTAs advocates a different approach to cooperation. This is what I propose to focus on in the following pages. But, first, let us start by drawing the perimeter of RC. I will then compare the chapters on RC in these three recent PTAs, focusing on three points: (1) principles and objectives; (2) institutional frameworks and (3) procedures.

THE SCOPE OF REGULATORY COOPERATION

The debate on RC has entered into trade negotiations on non-tariff barriers, leading to three important agreements at the WTO: on technical barriers to trade (TBT), on SPS measures and, more recently, on trade facilitation. These agreements are often presented as "technical" agreements, but RC today covers fields as diverse as intellectual property, public procurement, telecommunications, electronic commerce, professional qualifications, environment, etc. International cooperation aims to cover all public regulations and directives, giving priority to those affecting trade and investment.

International Regulatory Cooperation

Trade but also investment are privileged fields insofar as IRC aims to ensure that technical or non-technical regulations, standards and procedures are non-discriminatory and do not create unnecessary obstacles to trade.[4] The OECD,[5] in its own work, is going in the same direction: regulations, by their administrative and cumbersome nature, their variety and their divergences, come to affect trade and investment flows, but also the competitiveness of nations. For the OECD, as well as for the WTO, it is important to assess the usefulness of regulations and their impact, to bring national regulators together and to encourage the adoption of good practices between member countries. Let us avoid any misunderstanding: the field of action of IRC is not limited to trade, an area that it shares with the WTO,[6] it covers the whole range of regulatory areas.

The OECD defines IRC as follows:

> IRC can be defined as any step taken by countries (or jurisdictions), formal or informal, unilaterally, bilaterally or multilaterally, to promote some form of co-ordination / coherence in the design, monitoring, enforcement, or ex post management of regulation. (OECD 2013)

The Canadian perspective is very similar to that of the OECD. The Treasury Board Secretariat, responsible for RC for Canada, defines it as follows:

> Regulatory cooperation is a process where governments work together to: reduce unnecessary regulatory differences; eliminate duplicative requirements and processes; harmonize or align regulations; share information and experiences; and adopt international standards. (Canada 2020)

One of the main objectives of IRC is not only to bring national regulations closer—or even to harmonize them—but also procedures, methods and practices. Through dialogue between regulators, but also by using common governance frameworks. In many respects, RC draws inspiration from established practices in the area of industrial norms and standards. The scope of IRC is, of course, different since most regulations apply to human practices, but there is a very clear desire to adopt the same approach and to objectify as much as possible the whole approval process: from planning to implementation through monitoring. Great importance is also given to impact studies, performance analyses and other governance indicators, to the opinions of experts, to stakeholder consultation, *et cetera*. Essentially, five main performance criteria guide the whole process: usefulness, efficiency, transparency, predictability and temporality.

Good Regulatory Practices

A certain consensus has been established internationally to make "good (or better) regulatory practices" (GRPs) a principle of conduct in discussions between regulators. The OECD and most trade agreements openly refer to it (Basedow and Kauffmann 2016). However, as an EU document notes, there is no single definition of what is meant by GRPs[7]:

> There is no one definition or exhaustive list of GRPs. But the most commonly recognized ones include a commitment to: 1) provide information on our regulatory agendas; 2) consult stakeholders and the public; 3) assess potential impacts of future regulation before issuing regulations; and 4) after regulations have been in place for some time, evaluate their performance in delivering the intended outcomes. (European Commission 2016, p. 2)

What do trade agreements say? Nothing very clear in fact. USMCA and CETA make extensive use of the expression in the body of the text, but without defining it. CPTPP, on the other hand, gives a definition of "regulatory coherence" which covers GRPs:

[R]egulatory coherence refers to the use of good regulatory practices in the process of planning, designing, issuing, implementing and reviewing regulatory measures in order to facilitate achievement of domestic policy objectives, and in efforts across governments to enhance regulatory cooperation in order to further those objectives and promote international trade and investment, economic growth and employment. (art. 25.2)

USMCA does not give a definition of GRP, which is all the more astonishing. Not only Chapter 28 relates explicitly to GRPs, but it also affirms that they are fundamental to effective RC. This chapter nevertheless sets out "specific obligations with respect to good regulatory practices, including practices relating to the planning, design, issuance, implementation, and review of the Parties' respective regulations" (art. 28.2). This covers the entire decision-making process, from the planning stage to implementation.

The CETA chapter on RC does not refer to good practices (or best practices). However, GRPs can be traced in the text of the agreement when it comes to manufacturing, as well as in the agenda and the work plan of the Regulatory Cooperation Forum (RCF) (art. 21.6).

A memorandum of understanding (MOU) on GRPs reached between Canada and Mexico in 2018 provides some details on the concept. It gives the following definitions:

a. Good Regulatory Practices means internationally recognized processes, systems, tools and methods in areas like regulatory development, regulatory cooperation, stakeholder engagement, openness and transparency, and beyond, for improving the quality of regulations.

b. International Regulatory Cooperation means a good regulatory practice that is a process to find efficiencies across jurisdictions and reduce unnecessary regulatory differences. (MOU CAN-MEX, art. 2.a–b)

The 2018 MOU between Canada and the United States is a little different in that its purpose is to advance the work of the Regulatory Cooperation Council (RCC). Thus, it emphasizes the extent of cooperation and, above all, the initiative, review and follow-up processes. Annex 1 nevertheless specifies that the objectives of the RCC are to:

i. facilitate coordination between agencies and departments in both countries, enable engagement between stakeholders and regulators and promote opportunities for cooperation and

ii. foster alignment of existing federal regulatory activities where feasible and appropriate or, absent such alignment, explore the possibility of adopting other measures in order to reduce, eliminate or prevent unnecessary regulatory differences between both countries while maintaining high levels of protection for health, safety and the environment (MOU CAN-US, annex I, art. 1.i–ii).

Canada and IRC

A few words to complete this overview, on Canada's RC program.[8] It has two components. First, a national component. A Canadian free trade agreement (CFTA) has been signed between the federal, provincial and territorial governments.[9] It has been in effect since July 1, 2017. The objective of this agreement is to improve interprovincial trade and facilitate the free movement of people, goods, services and investment within Canada. Cooperation takes place through the Regulatory Reconciliation and Cooperation Table (CFTA, art. 404). Several conciliation agreements[10] have thus been concluded, covering fields as diverse as health and safety at work, transport, agricultural products, professional recognition, building codes, textiles, *et cetera*.

The international component covers Canada's participation in the work of large international organizations and fora, in particular the WTO and the OECD, as well as in the work of various committees set up under PTAs. I will come back to USMCA later, but I would like to emphasize that, although the United States and Canada have been cooperating for a long time, this took on a more formal character with the creation, in 2011, of the RCC.[11] The overall objective of this council is "to reduce the unnecessary regulatory burden on stakeholders, while continuing to protect the health and safety of citizens and the environment." More specifically, the objectives are to facilitate coordination between the two countries, to promote the harmonization of federal regulatory activities and to reduce, eliminate or prevent unnecessary divergences.[12] It is within this framework that a MOU was signed on June 4, 2018 between the two countries. And this with the objective of tightening RC between the two countries, resolving differences and promoting harmonization, especially with regard to new regulations and to sectors of deep integration or high integration potential.[13]

Bilateral cooperation is more modest with Mexico but on February 7, 2018, Canada nevertheless signed a MOU "for the advancement of good regulatory practices."[14] Its purpose is twofold: to promote GRP, including regulatory development, and advancing the adoption of GRPs across Latin America and the Caribbean. It should be noted about this memorandum (1) that it emphasizes good practices and (2) that the work plan focuses mainly on mutual exchange of information, data, experiences and best practices, technical visits and workshops training.

Regulatory cooperation in USMCA, CETA and CPTPP

Let us now see the provisions relating to IRC in these three PTAs.

Principles and Objectives

CETA came into force on September 21, 2017, on a temporary basis. It is the first PTA signed by Canada to include a specific chapter on RC (ch. 21). It bears the imprint of the EU, as we will see below. Three points should be emphasized.

First, by its title, "Regulatory Cooperation," CETA is clearly different from CPTPP and USMCA. The emphasis is clearly placed on cooperation, and not on "regulatory coherence" (CPTPP) or on "good practices" (USMCA).

Second, trade and investment are ranked third, and the competitiveness and efficiency of the industry fourth in the objectives of RC, behind: a) "the protection of human life, health or safety, animal or plant life or health and the environment"; and b) the goal "to build trust, deepen mutual understanding of regulatory governance and obtain from each other the benefit of expertise and perspectives" (CETA, art. 21.3).

Third, as already mentioned, the chapter does not refer to good practices, more precisely "best practices" as elsewhere in the text of the agreement. Partly out of prudence, partly to respect the EU vision of trade associated with sustainable development, the negotiators preferred to prioritize the principles and objectives of cooperation rather than to insist on practices and methods. Having said that, CETA is a trade agreement. We can therefore expect that RC will take place first and foremost in the areas that affect the production of goods and services and their trade, and that it is at this level that the use of "best practices" will take on its full significance. That said, the prioritization of objectives amounts to prioritizing rights. And this could be important in the future, especially in the event of differences of views between regulators.

In addition to focusing on GRPs, the USMCA's chapter on RC is different from CETA's one on a second point: it focuses clearly on trade and economic growth. Its definition of RC is quite explicit in this regard:

> [R]egulatory cooperation means an effort between two or more Parties to prevent, reduce, or eliminate unnecessary regulatory differences to facilitate trade and promote economic growth, while maintaining or enhancing standards of public health and safety and environmental protection. (USMCA, art. 28.1)

Article 28.2, entitled "Subject Matter and General Provisions," takes up and refines this definition:

> The Parties recognize that implementation of government-wide practices to promote regulatory quality through greater transparency, objective analysis, accountability, and predictability can facilitate international trade, investment, and economic growth, while contributing to each Party's ability to achieve its public policy objectives (including health, safety, and environmental goals) at the level of protection it considers appropriate. (USMCA, art. 28.2.1)

Admittedly, the text of the agreement guarantees the respect of collective choices in matters of health, public safety, environment, *et cetera*. Likewise, it recalls that the provisions of the chapter do not prevent a party from "a) pursuing its public policy objectives (including health, safety, and environmental goals) at the level it considers to be appropriate" (USMCA, art. 28.2.3.a). But in the end, trade and growth remain the top objectives of RC.

The chapter of the CPTPP devoted to RC is much more modest in scope. Its sole objective is to make more coherent the process of planning, designing, issuing, implementing and reviewing regulatory measures. This is meant to better achieve public policy objectives and to facilitate the work of intergovernmental RC initiatives. The emphasis, as we can see, is above all on awareness and commitment, which can be understood insofar as some of the contracting parties were not ready to commit too far, for strategic reasons or, more simply, for lack of capacity. The fact remains that this chapter commits and invites all parties not only to streamline their regulatory processes, but also (1) to implement "core regulatory practices" and (2) "to stimulate trade, international investment, and economic growth and job creation" (CPTPP, art. 25.5).

Institutional Frameworks

Of the three agreements under review, the USMCA is the one that most closely marks out the objectives and work of committees and other working groups. The agreement indeed provides for the establishment of four different levels of cooperation: (1) a national centralized regulatory coordination especially mandated to promote GRPs within governmental and quasi-governmental agencies; (2) the creation of a trilateral committee on good practices; (3) an intergovernmental consultation mechanism and ministerial contact points and (4) the constitution of subcommittees and working groups as well as the use of expert advisory groups or bodies.

The role of the trilateral committee essentially consists of coordinating activities, monitoring the implementation and follow-up of decisions, carrying out consultations and investigations, coordinating the activities of subcommittees and other working groups. It should also be noted that reference is made to RC in several of the chapters of the USMCA, in particular those dealing with energy, telecommunications, SPS standards or even the environment.

In comparison, the institutional framework of the CPTPP is consistent with the objectives of its RC chapter. The first objective of this chapter is to urge the contracting parties to "bring order" to their regulations and regulatory practices, thus paving the way to cooperation. In addition to good practices, reference is made to the need for the parties to set up a centralized regulatory governance structure. A second objective is to promote consultation, the exchange of information, dialogue and experiences between the parties.[15] The third objective, perhaps the most distant, is to bring the regulations closer and involve all stakeholders in this process. It will be the purpose and role of the Committee on Regulatory Coherence: proceeding in small steps, at the rhythm of each but in the same direction, as in the Association of Southeast Asian Nations.[16]

The institutional framework for CETA, on the other hand, is very unique. The negotiators had to deal with very different institutional realities on both sides of the Atlantic. Besides, the trade negotiations conducted by Europe are always coupled with a strategic framework that

engages the partners in terms of human rights, social rights, environment, *et cetera*. These realities are reflected in the statement of objectives
of the RC chapter but also in the way in which the cooperation bodies
were designed. There are contact points as well as working and consultation groups, in particular with "Private Entities," but, fundamentally,
cooperation revolves around the RCF.

The functions entrusted to this forum are very numerous (art. 21.6)
but, essentially, they revolve around four points: (1) discuss regulatory
policy issues of mutual interest that the parties have identified; (2) assist
individual regulators to identify potential partners for cooperation activities and provide them with appropriate tools; (3) review regulatory
initiatives and (4) encourage the development of bilateral cooperation
activities. Consultations and calls for proposals are not limited to the sole
private sector, but are also aimed at civil society. This opens up many
perspectives for non-governmental organizations, trade unions and other
civil society actors.[17]

Procedures

In the case of technical standards, obviously the main objective is harmonization but, failing that, mutual recognition remains a second-best
option.[18] The EU has a long history in this area; it is therefore not
surprising that several mutual acceptance protocols can be found in
CETA.[19] Mutual acceptance and certification procedures should reduce
delays and administrative formalities and facilitate the entry of products.
They complement what is covered, and in great length, in Chapter 4 on
TBT, which is itself very detailed.[20] The same goes for USMCA and its
Chapter 11 that also deals with TBT. That said, let us now see what the
texts say about the procedures and modus operandi of RC.

First of all, within CETA, RC is on a voluntary basis. A party is not
required to participate in an activity and can refuse or cease to cooperate.
At most, it may be asked to explain the reasons for its decision. It is
also reaffirmed, as in the case of the other two PTAs, that RC in no
way limits "each Party to carry out its regulatory, legislative and policy
activities" (art. 21.2.4). The objective is not to harmonize regulations,
but to improve their efficiency and compatibility.

Three other points are important to highlight about CETA. First,
the importance placed on trust, understanding and expertise. It is no
coincidence that this point is second among the four objectives of RC.

This acknowledges the collective choices of each party and, in so doing, averts disputes over principles.[21] Next, the list of cooperation activities (art. 21.4) is as long as it is very wide, with no less than 19 points! It is also expected that the parties will exchange information between themselves about planned or ongoing regulatory projects. Finally, the provisions of Chapter 21 are not subject to the agreement's dispute settlementmechanism.

In fact, the chapter was seemingly designed to meet the needs of governments, industry and civil society by entrusting the RCF with the mandate to give itself a work plan and to organize consultation, information exchange and dialogue between regulators and stakeholders. One may wonder, however, whether there is not also an intention, no doubt more ambitious, of bringing regulatory systems closer together at a level more fundamental than practices, to that of principles.[22] This would make sense of the first part of the second objective: "build trust, deepen mutual understanding of regulatory governance" (CETA, art. 21.3.b).

The approach, procedures and working methods in USMCA are different from those found in CETA. In this regard, it should be recalled that it was under the presidency of Barak Obama that the United States made a real commitment not only to bring order to its own regulations, but also to make IRC one of its top priorities.[23] Five guidelines can be found: (1) centralization of the regulatory process; (2) transparency, predictability and accountability; (3) the use of impact studies; (4) reduction of regulatory costs (5) and regulatory impact on international trade (see Deblock and Wells 2017).

Even if the North American Free Trade Agreement (NAFTA) already addressed RC through committees or working groups, in particular on agricultural products, SPS measures or measures linked to standards, discussions remained limited to the areas that had been identified. Those relating to other fields were referred either to specialized bilateral cooperation agreements or, more broadly, to the work of the RCC mentioned above. With USMCA and its chapter devoted to RC, the latter takes on another dimension.

First, the methodological approach repeats, in fact, that already adopted within the framework of the RCC,[24] but the procedures are presented in great detail and long exposed. There are no less than 15 successive articles dealing with them, presented according to a logic that closely follows the entire regulatory process, from the initial planning of regulations to their implementation and their retrospective review, including their development, consultation experts, impact studies, publicization, *et cetera.* Two articles are particularly important: that on the "transparent development of regulations" (USMCA, art. 28.9) and that on "regulatory impact assessment" (art. 28.11). Article 28.9 insists on the transparency of the process, the dissemination of information and the impact study but also on the possibility of any interested person—regardless of domicile—to provide comments. Regulations that have a significant impact on trade are the subject of particular attention. Note also that it is expected from each of the parties that it publishes, annually, the list of regulations that it intends to adopt or propose during the next 12 months. In addition to the advisory opinion of expert groups, USMCA stipulates that all regulations must be subject not only to an impact study (art. 28.11), but also to a retrospective review (art. 28.13).

Second, including IRC in a trade agreement gives it more strength. In this regard, the possibility of having recourse to dispute settlement must be noted. Article 28.20 is very convoluted but it nevertheless breaks with the established practice of not resorting to the dispute settlement mechanism for RC. Indeed, after recognizing that it is often possible to find a mutually satisfactory solution, the text appeals to the discernment of the parties to assess the usefulness of using it (USMCA, art. 28.20.1), to then specify that:

> No Party shall have recourse to dispute settlement under Chapter 31 … for a matter arising under this Chapter except to address a sustained or recurring course of action or inaction that is inconsistent with a provision of this Chapter. (art. 28.20.3)

Let us finish with a few words on the CPTPP. The main purpose of its RC chapter (ch. 25), I recall, is to encourage the parties to establish structured, transparent and predictable procedures for the development of regulations. The parties are also invited to take into account, in their planning, the regulatory measures of the other parties, as well as any relevant development in international bodies. As for cooperation, it is mainly limited to the exchange of information, the encouragement to adopt good practices and the review of progress made. Nothing very restrictive, therefore, confirmed by the fact that the parties cannot have recourse to dispute settlement. Yet, there is a general orientation: improving regulatory coherence with a view to increasing trade and investment between the parties.

CONCLUSION

I would conclude this chapter with three remarks. First, the literature on IRC places great emphasis on pragmatism and trust in relations between regulators (Hale 2019), but gives little importance to political principles and priorities. Even if the common objective is to improve the efficiency of regulatory processes and to bring them closer, or even to harmonize them, there is still a fundamental difference between an approach geared to stimulate trade under the constraint of respecting public rights (USMCA), and an approach which makes the respect of public rights a top priority, moreover ranked before trade and growth (CETA).

Second, NAFTA established a contractual integration model in North America and set up an institutional framework very different from the EU model. USMCA reinforces this North American model by integrating RC, and, above all, by judicialized practices hitherto established within a dialogue between regulators. Several of the peculiarities of this model have been highlighted as well as what distinguishes it from CETA's approach. Despite all the precautions taken by Canada during the negotiations, the convergence of regulatory practices and systems, with some exceptions, is expected to go in one direction: that of the dominant market, in other words the United States.

Third, having signed CETA, CPTPP and USMCA, Canada will have to manage three regimes which are, ultimately, very different. Too far from Asia, having little influence there, it is hard to imagine that it could take a close interest in the RC that CPTPP is opening up. More experienced in cooperation within North America than with Europe, Canadian regulators are likely to struggle to understand EU practices and get closer to their European counterparts. We can therefore expect that, once again, transatlantic regulatory dialogue, even enshrined in a PTA, will be a source of misunderstanding and disillusionment for both Canadians and Europeans. On the other hand, given the gravity effect that weighs on Canada's trade, there is every reason to believe that RC will continue to develop in North America, in favor of the United States.

NOTES

1. See, in particular, the recommendation of the Council on Regulatory Policy and Governance (OECD 2012).
2. Divergence comes at a cost. The Organization for Economic Cooperation and Development (OECD) distinguishes four categories of costs: information, specification, compliance and customs procedure.

3. For a critical perspective, see Trew (2019).
4. An OECD study shows that agreements that contain provisions on TBT and SPS standards have greater trade effects than others (Disdier et al. 2019). For more information about TBT and the WTO agreement on the subject, see WTO (n.d.).
5. The work at the OECD is the responsibility of the Regulatory Policy Committee.
6. Witness the joint study *Facilitating trade through regulatory cooperation: The case of the WTO's TBT/SPS Agreementsand Committees* (WTO/OECD 2019).
7. The Standards Application and Trade Development Facility (STDF) adopts the definition of the World Bank: "Good Regulatory Practices (GRPs) are defined as internationally recognized processes, systems, tools and methods to improve the quality of regulations and ensure that regulatory outcomes are effective, transparent, inclusive and sustained" (STDF 2018, p. 6).
8. The rules to be observed in terms of regulation are defined in Canada by the Cabinet Directive on Regulation.
9. For more information about the CFTA, see: https://www.cfta-alec.ca/canadian-cfta/-free-trade-agreement.
10. A conciliation agreement is an agreement intended to ensure that the regulatory measures identified in that agreement no longer constitute an obstacle to trade, investment or labor mobility within Canada.
11. For a historical regard, see Heynen (2013).
12. See the very detailed joint action plans for 2011 and 2014 (RCC 2011, 2014).
13. The Canada–US Regulatory Cooperation Council Stakeholder Forum brings together senior regulators, industry and other members of the public from both sides of the Canada-US border.
14. Since 2010, the United States has also had a similar council with Mexico: the US–Mexico High Level Regulatory Cooperation Council.
15. According to the OECD, no country has yet a centralized legal base for RC.
16. Four of the contracting parties are members of ASEAN: Brunei, Malaysia, Singapore and Vietnam.
17. It is still too early to assess the work of this forum. It started in 2018 and the parties have adopted a work plan. Key areas include: consumer product safety, cosmeceuticals, pharmaceutical inspection, cybersecurity and animal welfare.
18. A third option is nevertheless possible: regulatory equivalence or enhanced mutual recognition. It implies a reciprocal examination of regulatory systems.

19. It includes a specific protocol for the manufacture of pharmaceutical products and a general protocol that targets a long list of products.
20. Mention should also be made of Chapter 12—Domestic Regulation, which deals, among other things, with certification and qualification procedures.
21. Ideological conflicts, as the United States describes them.
22. Mutual understanding and the approximation of regulatory systems have been central to the transatlantic dialogue and cooperation agreements between Canada and the EU for a very long time, but the results have hardly lived up to expectations. CETA negotiations were conducted with a view to bring this dialogue out of deadlock.
23. To be quite exact, it was under the presidency of Bill Clinton that the first directives were taken to improve regulatory efficiency and define working methods.
24. This explains why the three countries very quickly agreed on the directions and content of this chapter.

References

Ahmed, Usman. 2019. The Importance of Cross-Border Regulatory Cooperation in an Era of Digital Trade. *World Trade Review* 18 (1): 99–120.

Basedow, Robert, and Céline Kauffmann. 2016. *International Trade and Good Regulatory Practices: Assessing The Trade Impacts of Regulation*. OECD Regulatory Policy Working Papers, No. 4. https://www.oecd-ilibrary.org/govern ance/international-trade-and-good-regulatory-practices_5jlv59hdgtf5-en.

Canada. 2020. *Regulatory Cooperation in Canada*. Last modified November 19, 2020. https://www.canada.ca/en/government/system/laws/develo ping-improving-federal-regulations/regulatory-cooperation/learn-about-reg ulatory-cooperation.html.

Canadian Free Trade Agreement (CFTA), signed April 7, 2017, entered into force, July 1, 2017. https://www.cfta-alec.ca/wp-content/uploads/2017/ 07/CFTA-Consolidated-Text-Final-Print-Text-English.pdf.

Comprehensive and Progressive Agreement for Trans-Pacific Partnership (CPTPP), signed March 8, 2018, entered into force December 30, 2018. https://www.international.gc.ca/trade-commerce/trade-agreements-accords-commerciaux/agr-acc/cptpp-ptpgp/agreement-entente.aspx?lang=eng.

Comprehensive Economic and Trade Agreement (CETA), signed October 30, 2016, entered provisionally into force September 21, 2017. https://www.int ernational.gc.ca/trade-commerce/trade-agreements-accords-commerciaux/ agr-acc/ceta-aecg/text-texte/toc-tdm.aspx?lang=eng.

Deblock, Christian, and Guy-Philippe Wells. 2017. Coopération réglementaire et accords de commerce.*Études internationales* 48 (3–4): 319–345.

Disdier, Anne-Celia, Susan F. Stone, and Frank van Tongeren. 2019. *Trade and Economic Effects of IRC: Further Empirical Evidence from SPS and TBT Provisions*. OECD Trade Policy Papers, No. 224. https://www.oecd-ilibrary.org/trade/trade-and-economic-effects-of-irc_8648b6ca-en.

European Commission. 2016. *Good Regulatory Practices (GRPs) in TTIP: An Introduction to the EU's Revised Proposal*. March 21. http://trade.ec.europa.eu/doclib/docs/2016/march/tradoc_154381.pdf.

Hale, Geoffrey. 2019. Regulatory Cooperation in North America: Diplomacy Navigating Asymmetries. *American Review of Canadian Studies* 49 (1): 123–149.

Heynen, Jeff. 2013. The Canada-U.S. Regulatory Cooperation Council. In *International Regulatory Co-operation: Case Studies, Vol. 2: Canada-US Cooperation, EU Energy Regulation, Risk Assessment and Banking Supervision*, ed. OCDE, 9–19. Paris: OECD.

Memorandum of Understanding Between the Treasury Board of Canada Secretariat and the United States Office of Information and Regulatory Affairs regarding the Canada-United States Regulatory Cooperation Council (MOU CAN-US), signed June 4, 2018. https://www.canada.ca/en/government/system/laws/developing-improving-federal-regulations/regulatory-cooperation/memorandum-understanding-between-canada-united-states-advance-regulatory-cooperation-council.html.

Memorandum of Understanding Between the Treasury Board Secretariat of Canada and the Ministry of Economy of the Mexican United States for the Advancement of Good Regulatory Practices (MOU CAN-MEX), signed February 7, 2018. https://www.canada.ca/en/government/system/laws/developing-improving-federal-regulations/regulatory-cooperation/memorandum-understanding-between-treasury-board-secretariat-ministry-economy-mexican-united-states.html.

North American Free Trade Agreement (NAFTA), signed December 17, 1992, entered into force January 1, 1994. https://www.international.gc.ca/trade-commerce/trade-agreements-accords-commerciaux/agr-acc/nafta-alena/fta-ale/index.aspx?lang=eng.

OECD. 2012. *Recommendation of the Council on Regulatory Policy and Governance*. Paris: OECD.

OECD. 2013. *International Regulatory Co-operation: Addressing Global Challenges*. Paris: OECD.

OECD. 2018. *OECD Regulatory Policy Outlook 2018*. Paris: OECD.

Standards and Trade Development Facility (STDF). 2018. *Good Regulatory Practice to Support the Development and Implementation of SPS Measures*. STDF/Coord/588/Concept Note (Revised March 6, 2018). https://www.standardsfacility.org/sites/default/files/Revised_STDF_concept_note_GRP_Mar18.pdf.

Trew, Stuart. 2019. *International Regulatory Cooperation and the Public Good. How "Good Regulatory Practices" in Trade Agreements Erode Protections for the Environment, Public Health, Workers and Consumers.* Ottawa: Canadian Centre for Policy Alternatives. https://www.iatp.org/sites/default/files/2019-05/International%20regulatory%20cooperation-web300.pdf.

United States-Canada Regulatory Cooperation Council (RCC). 2011. *Joint Action Plan.* December. https://obamawhitehouse.archives.gov/sites/def ault/files/omb/oira/irc/us-canada_rcc_joint_action_plan.pdf.

United States-Canada Regulatory Cooperation Council (RCC). 2014. *Joint Forward Plan.* August. https://obamawhitehouse.archives.gov/sites/def ault/files/omb/oira/irc/us-canada-rcc-joint-forward-plan.pdf.

United States-Mexico-Canada Agreement (USMCA), signed November 30, 2018, entered into force July 1, 2020. https://ustr.gov/trade-agreements/free-trade-agreements/united-states-mexico-canada-agreement/agreement-between.

Von Lampe, Martin, Koen Deconinck, and Veronique Bastien. 2016. *Trade-Related International Regulatory Co-operation: A Theoretical Framework.* OECD Trade Policy Papers, No. 195. https://www.oecd-ilibrary.org/doc server/3fbf60b1-en.pdf?expires=1612808595&id=id&accname=guest&che cksum=E6A6E10D0EA04A55C08F3A942BAE1650.

WTO/OECD. 2019. *Facilitating Trade Through Regulatory Cooperation. The Case of the WTO's TBT/SPS Agreementsand Committees.* Geneva/Paris: WTO/OECD.

WTO. n.d. *Technical Barriers to Trade. Trade topics.* https://www.wto.org/eng lish/tratop_e/tbt_e/tbt_e.htm.

CHAPTER 13

Settlement of State-To-State and Unfair Trade Disputes Under the USMCA

David A. Gantz

INTRODUCTION

The North American Free Trade Agreement (NAFTA) incorporated three distinct dispute settlement mechanisms (DSMs). These address (1) investor-state disputes (ISDS) between foreign investors and host states; (2) binational panel review of national administrative agency rulings under domestic anti-dumping (AD) and subsidy/countervailing duty (CVD) laws; and (3) state-to-state disputes challenging another party's application or interpretation of the agreement. These mechanisms figured in NAFTA's Chapters 11, 19, and 20, respectively. The United States–Mexico–Canada Agreement (USMCA) incorporates the same three mechanisms.

D. A. Gantz (✉)
Center for the United States and Mexico, Baker Institute for Public Policy, Rice University, Houston, TX, USA
e-mail: dagantz@arizona.edu

James E. Rogers College of Law, University of Arizona, Tucson, AZ, USA

© The Author(s), under exclusive license to Springer Nature Switzerland AG 2022
G. Gagné and M. Rioux (eds.), *NAFTA 2.0*, Canada and International Affairs,
https://doi.org/10.1007/978-3-030-81694-0_13

199

Retention of these three mechanisms was not a US objective in the NAFTA renegotiation. Rather, the original proposals made to Canada and Mexico contemplated:

- A provision that would allow a party (e.g., the United States) to opt out of ISDS protection for foreign investment, without necessarily providing reciprocal protection for investors from Mexico and Canada;
- Elimination of Chapter 19 (AD/CVD binational panel) reviews of unfair trade practice remedies imposed by national agencies;
- Converting state-to-state dispute settlement (Chapter 20) into a less legal and more diplomatic means for resolving disputes over the interpretation and application of NAFTA provisions, by allowing the United States to disregard panel decisions the US views as "clearly erroneous" (Wingrove and Martin 2017).

Wisely, in my view, the US negotiators demonstrated a significant degree of flexibility in modifying or abandoning these objectives, without which the renegotiation probably would not have been successfully concluded and the US House of Representatives would not have approved the USMCA.

This chapter addresses reviews of unfair trade practice remedies and state-to-state disputes.[1] Chapter 6 discusses investment disputes.

RESOLUTION OF "UNFAIR" TRADE DISPUTES

The NAFTA Chapter 19 DSM has been a nonnegotiable "red line" for Canada since 1987. It was critical to Canada's acceptance of the United States–Canada Free Trade Agreement (USCFTA) (Panetta 2017). The Chapter 19 binational panel process is an alternative to federal court review of AD and CVD determinations by the US Department of Commerce and the US International Trade Commission (and parallel agencies in Canada and Mexico). Under the USCFTA and again under NAFTA, administrative determinations in AD and CVD cases—whether related to the existence and/or amount of dumping or subsidies, or the existence (or threat) of material injury—have been reviewable by binational panels composed of private citizens from the two countries involved, appointed from a roster of at least 25 citizens of each country, primarily trade lawyers and academics, but occasionally sitting or retired judges. The reviews are subject to the national unfair trade laws of the country that imposed the duties, not to World Trade Organization (WTO) or other international legal rules, but the process is international in that the panelists are nationals of two countries (i.e., the US and Canada) in a dispute involving the imposition of import duties on the goods of either party (NAFTA, art. 1904).

The maintenance of Chapter 19 procedures was apparently not a critical issue for Mexico in the USMCA negotiations (although the final provisions apply to Mexico as well as to Canada and the United States),[2] but it was politically essential for Canada. As Prime Minister Justin Trudeau said in early September 2018, "we will not sign a deal that is bad for Canadians and, quite frankly, not having a Chapter 19 to ensure that the rules [governing unfair trade rulings by administrative agencies] are followed would be bad for Canadians" (Siripurapu 2018). This statement reflected a long-held belief by Canada that US federal courts (such as the Court of International Trade and the Court of Appeals for the Federal Circuit) are not sufficiently independent from the executive branch (despite, in my view, little or no evidence of any such bias).

It is safe to conclude that without US willingness to carry Chapter 19 provisions into the USMCA with only minor changes, Canada would not have adhered to the USMCA. The fact that the United States was willing to continue Chapter 19 provisions suggests perhaps—more than any other aspect of the negotiations with Canada—how important it was for the United States to assure that Canada became a USMCA party along with Mexico. Chapter 19 has never been popular with US officials or stakeholders. As I observed after an extensive review 13 years ago,

> The panel process has been criticized (mostly by U.S. NGOs and others who have opposed NAFTA generally) in several respects. First, it has been attacked for putting decision-making power in the hands of individuals, including foreign nationals, without judicial experience, who are not accountable for their performance, who have not been appointed in accordance with Article III of the U.S. Constitution, and who may disregard the requirement that they behave as would local courts and apply U.S. law. The complexities and costs of a largely ad hoc system, which substitutes for what most believe is an acceptable national court system, have also been cited. (Gantz 2009, pp. 356, 381)

This unhappiness is reflected in the fact that a mechanism similar to NAFTA Chapter 19 has never been incorporated in any new US preferential trade agreement (PTA) prior to the USMCA. Canada and Mexico similarly have not used an unfair trade DSM in any of their post-NAFTA PTAs. Perhaps they were willing to rely on the WTO's DSM for AD and CVD disputes, or it may be that Canada and Mexico, like many other WTO members, uniquely feared US use of its own AD and CVD laws.

For Canada, Chapter 19 has a long history rooted in a dispute over softwood lumber exports to the United States, which has generated multiple Chapter 19 reviews under the USCFTA[3] and again under NAFTA.[4] The dispute also generated one of three Chapter 19 "extraordinary challenges" (ECs), a very limited review process in which Canada ultimately prevailed, as it did in the bulk of Chapter 19 binational panel disputes.[5] In retrospect, the EC procedure appears to make it virtually impossible for any complaining party to prevail. The EC procedure only applies where one party alleges that:

> (a) (i) a member of the panel was guilty of gross misconduct, bias, or a serious conflict of interest, or otherwise materially violated the rules of conduct, (ii) the panel seriously departed from a fundamental rule of procedure, or (iii) the panel manifestly exceeded its powers, authority or jurisdiction set out in this Article, for example by failing to apply the appropriate standard of review, and (b) any of the [above] actions ... has materially affected the panel's decision *and threatens the integrity of the binational panel review process* ... (emphasis added) (NAFTA, art. 1904.13).

While it is conceivable that a binational panel might have violated one or more of the elements of paragraph (a) above, and even that said violation could have materially affected the panel's decision in paragraph (b) (why else would the aggrieved party have initiated the extraordinary challenge in the first place?), the further requirement that the moving party demonstrates that the violation "threatens the integrity of the binational panel review process" as a whole has proved impossible to meet over the 32 years in which the binational panel process has been in force. Nevertheless, perhaps for the reasons noted below, the EC procedure language in the USMCA is word for word identical to NAFTA's. (USMCA, art. 10.12.13)

Thus, as Canada asserted after the USMCA negotiations were completed,

> Given the integrated nature of the North American economy, it is important to minimize the disruptions that can result from the imposition of trade remedies. This outcome ensures that trade remedies are applied in a fair, transparent, and responsible way while maintaining recourse, when necessary, to an impartial binational panel dispute settlementmechanism to review anti-dumping and countervailing duty measures imposed by CUSMA partners. (Canada 2019)

At the same time, there is little evidence that Canada, despite insisting on the inclusion of a Chapter 19-style mechanism in the USMCA, would have been unwilling to consider modifications that might have made Chapter 19 less controversial in the US and more effective. The timing of the negotiations, when Mexico and the United States concluded what was effectively a bilateral agreement in August 2018 and Canada rushed to be brought into the accord by the end of September, effectively precluded a detailed review of Chapter 19.[6] Had the parties been afforded more time, it is at least possible that the limited review of binational panel determinations under NAFTA's EC procedure could have been addressed and modified.

Also, the parallel remedies provided in the event of challenges to AD and CVD orders available to private parties under NAFTA Chapter 19 and to governments under the WTO's DSM might have been discussed. NAFTA and USMCA allow parties to choose between regional or WTO forums for most state-to-state disputes, but neither addresses parallelism with unfair trade disputes (NAFTA, art. 2005.1; USMCA, art. 31.3.1). The absence, as of December 11, 2019, of the fully functioning WTO adjudication option, as discussed below, presumably makes this binational panel system under the USMCA even more important to Canada and Mexico.

State-to-State Dispute Settlement

US Ambivalence Regarding Third Party Dispute Settlement

US efforts to undercut the WTO's Appellate Body are apparently due to dissatisfaction with both its procedures and substantive actions (the latter of which did not originate with the Trump administration) (see

Elliott 2018) and the Trump administration's commitment to "defending our national sovereignty over trade policy" (USTR 2017, p. 3). As of December 11, 2019, the Appellate Body ceased to function, since only one of the seven members remained active (see Keaten and Wiseman 2019), even though efforts were made to carry over to conclusion three cases that were pending at that time.[7] Some but not all of these US objections are applicable *mutatis mutandis* to other third-party DSMs that affect the application of US trade laws and policies, such as those in PTAs.

The United States–China "Phase One" trade agreement, concluded on January 15, 2020, omits third-party dispute settlement including recourse to the WTO entirely, replacing it with a "bilateral evaluation and dispute resolution mechanism" that permits unilateral action by the United States in the event of alleged failure by China to comply with the agreement (US–China Economic and Trade Agreement, ch. 7). The United States' proposed objectives for PTA negotiations with the United Kingdom suggest that a chapter on state-to-state dispute settlement by panel may be included, but provide little detail beyond transparency provisions and a cryptic suggestion that the agreement should "provide mechanisms for ensuring that the Parties retain control of disputes and can address situations when a panel has clearly erred in its assessment of the facts or the obligations that apply" (USTR 2019, p. 14). Since those objectives were issued two years ago it is not clear whether they will be reflected if and when those negotiations actually move forward.

Relatively little public discussion of US objections to NAFTA's Chapter 20 DSM exists for what I believe are several obvious reasons. First, it has been possible for the United States (and in theory the other parties) to indefinitely delay panel proceedings simply by refusing to appoint individuals to the Chapter 20 roster.[8] Instead of panel members being more or less automatically appointed to adjudicate a dispute, each panel member is selected only after extensive bilateral consultations among the states party to the dispute. For example, in the most recently completed Chapter 20 proceeding, Cross-Border Trucking Services, 15 months passed between Mexico's first panel request and when proceedings actually began.[9] Distrust from Mexico and Canada was strongly reinforced when the United States refused to cooperate for more than four years on the formation of a panel requested by Mexico to adjudicate related disputes over high-fructose corn syrup and US sugar quotas under NAFTA. Mexico effectively reciprocated a few years later by refusing the United States' request to adjudicate the latest chapter in the dispute over tuna under NAFTA Chapter 20, insisting instead that the case be pursued at the WTO.[10]

Despite this history of US stonewalling Mexico, the initial state-to-state DSM of the USMCA was only slightly altered from NAFTA's Chapter 20, with no guaranty that stonewalling would not occur in the future (see Lester 2018). Fortunately, as explained below, the final version of USMCA Chapter 31 greatly reduces the risk that any party will refuse the appointment of panelists.

Second, all three NAFTA parties appear to have generally preferred the WTO's DSM to NAFTAs for the review of trade disputes among them. They could be confident that WTO panels would be promptly appointed by the WTO Secretariat, that panel and Appellate Body time limits for each stage of the dispute resolution process would be more or less observed, that other members could intervene in cases (often a benefit for Mexico and Canada that was not available in NAFTA dispute settlement), and that procedures to enforce rulings would be effective.[11] Unfortunately, delays in WTO adjudication have increased in recent years, in part due to US refusal to appoint and reappoint Appellate Body members at the WTO (Elliott 2018). The demise of the WTO DSM makes the DSMs under Chapter 10 (unfair trade) and Chapter 31 (state-to-state) of the USMCA all the more important to Canada and Mexico. The Democrats in the US Congress forced the Trump administration to improve the functioning of the USMCA state-to-state DSM.

State-to-State Dispute Settlement under the USMCA

Mexico and Canada faced an unpleasant choice in the negotiations: they could either support a NAFTA-type mechanism in the USMCA despite its imperfections or accept a mechanism that likely would have posed even fewer restraints on the United States than NAFTA Chapter 20. Faced with this dilemma, Mexican negotiators beat back US efforts to formally grant veto power to parties that object to adverse panel decisions. As one of Mexico's negotiators noted, "Dispute resolution is for the small country. So, Mexico is particularly interested" (Lester 2018). Simultaneously, the negotiator admitted that USMCA Chapter 31, as originally negotiated, did not address effectively the root problem behind the delays in establishing panels (i.e., the United States' failure to agree to designate panel rosters in advance). However, he argued that this was a necessary compromise to avoid the US veto proposal. In so doing, Mexico suggested—perhaps overly optimistically—that instances of blocked panels had been limited to a single case involving sugar, and "it's not something that will happen frequently, so we said okay" (Lester 2018). As indicated earlier, the sugar case was not the only instance in which long delays in appointing panelists had occurred, but it may well have been the only one in which the United States acted in bad faith rather than simply exercising extraordinary care in choosing objective panelists.

The result in the initial signed version of the USMCA was a state-to-state DSM that made few substantive changes compared to NAFTA and more closely resembled NAFTA than the corresponding provisions (art. 28.9) of the Trans-Pacific Partnership (TPP). A few possibly significant differences existed in the original USMCA language. For example, NAFTA Article 2018.1 states that "[o]n receipt of the final report of a panel, the disputing parties shall agree on the resolution of the dispute, which normally shall conform with the determinations and recommendations of the panel, and shall notify their Sections of the Secretariat of any agreed resolution of any dispute." The USMCA, in Article 31.18, simply mandates that "[w]ithin 45 days from receipt of a final report … the disputing parties shall endeavor to agree on the resolution of the dispute." The USMCA provides more specific directions for the function of panels.

> A panel's function is to make an objective assessment of the matter before it and to present a report that contains: (a) findings of fact; (b) determinations as to whether: (i) the measure at issue is inconsistent with obligations in this Agreement, (ii) a Party has otherwise failed to carry out its obligations in this Agreement, (iii) the measure at issue is causing nullification or impairment …, or (iv) any other determination requested in the terms of reference; (c) recommendations, if the disputing Parties have jointly requested them, for the resolution of the dispute; and (d) the reasons for the findings and determinations. (USMCA, art. 31.13.1)

Also, reflecting technological changes, USMCA (art. 31.12) allows for electronic filing of documents. Still, in the event a party wishes to challenge another party's application or interpretation of the agreement, the USMCA, like NAFTA, provides for mandatory consultations and optional "good offices" (conciliation, mediation, or other instances where a third party seeks to help the disputing parties resolve their differences) before resorting to the panel procedures (USMCA, arts 31.4, 31.5). Roster appointment requirements initially were essentially unchanged from NAFTA and five-person panels remain the rule (arts 31.6, 31.8, 31.9). Appointed panelists must "have expertise or experience in international law, international trade, other matters covered by this Agreement, or the resolution of disputes arising under international trade agreements." Members must be selected objectively, be independent of the governments involved, and follow a code of conduct designed to avoid actual or apparent conflicts of interest (art. 31.8.2). Critically, under the initial version of the USMCA (as was the case with NAFTA), "The roster shall be appointed by *consensus* and remain in effect for a minimum of three years or until the parties constitute a new roster" (emphasis added). However, as noted below, the amended version provides that in the event that consensus cannot be achieved on the initial 30 roster members within 30 days after the entry into force of the USMCA (i.e., by July 31, 2020), "the roster shall be comprised of the designated individuals" (art. 31.8.1).

As in NAFTA, no appellate mechanism exists in the USMCA, and trade penalties (e.g., additional tariffs or quotas) are available if the losing party fails to implement the final report or otherwise "to agree on the resolution of the dispute" (arts 31.18, 31.19).

Whether the Mexico negotiator's optimism (in my view misplaced) that parties (read the United States) would refrain from blocking roster and panel appointments under the USMCA was justified will never be known because, as of December 2019, it became a much less significant threat. Changes in the mechanism were demanded by the Democrats in Congress (presumably because of their concerns over enforcement of the USMCA's labor and environmental obligations) and accepted by the Trump administration. The resulting Protocol of Amendment to the USMCA was welcomed by both Mexico and Canada.

The changes secured by the Democratic Congress focus primarily on appointment of roster members and selection of roster members when a complaint is lodged, although they also make the dispute settlement process more predictable by adding rules of evidence to the rules of procedure (USMCA, art. 31.11.2). First, blocking of or failure to appoint roster members should be significantly less feasible:

> The Parties shall establish, by the date of entry into force of this Agreement, and maintain a roster of up to 30 individuals who are willing to serve as panelists. Each Party shall designate up to 10 individuals. The

Parties shall endeavor to achieve consensus on the appointments. If the Parties are unable to achieve consensus by one month after the date of entry into force of this Agreement, the roster shall be comprised of the designated individuals. The roster shall remain in effect for a minimum of three years or until the Parties constitute a new roster. If a Party fails to designate its individuals to the roster, the Parties may still request the establishment of panels under Article 31.6 (Establishment of a Panel). The Rules of Procedure, which shall be established by the date of entry into force of this Agreement, shall provide for how to compose a panel in such circumstances. Members of the roster may be reappointed. In the event that an individual is no longer able or willing to serve as a panelist, the relevant Party shall designate a replacement. The Parties shall endeavor to achieve consensus on the appointment. If the Parties are unable to achieve consensus by one month after the date the replacement is designated, the individual shall be added to the roster. (USMCA, art. 31.8.1)

In other words, if the United States had declined to agree on the initial roster nominees of Canada and Mexico, after 30 days panelists would still be designated, and could be drawn upon to staff panels under the circumstances set out in subparagraph c), below. These additional revisions provide detailed procedures for choosing the five panelists (in this quotation where there are two disputing parties) and would presumably prevail in the event of a conflict of the USMCA text with the rules of procedure:

a. The panel shall comprise five members, unless the disputing Parties agree to a panel comprised of three members.
b. The disputing Parties shall endeavor to decide on the chair of the panel within 15 days of the delivery of the request for the establishment of the panel. If the disputing Parties are unable to decide on the chair within this period, the disputing Party chosen by lot shall select within five days as chair an individual who is not a citizen of that Party.
c. If the responding Party refuses to participate in or fails to appear for the choosing by lot procedure, the complaining Party shall select an individual from the roster who is not a citizen of that Party ....
d. Within 15 days of selection of the chair, each disputing Party shall select two panelists who are citizens of the other disputing Party.

e. If a disputing Party fails to select its panelists within that period, those panelists shall be selected by lot from among the roster members who are citizens of the other disputing Party.

f. If the responding Party refuses to participate in or fails to appear for the choosing by lot procedure, the complaining Party shall select two individuals from the roster who are citizens of the complaining Party ... (USMCA, art. 31.9.1).

The detailed rules of procedure for dispute settlement under Chapter 31 were available as of June 29, 2021 (USTR 2021). However, in contrast with its practices under NAFTA, the United States had appointed ten potential panelists to its roster, as required by USMCA, on July 1, 2020 (USTR 2020). (Canada and Mexico had also done so.) For many observers, including the author, this was an important test of whether the USMCA mechanism will be a significant improvement over the failed NAFTA Chapter 20. The fact that the United States, typically the recalcitrant party in the past, has strictly met this USMCA requirement is grounds for optimism that the USMCA Chapter 31 mechanism will function more effectively, without the long delays and occasional stonewalling that occurred under NAFTA. Optimism is further justified by the provision, noted above, which provides that roster members appointed for a three-year term can remain on the roster beyond that period, until their replacements are installed.

Only time will tell whether this language, and the rules of procedure, will completely eliminate stonewalling, but the mechanism provides powerful incentives for parties to appoint and continue to appoint their own rosters of potential panelists. It seems unlikely that any party would risk the selection of a panel chair by the complaining party in which it had no role in selecting. Similarly, why would a party risk the selection of two panelists who are citizens of another party by that party rather than on its own behalf? With five-person panels, two of the panelists are each to be chosen from citizens of the opposing party. Thus, in a dispute between the United States and Mexico, the United States is to choose two Mexican citizens from the rosters, and Mexico is to choose two US citizens, as was the case under NAFTA. It is unclear why the USMCA negotiators chose to maintain the five-panelist approach rather than following the Comprehensive and Progressive Agreement for Trans-Pacific Partnership (CPTPP)[12] and other mechanisms that have opted for three panelists.

Still, the more sensible approach to addressing a situation where the responding party refuses to appoint its panelists or cooperate in the choice of the chairperson was apparently never seriously considered. In USMCA, for example, when the parties to an investment dispute are unable to agree on the choice of arbitrators, the Secretary-General of the International Centre for Settlement of Investment Disputes (ICSID) makes the appointments in consultation with the parties (USMCA, annex 14-D, art. 14.D.6.2). It would have been preferable under Chapter 31 to designate an appointing authority such as the ICSID Secretary-General, the Director-General of the WTO, or the head of some similar body, to avoid lengthy disputes over panel selections. Unfortunately, the Trump administration is not the only current or past US or foreign government that has shied away from giving such responsibility to an independent official of an international organization.[13]

While neither NAFTA nor the USMCA addresses alternative dispute resolution between private parties in any detail, both provide for a mandatory advisory committee on private commercial disputes (NAFTA, art. 2022; USMCA, art. 31.22.4). Some may consider this potentially significant, since the TPP called for no similar advisory committee (TPP, art. 28.23). The "NAFTA 2022" committee has met periodically throughout the agreement's history (See USMCA Secretariat n.d.). Similar committees were contemplated in post-NAFTA PTAs negotiated by the United States, but typically their formation was discretionary; to the best of my knowledge, none was ever formed (see, e.g., CAFTA-DR, art. 20.22.4).

NOTES

1. This text is based on Gantz (2019, 2020).
2. USMCA, Chapter 10, Sections B, C, D, Annexes 10-B.1, 10-B.2, 10-B.3, 10-B.4 and 10-B.5.
3. See *Certain Softwood Lumber Products from Canada*, Case nos. USA-CDA-1992–1904-01, USA-CDA-1992–1904-02 (NAFTA Secretariat, n.d.) The dispute started prior to the USCFTA. For a historical discussion of the softwood lumber dispute, through 2010, see Chapter 13 in *Trade remedies in North America* (Bowman et al. 2010, pp. 553–88).
4. See *Certain Softwood Lumber Products from Canada*, Case nos. USA-CDA-2002–1904-02, USA-CDA-2002–1904-03, USA-CDA 2002–1904-07, USA-CDA-2005–1904-01, USA-CDA-2006–1904-04, USA-CDA-2006–1904-05 (NAFTA Secretariat, n.d.).

5. See NAFTA (art. 1904.13, annex 1904.13); and *Softwood Lumber Products from Canada*, Case no. ECC-2004–1904-01USA(NAFTA Secretariat, n.d.).
6. It was critical for Mexico to be able to sign the USMCA before President Lopez Obrador took office on December 1, 2018. President Trump under the Trade Promotion Authority could not sign in less than 90 days after the text was made public.
7. *Russia—Measures Affecting the Importation of Railway Equipment and Parts Thereof*, WTO/DS499/AB/R, adopted March 5, 2020; *United States—Countervailing Measures on Supercalendered Paper from Canada*, WTO/DS505/AB/R, adopted March 5, 2020; *Australia—Certain Measures Concerning Trademarks, Geographical Indications and Other Plain Packaging Requirements Applicable to Tobacco Products and Packaging*, WT/DS435/AB/R, adopted June 29, 2020.
8. NAFTA (arts. 2008, 2009). On a few occasions, NAFTA panelist rosters were designated but when they expired after three years they often were not replaced. USMCA provides in Article 31.8.1 that roster members once appointed remain in place until their successors are appointed, and that the initial roster of 30 persons must be in place as of the entry into force of USMCA. However, similar language in NAFTA (art. 2009.1) providing for appointment of roster members by January 1, 1994 (the date NAFTA entered into force) was apparently not complied with.
9. *In the Matter of Cross-Border Trucking Services*, USA-Mex-1998–2008-01 (NAFTA Secretariat n.d.).
10. See *United States—Measures Concerning the Importation, Marketing and Sale of Tuna and Tuna Products*, WTO/AB/DS381/AB/R, adopted June 3, 2012.
11. See Understanding on Rules and Procedures Governing the Settlement of Disputes, especially Articles 4, 6, 10, 11, 12, 16, 17, 19, 20 and 22. In fairness, a significant majority of the nearly three dozen WTO actions involving NAFTA parties addressed unfair trade, i.e., AD and CVD, actions, where NAFTA Chapter 20jurisdiction is excluded. See: NAFTA (art. 2004); WTO (n.d.).
12. After the US withdrawal from the TPP, the latter gave place to the CPTPP.
13. Interestingly, the panel appointment process in Chapter 28 of the CPTPP contemplates the use of an unspecified "independent third party" under certain circumstances when the parties cannot agree on the chairperson. However, the parties to the dispute must "jointly" choose the independent third party! See CPTPP (art. 28.9.2.d.v.B).

REFERENCES

Bowman, Gregory W., Nick Covelli, David A. Gantz, and Ihn Ho Uhm. 2010. *Trade Remedies in North America*. Alphen aan den Rijn: Kluwer Law International.

Elliott, Kimberly Ann. 2018. Can the World Trade Organization be Saved? *World Politics Review*, October 16. http://bit.ly/2YMiffY.

Gantz, David A. 2009. The United States and Dispute Settlement Under the North American Free Trade Agreement: Ambivalence, Frustration and Occasional Defiance. In *The Sword and the Scales: The United States and International Courts and Tribunals*, ed. Cesare P. R. Romano, 356–394. New York: Cambridge University Press.

Gantz, David A. 2019. *The United States-Mexico-Canada Agreement: Settlement of Disputes*. Baker Institute for Public Policy, Report 05.02.19. https://www.bakerinstitute.org/media/files/files/d14a5a86/bi-report-050219-mex-usmca-3.pdf.

Gantz, David A. 2020. *An Introduction to the United States-Mexico-Canada Agreement: Understanding the New NAFTA*. Cheltenham, UK/Northampton, MA: Edward Elgar.

Keaten, Jamey, and Paul Wiseman. 2019. World Trade Without Rules? U.S. Shuts Down WTO Appeals Court. *The Associated Press*, December 10. https://apnews.com/article/a08cc387ff5c1af859e6f17020e29a91.

Lester, Simon. 2018. "Mexico's View of the Problems with the NAFTA Panel Appointment Process. *International Economic Law and Policy Blog*, October 12. http://bit.ly/2uR2tm5.

Panetta, Alexander. 2017. NAFTA's Third-Party Arbitration System was Canada's Big Prize...Is It Worth Fighting For? *Toronto Star*, August 23. Last Updated April 13, 2018. http://bit.ly/2K5W4hr.

Siripurapu, Anshu. 2018. Trudeau: Chapter 19, Cultural Exemptions are NAFTA Red Lines for Canada. *World Trade Online*, September 4. http://bit.ly/2OOcXMo.

Wingrove, Josh, and Eric Martin. 2017. U.S. Proposes Gutting Nafta Legal Dispute Tribunals. *Bloomberg*, October 14. https://bloom.bg/2Uo23Cr.

OFFICIAL DOCUMENTS

Canada. 2019. *Trade Remedies and Related Dispute Settlement (Chapter 19) Summary*. Last Modified June 10, 2019. http://bit.ly/2Vp7WfU.

Comprehensive and Progressive Agreement for Trans-Pacific Partnership (CPTPP), Signed March 8, 2018, Entered into Force December 30, 2018. https://www.international.gc.ca/trade-commerce/trade-agreements-accords-commerciaux/agr-acc/tpp-ptp/text-texte/toc-tdm.aspx?lang=eng.

Dominican Republic-Central America-United States Free Trade Agreement (CAFTA-DR), Signed August 5, 2004, Entered into Force March 1, 2006. https://ustr.gov/trade-agreements/free-trade-agreements/cafta-dr-dominican-republic-central-america-fta/final-text.

Economic and Trade Agreement Between the Government of the United States of America and the Government of the People's Republic of China (US-China Economic and Trade Agreement), Signed January 15, 2020. https://ustr.gov/sites/default/files/files/agreements/phase%20one%20a greement/Economic_And_Trade_Agreement_Between_The_United_States_ And_China_Text.pdf.

NAFTA Secretariat. n.d. *Dispute Settlement. Decisions and Reports*. https:// web.archive.org/web/20161121010237/, https://www.nafta-sec-alena.org/ Home/Dispute-Settlement/Decisions-and-Reports. Accessed January 29, 2021.

North American Free Trade Agreement (NAFTA), Signed December 17, 1992, Entered into Force January 1, 1994. https://www.international.gc.ca/trade-commerce/trade-agreements-accords-commerciaux/agr-acc/nafta-alena/fta-ale/index.aspx?lang=eng.

Protocol of Amendment to the United States-Mexico-Canada Agreement (USMCA), Signed December 10, 2019. https://ustr.gov/sites/default/ files/files/agreements/FTA/USMCA/Protocol-of-Amendments-to-the-Uni ted-States-Mexico-Canada-Agreement.pdf.

Trans-Pacific Partnership (TPP), Signed February 4, 2016. https://ustr.gov/ sites/default/files/TPP-Final-Text-Dispute-Settlement.pdf.

Understanding on Rules and Procedures Governing the Settlement of Disputes, Annex 2 to the Marrakesh Agreement Establishing the World Trade Organization, Signed April 15, 1994, Entered into Force, January 1, 1995. http:// bit.ly/2uR2x5j.

United States – Canada Free Trade Agreement (USCFTA), Signed January 2, 1988, Entered into Force January 1, 1989. http://www.international.gc.ca/ trade-agreements-accords-commerciaux/assets/pdfs/cusfta-e.pdf.

United States-Mexico-Canada Agreement (USMCA), Signed November 30, 2018, Entered into Force July 1, 2020. https://ustr.gov/trade-agreements/ free-trade-agreements/united-states-mexico-canada-agreement/agreement-between.

USMCA Secretariat. n.d. *NAFTA 2022 Committee*. Last Modified June 24, 2020. https://can-mex-usa-sec.org/secretariat/ard-red-masc/commit tee-comite-comite.aspx?lang=eng&.

USTR. 2017. *The President's 2017 Trade Policy Agenda*. http://bit.ly/2WIGSs4.

USTR. 2019. *United States-United Kingdom Negotiations: Summary of Specific Negotiating Objectives*. February. https://ustr.gov/sites/default/files/Sum mary_of_U.S.-UK_Negotiating_Objectives.pdf.

USTR. 2020. *U.S. Names Panelists for USMCA Enforcement*. July 1. https://ustr.gov/about-us/policy-offices/press-office/press-releases/2020/july/us-names-panelists-usmca-labor-enforcement.

USTR. 2021. Rules of Procedure for Chapter 31. *USMCA Secretariat*, June 29.

WTO. n.d. *Chronological List of Disputes Cases*. http://bit.ly/2TXpIoO.

CHAPTER 14

Macroeconomic Policies and Exchange Rate Matters

Delphine Ducasse, Micheline B. Somda, and David Pavot

The penultimate chapter of the United States–Mexico–Canada Agreement (USMCA) concerns, as its title hints, macroeconomic policies and exchange rate matters. It has no equivalent chapter in the North American Free Trade Agreement (NAFTA) and contains therefore entirely new provisions that do not correspond to previous articles. The USMCA is even the first trade agreement to contain a chapter on macroeconomic policies and exchange rate matters. What prompted the parties to include such a chapter during the NAFTA renegotiation? The currency manipulations done in the past, the inability of the International Monetary Fund (IMF) to effectively regulate competitive devaluations, and the will of the

D. Ducasse · M. B. Somda
Faculty of Law, Université de Sherbrooke, Sherbrooke, QC, Canada

D. Pavot (✉)
Department of Marketing, Business School on Antidoping in Sports, Université de Sherbrooke, Sherbrooke, QC, Canada
e-mail: David.Pavot@USherbrooke.ca

215
G. Gagné and M. Rioux (eds.), *NAFTA 2.0*,
Canada and International Affairs,
https://doi.org/10.1007/978-3-030-81694-0_14

United States to create model clauses for future agreements are among the key drivers.

The content of USMCA's Chapter 33 resembles certain non-binding provisions (see Canada 2020) fsound in the IMF Articles of Agreement, but it distinguishes itself by subjecting the transparency requirements to the dispute settlement mechanism of the agreement. Although this chapter will not change the parties' monetary policies, as they already comply with all its obligations, the inclusion of such a chapter in itself is a step forward in better regulating currency transactions internationally.

The Reasons Behind Chapter 33

When the NAFTA was initially concluded in 1992, macroeconomic policies and exchange rate matters were not part of the negotiation agenda, and, thus, no chapter on these issues was included in the agreement. More broadly, while the use of money for commercial purposes had been well known since the currency war of the inter-war period, the early 1990s saw the structuring of trade in a more compartmentalized way in relation to money or finance. The question arises then of why Mexico, Canada and, more importantly, the United States agreed to incorporate such a chapter in a renewed version of NAFTA. The United States seems to be the country that pushed the issue, having as a trade negotiation objective "[t]hrough an appropriate mechanism, [to] ensure that the NAFTA countries avoid manipulating exchange rates in order to prevent effective balance of payments adjustment or to gain an unfair competitive advantage" (USTR 2017, p. 17).

The United States had already tried to link monetary policy issues with international trade during the negotiation of the Trans-Pacific Partnership (TPP), succeeding in having a Joint Declaration of the Macroeconomic Policy Authorities attached to the agreement.[1] An indication that the United States was the true initiator of such a declaration, it was not taken up in the Comprehensive and Progressive Agreement for Trans-Pacific Partnership (CPTPP) concluded after the withdrawal of the United States by President Trump. The USMCA is consequently the first preferential trade agreement (PTA) to cover macroeconomic and exchange rate policies (Segal 2018).

Currency Manipulations

This negotiation aim from the United States can be explained by the multiple currency manipulations that happened between 2003 and 2013, where certain countries kept their currencies undervalued to gain international competitiveness and trade surpluses. During this period, manufacturing countries in Asia, oil exporters and financial centers like Switzerland and Singapore, intervened heavily in the foreign exchange markets, China being the largest manipulator (Bergsten 2018). According to the Peterson Institute for International Economics, the United States was the biggest loser, seeing its trade deficit increase by US$200 billion to US$500 billion per year (Bergsten and Gagnon 2012, p. 1). Under President Obama, when the Trade Promotion Authority (TPA) was renewed in 2015,[2] two trade negotiating objectives related to currency were therefore added (Bergsten 2018). Specifically, the 11th and 12th objectives specify that:

> parties to a trade agreement with the United States [shall] avoid manipulating exchange rates in order to prevent effective balance of payments adjustment or to gain an unfair competitive advantage over other parties to the agreement [and that the United States will] seek to establish accountability through enforceable rules, transparency, reporting, monitoring, cooperative mechanisms, or other means to address exchange rate manipulation involving protracted large scale intervention in one direction in the exchange markets and a persistently undervalued foreign exchange rate to gain an unfair competitive advantage in trade over other parties to a trade agreement (TPA 2015, sec. 102).

This partly explains why the United States has been prone to promote currency provisions in the PTAs negotiated post-2015, like TPP, USMCA, but also the trade agreements with South Korea and China.[3]

The International Monetary Fund

Another reason for the United States to include currency provisions in PTAs, which typically do not deal with such theme, is the inability of the IMF to effectively enforce the member states' obligations regarding exchange arrangements. Indeed, even if a country is deemed a currency manipulator by the IMF, the only sanctions available are the suspension of the country's voting rights in the IMF, or at the extreme an expulsion from the IMF (Articles of Agreement, art. 26.2.b.c). As those sanctions require either a 70 or 85% majority vote, they would be difficult to enact and would not economically pressure the country to stop its currency manipulation (Bergsten and Gagnon 2012, p. 11). In any case, the decision-making practice at the IMF is consensus-based (Lowenfeld 2009, p. 604). It is therefore hard to see a member admitting that it may have committed an unlawful act. As a result, no monetary manipulation has been officially noted by the IMF. Moreover, the sanctions available to the IMF are totally unsuitable for such actions classified as competitive devaluations. Indeed, they range from suspension of access to Fund resources to exclusion, and do not provide for any corrective mechanism or effective sanction to induce the offending member to correct its unlawful act. By including monetary provisions in PTAs that contain robust dispute settlement mechanisms, the United States ensures it possesses sufficient trade leverage to apply economic pressure on countries that manipulate their currencies.

Template for Future Agreements

Apart from its general trade negotiating objective inscribed in the TPA and the fact that the IMF does not have the necessary tools to regulate competitive devaluations, the United States seems to have pushed for Chapter 33 in the USMCA in order to create a model for future trade agreements. Indeed, as the United States, Canada and Mexico all have floating exchange rate regimes and already meet the transparency requirements enacted in the chapter, the real impact of such chapter on current policies and practices in the three countries is almost non-existent (Bergsten 2018; Segal 2018). In its Statement on Implementation, Canada even mentions in relation to Chapter 33 that "[n]o amendments to Canadian legislation arise from this Chapter" (Canada 2020).

The phenomenon of conventional modelling is becoming more and more widespread in international economic law. It can be defined as adopting a set of provisions, on an indicative basis, in order to provide a framework for future bilateral negotiation (Juillard 1994, p. 120). This technique is particularly present in the field of investment law with model bilateral investment treaties (BITs). The United States developed its first model BIT in 1981 in response to the expansion of international trade and the lack of international investment protection. It was used in the negotiations of agreements with Egypt and Panama (Vandevelde 1988, p. 210).

Since then, the US model BIT has been revised several times, including in 2004 and 2012 (US Department of State 2012). One of the reasons that led to the 2004 revision was the need to ensure the model's consistency with recently negotiated PTAs, particularly NAFTA, which contained a chapter on investment. While the model BIT has been used frequently by the United States in bilateral negotiations, there is now a global trend toward conventional modelling. Indeed, in addition to developed countries such as Canada, France and the Netherlands, many countries such as Morocco, Brazil, Colombia, Ecuador, India and Nigeria have recently adopted model BITs (Nikièma 2018).

The concept of conventional modelling has also been used by the United States in PTAs. Following the stalemate of the negotiations on agriculture during the Uruguay Round, the United States started negotiating PTAs with Israel and Canada, and later with Mexico (NAFTA). This propensity of the United States for regionalism has been perceived as a strategy to offer a model of what could be negotiated at the multilateral level, especially regarding trade in services and intellectual property rights (Taylor 2009, p. 571). After NAFTA's entry into force in 1994, the negotiation of regional and bilateral PTAs became the primary US means for securing trade liberalization, as this could not be achieved at the multilateral level. The approach of "competitive liberalization" was then developed, with the view that regional and bilateral efforts would energize and focus WTO negotiations. In order to achieve this goal and impose its trade agenda worldwide, the PTAs concluded by the United States had to be fairly similar, hence the model PTAs (Taylor 2009, pp. 576–77).

As stated above, USMCA Chapter 33 has limited impact on the three parties, in view of their already existing floating exchange rates and meeting transparency requirements. Rather, it is reasonable to assume that this chapter would serve as a template for future agreements negotiated between the United States and countries that are on the US Treasury's monitoring list of major trading partners deserving close attention to their currency practices, such as Japan, China, South Korea and Germany (Gantz 2020, p. 217; Segal 2018; US Department of the Treasury 2020b).[4] USMCA Chapter 33 has already been used as a template in the Phase One Agreement with China, which had been designated as a "currency manipulator" by the US Treasury Department in 2019.[5] Indeed, Chapter 5 of the agreement with China, entitled "Macroeconomic Policies and Exchange Rate Matters and Transparency," is extremely similar to Chapter 33 of the USMCA except for a few minor differences. The parties

undertake in the general provisions "to refrain from competitive devaluations and the targeting of exchange rates for competitive purposes"
(US-China Agreement, art. 5.1.4). The commitments regarding exchange
rate practices are substantially identical (art. 5.2), save for the obligation
to inform other parties of when an intervention has been carried out,
only present in USMCA (art. 33.4). Transparency requirements in both
agreements are also analogous.[6]

The agreement with China remains the only example of the use of
Chapter 33 of the USMCA as a model as of January 2021, although
it was expected that the agreements with Korea and Japan were to
include currency provisions since both countries are on the US Treasury's list of currency manipulating countries (US Department of the
Treasury 2020a, p. 5). During the negotiation with Korea, the issue of
currency manipulation was indeed discussed. The US Trade Representative even said in 2018 that "an agreement is being finalized on robust
provisions to prohibit competitive devaluation and exchange rate manipulation in order to promote a level playing field for trade and investment"
(USTR 2018). While the final agreement does not contain such provisions, Korea did start in March 2019 to report publicly on its foreign
exchange intervention (US Department of the Treasury 2020a, p. 1).

In light of the past conventional US modelling practice and the limited
impact of Chapter 33 on USMCA parties, this chapter appears to have
been created to serve as a model for future US negotiations, particularly with countries that may manipulate their currencies for competitive
purposes.

Content of Chapter 33: Exchange Rate Policies and Transparency

As described by the Canadian government, USMCA's Chapter 33
"includes non-binding commitments relating to exchange rate policy and
continued dialogue between the Parties on macroeconomic and exchange
rate policies, as well as enforceable commitments for a high level of transparency and public reporting on certain factors that may affect exchange
rates and other macroeconomic issues" (Canada 2020). The parties,
however, have limited the scope of the chapter by excluding "regulatory or supervisory activities or monetary and related credit policy and
related conduct of an exchange rate or fiscal or monetary authority of a
Party" (USMCA, art. 33.3), thus carving out global monetary policies.

This was necessary for the American Federal Reserve to maintain flexibility on conducting expansionary monetary policies to stimulate the economy, if needed (Bergsten 2018).

Three areas covered by USMCA's Chapter 33 deserve further attention: a definition of competitive devaluation, obligations related to the manipulation of exchange rates, and transparency requirements.

Definition of Competitive Devaluation

One of the innovations of USMCA's Chapter 33 is the definition of competitive devaluation. Indeed, while competitive devaluation naturally falls within the IMF's scope of competence, the IMF has never explicitly defined competitive devaluation, nor has it ever officially qualified an actual devaluation as competitive. Apart from the lack of definition in the IMF Articles of Agreement in themselves, the implementation of a regime of "generalized currency floating" in 1978 makes it difficult to qualify a devaluation as competitive (Dufour 2019, p. 239; Carreau 2009, p. 82). More importantly, the decision-making procedure that prevails at the IMF makes it almost impossible to qualify a devaluation as competitive, although such qualification would at least give hints on currency manipulation (Bergsten and Gagnon 2012, p. 11).

In principle, the Executive Board is the competent body to deal with currency manipulation (Articles of Agreement, arts 12.2–12.3), since it examines all aspects of the IMF's work, from the economic health assessments prepared each year by the institution's staff for all member countries to economic policy issues that concern the global economy as a whole. Normally, the Executive Board makes decisions by consensus, although it sometimes takes formal votes (IMF n.d.). Consensus as a method of decision-making prevents any qualification of devaluation as competitive, since the mere opposition of the country concerned could prevent a decision (Dufour 2019, p. 239). Even if a formal vote is requested, the qualification of a devaluation as competitive would be at the mercy of the political interests at stake. For example, a country like China, whose weighted voting power at the IMF reaches more than 6% (IMF 2020), could easily mobilize institutional opposition to such a qualification (Bergsten and Gagnon 2012).

Unlike the IMF, USMCA Chapter 33, in Article 33.1, defines competitive devaluation as "an action undertaken by an exchange rate authority of a Party for the purpose of preventing effective balance of payments adjustment or gaining an unfair competitive advantage in trade over another Party." This is a major step forward, as it will be easier to qualify a devaluation as competitive, by analyzing the objectives pursued by the measures taken by the exchange rate authority following objective criteria.

Manipulation of Exchange Rates and Macroeconomic Policies

In USMCA's Article 33.4, the parties confirm that they are bound by the IMF Articles of Agreement to avoid manipulating exchange rates. The article also adds hortatory obligations, including achieving and maintaining market-determined exchange rates, refraining from competitive devaluation, and pursuing sound macroeconomic policies (Canada 2020). These commitments, however, resemble greatly the "Obligations Regarding Exchange Arrangements" contained in Article 4 of the IMF Articles of Agreement, and, therefore, do not constitute in themselves a legal innovation, especially as the provisions are not imperative.[7] Interesting though is the provision requiring the parties to inform each other when an intervention has been carried out with respect to the currency of another party to the agreement (USMCA, art. 33.4.3).

Transparency Requirements

The United States, Canada and Mexico agree to disclose publicly a variety of economic data, including monthly foreign exchange reserves data and forward positions, monthly interventions in spot and forward exchange markets, quarterly balance of payments portfolio capital flows, and quarterly exports and imports. Moreover, the parties agree to the public disclosure by the IMF of IMF Staff Reports on their respective country, as well as the confirmation of each party's participation to the IMF Currency Composition of Official Foreign Exchange Reserves (COFER) database (USMCA, art. 33.5).

As already stated, these transparency requirements were already met by the United States, Canada and Mexico before the USMCA's entry into force. The innovation of Chapter 33 in this respect stems from the fact that these provisions are subject to the agreement's dispute settlement mechanism, provided that a party has failed to carry out its obligations in a recurrent or persistent manner and has not remedied the situation in prior consultations between parties' representatives (USMCA, art. 33.8). Consequently, these transparency requirements are for the first time enforceable under an international agreement.

Concluding Remarks

While Chapter 33 has most likely been included in USMCA in order to serve as a model for future trade agreements to prevent competitive currency manipulations, it still represents a revolutionary step in the world of international trade (Bergsten 2018). It demonstrates the will of some states to include more and more non-trade issues in PTAs and to make such issues subject to the strong dispute settlement mechanisms generally contained in such agreements. It remains to be seen if Chapter 33 of the USMCA will in fact be reproduced in PTAs to come.

Notes

1. USMCA's Chapter 33 is extremely similar to the Joint Declaration, reiterating similar commitments. See *Joint Declaration of the Macroeconomic Policy Authorities of Trans-Pacific Partnership Countries*. https://www.tre asury.gov/initiatives/Documents/TPP_Currency_November%202015.pdf.
2. The previous act had been enacted in 2002.
3. The agreement with China is not a PTA per se, as the vast majority of tariffs between both countries will remain, and the fundamental principles of free trade are not included in the agreement. See Dufour and Ducasse (2019, pp. 234–235).
4. The full list includes: China, Japan, Korea, Germany, Italy, Singapore, Malaysia, Thailand, Taiwan and India.
5. This designation was rescinded a few days before the signing of the agreement between China and the United States. The US Treasury said at the time that "China has made enforceable commitments to refrain from competitive devaluation and not target its exchange rate for competitive purposes and has also agreed to publish relevant information related to exchange rates and external balances." US Department of the Treasury (2019). See also: Shalal and Alper (2020); US Department of the Treasury (2020a, pp. 1–2).
6. US-China Agreement (art. 5.3); USMCA (art. 33.5). The only difference between the two articles on transparency is the added obligation in USMCA to disclose monthly interventions in spot and forward foreign exchange markets.
7. The word "should" is used instead of the word "shall," which would have imposed a greater obligation on the parties. Moreover, except for Article 33.5 (Transparency and Reporting), all articles of Chapter 33 are not subject to the dispute settlement mechanism.

References

Bergsten, C. Fred. 2018. *A Positive Step in the USMCA: Countering Currency Manipulation*. Peterson Institute for International Economics, October 4. https://www.piie.com/blogs/trade-investment-policy-watch/positive-step-usmca-countering-currency-manipulation.

Bergsten, C. Fred, and Joseph E. Gagnon. 2012. *Currency Manipulation, the US Economy and the Global Economic Order*. Peterson Institute for International Economics, Policy Brief No. PB12–25, December. https://www.piie.com/sites/default/files/publications/pb/pb12-25.pdf.

Carreau, Dominique. 2009. *Le Fonds monétaire international*. Paris: Pedone.

Dufour, Geneviève. 2019. La compétence de l'OMC en matière de change: Le cas des dévaluations monétaires compétitives au regard de l'article XV du GATT. *Revue De Droit International Et De Droit Comparé* 96 (2): 237–257.

Dufour, Geneviève, and Delphine Ducasse. 2019. 'America First' and the Return of Economic Isolationism and Nationalism to the United States: A Historic Turning Point for International Trade Law. *Canadian Yearbook of International Law* 57: 223–255.

Gantz, David A. 2020. *An Introduction to the United States-Mexico-Canada Agreement: Understanding the New NAFTA*. Cheltenham, UK/Northampton, MA: Edward Elgar.

Juillard, Patrick. 1994. L'évolution des sources du droit des investissements. *Collected Courses of the Hague Academy of International Law* 250: 9–216.

Lowenfeld, Andreas F. 2009. *International Economic Law*. Oxford: Oxford University Press.

Nikièma, Suzy. 2018. *Élaborer un modèle de traité d'investissement: opportunités et défis*. International Institute for Sustainable Development, December. https://www.iisd.org/system/files/meterial/model-investment-treaty-webinar-note-fr.pdf.

Segal, Stephanie. 2018. *USMCA Currency Provisions Set a New Precedent*. Center for Strategic and International Studies, October 5. www.csis.org/analysis/usmca-currency-provisions-set-new-precedent.

Shalal, Andrea, and Alexandra Alper. 2020. U.S. Treasury drops China currency manipulator label ahead of trade deal signing. *Reuters*, January 13. https://www.reuters.com/article/us-usa-trade-china-idUSKBN1ZC2FV.

Taylor, C. O'Neal. 2009. Of Free Trade Agreements and Models. *Indiana International & Comparative Law Review* 19 (3): 569–609.

Vandevelde, Kenneth J. 1988. The Bilateral Investment Treaty Program of the United States. *Cornell International Law Journal* 21 (2): 201–276.

OFFICIAL DOCUMENTS

Articles of Agreement of the International Monetary Fund, Signed July 22, 1944, Entered into Force December 27, 1945. https://www.imf.org/external/pubs/ft/aa/pdf/aa.pdf.

Canada. 2020. *Canada-United States-Mexico Agreement—Canadian Statement on Implementation.* https://www.international.gc.ca/trade-commerce/trade-agreements-accords-commerciaux/agr-acc/cusma-aceum/implementation-mise_en_oeuvre.aspx?lang=eng#137. Accessed October 14, 2020.

Comprehensive and Progressive Agreement for Trans-Pacific Partnership (CPTPP), Signed March 8, 2018, Entered into Force December 30, 2018. https://www.international.gc.ca/trade-commerce/trade-agreements-accords-commerciaux/agr-acc/tpp-ptp/text-texte/toc-tdm.aspx?lang=eng.

Economic and Trade Agreement Between the Government of the United States of America and the Government of the People's Republic of China (US-China Agreement), Signed January 15, 2020. https://ustr.gov/sites/default/files/files/agreements/phase%20one%20agreement/Economic_And_Trade_Agreement_Between_The_United_States_And_China_Text.pdf.

International Monetary Fund (IMF). 2020. *IMF Members' Quotas and Voting Power, and IMF Board of Governors.* https://www.imf.org/external/np/sec/memdir/members.aspx#3. Accessed October 14, 2020.

International Monetary Fund (IMF). n.d. *About the IMF. Governance Structure.* https://www.imf.org/external/about/govstruct.htm. Accessed October 14, 2020.

North American Free Trade Agreement (NAFTA), Signed December 17, 1992, Entered into Force January 1, 1994. https://www.international.gc.ca/trade-commerce/trade-agreements-accords-commerciaux/agr-acc/nafta-alena/fta-ale/index.aspx?lang=eng.

Office of the United States Trade Representative (USTR). 2017. *Summary of Objectives for the NAFTA Renegotiation,* November. https://ustr.gov/sites/default/files/files/Press/Releases/Nov%20Objectives%20Update.pdf.

Office of the United States Trade Representative (USTR). 2018. *New U.S. Trade Policy and National Security Outcomes with the Republic of Korea. Fact Sheet.* https://ustr.gov/about-us/policy-offices/press-office/fact-sheets/2018/march/new-us-trade-policy-and-national.

Trans-Pacific Partnership (TPP), Signed February 4, 2016. https://ustr.gov/sites/default/files/TPP-Final-Text-Dispute-Settlement.pdf.

Trade Promotion Authority (TPA). 2015. Trade Priorities and Accountability Act of 2015, 19 USC 4201.

United States – Mexico – Canada Agreement (USMCA), Signed November 30, 2018, Amended December 10, 2019, Entered into Force July 1, 2020. https://www.international.gc.ca/trade-commerce/trade-agreements-accords-commerciaux/agr-acc/cusma-aceum/text-texte/toc-tdm.aspx?lang=eng.

US Department of State. 2012. *United States Concludes Review of Model Bilateral Investment Treaty*, April 20. https://2009-2017.state.gov/r/pa/prs/ps/2012/04/188198.htm.

US Department of the Treasury. 2019. *Treasury Designates China as a Currency Manipulator*, August 5. https://home.treasury.gov/news/press-releases/sm751.

US Department of the Treasury. 2020a. *Macroeconomic and Foreign Exchange Policies of Major Trading Partners of the United States. Report to Congress*, January. https://home.treasury.gov/system/files/136/20200113-Jan-2020-FX-Report-FINAL.pdf.

US Department of the Treasury. 2020b. *Macroeconomic and Foreign Exchange Policies of Major Trading Partners of the United States. Report to Congress*, December. https://home.treasury.gov/system/files/206/December-2020-FX-Report-FINAL.pdf.

CHAPTER 15

Exceptions, General Provisions, the Review and Term Extension Clause

Richard Ouellet

Many practitioners, scholars and business people wonder if the United States–Mexico–Canada Agreement (USMCA) will become the 2020s gold standard for preferential trade agreements (PTAs), as the North American Free Trade Agreement (NAFTA) was in the 1990s. As I write these lines, the legal texts of the newly concluded Regional Comprehensive Economic Partnership (RCEP)[1] are being published. Obviously, the negotiators and the officials responsible for the legal scrub of this mega-PTA have not been strongly inspired by the novelties of USMCA.

USMCA is not meant to be a model. NAFTA 2.0 is specifically adapted to the North American economic and political context, to the particular interests of the parties at the time it was concluded, to the values that

R. Ouellet (✉)
Faculty of Law, Centre for Interdisciplinary Studies in International Trade and Investment, Université Laval, Quebec City, QC, Canada
e-mail: Richard.Ouellet@fd.ulaval.ca

© The Author(s), under exclusive license to Springer Nature Switzerland AG 2022
G. Gagné and M. Rioux (eds.), *NAFTA 2.0*, Canada and International Affairs, https://doi.org/10.1007/978-3-030-81694-0_15

227

unite or split the three trading partners. The exceptions, the general provisions and the mechanism of revision of the agreement are revealing and eloquent examples of this intent to devise a tailor-made PTA.

GENERAL EXCEPTIONS (ARTICLE 32.1)

World Trade Organization (WTO) general exceptions are incorporated into USMCA. For the purposes of the USMCA chapters related to trade in goods, Article XX of the General Agreement on Tariffs and Trade (GATT) is made part of the agreement. Similarly, for the purposes of the USMCA chapters related to trade in services, paragraphs (a), (b) and (c) of Article XIV of the General Agreement on Trade in Services are made part of USMCA.

Article 32.1 of the USMCA preserves the ability of the parties to adopt, maintain and apply measures necessary to fulfil any of the legitimate objectives listed in the GATT and GATS exceptions. "Subject to the requirement that such measures are not applied in a manner which would constitute a means of arbitrary or unjustifiable discrimination between countries where the same conditions prevail, or a disguised restriction on international trade" (GATT, art. XX). Article 32.1 notably protects the leeway of the parties to apply the environmental measures necessary to protect human, animal or plant life or health or the measures relating to the conservation of living and non-living exhaustible natural resources.

Article 32.1 is a modernized version of Article 2101 of NAFTA and a copy of Article 29.1 of the Comprehensive and Progressive Agreement for Trans-Pacific Partnership (CPTPP).

ESSENTIAL SECURITY (32.2)

The idea of a national security exception is an old one. Many of the first Friendship and Commerce Treaties signed between 1850 and the beginning of the Second World War included this kind of exception. In 1946, the GATT contracting parties enshrined it in Article XXI. Until recently, most PTAs copied or incorporated the exact wording of Article XXI.

In short, the national security exception, as it is phrased in Article XXI, states that, under different circumstances—that are more or less subjective and left to the appreciation of each country—a party is not prevented by trade rules to take any action which it considers necessary for the protection of its essential security interests.

Trading nations have long been reluctant to invoke this exception because of its debatable scope of application and its self-judging nature. With very few interpretations from the GATT bodies, and without any dispute settlement report dealing with Article XXI, the limits of this exception remained untested for almost 70 years. For the last five years, however, the debate over the nature and the contours of the national security exception has been raging.

In 2016, Russia denied the liberty of transit to the goods originating in Ukraine and destined to countries like Kazakhstan, the Kyrghyz Republic and others. In 2017, Ukraine requested the WTO Dispute Settlement Body to establish a panel. Russia admitted that its transit measures were inconsistent with the disciplines of the GATT, but asserted that these measures were necessary for the protection of its essential security interests. More importantly, Russia argued that the panel lacked the jurisdiction to address the matter because the very specific paragraph invoked by Russia was "totally self-judging" and that the measures taken by Russia fell under its discretion. In its report adopted in April 2019, the panel rejected this last argument and found that, under some subparagraphs of Article XXI, the discretion left to each country is limited by circumstances that can be objectively found and appreciated by a panel (Russia—Traffic in Transit).

In 2018, the US Department of Commerce published reports in which it argued that the national security of the country could be endangered by too massive imports of steel and aluminum (US Department of Commerce 2018a, 2018b). Using these reports as a basis, the Trump administration invoked Section 232 of the US Trade Expansion Act and decreed the imposition of punitive tariffs on imported steel and aluminum. A dozen WTO members responded by countermeasures and by complaints before the WTO Dispute Settlement Body. As of today, the US is involved in at least 10 pending disputes where the interpretation of Article XXI is at stake.

The wording of the USMCA security exception is very different from the one of Article XXI of the GATT. Article 32.2 is a repetition of Article 29.2 of the CPTPP, negotiated while the United States still intended to be a party to this PTA. Bad news for Canada and for Mexico, the phrasing of Article 32.2 suggests that the essential security exception of USMCA is much more self-judging than the one spelt in the GATT.

Indigenous Peoples Rights (Article 32.5)

During the USMCA negotiations, many wished for a chapter dedicated to the rights of indigenous peoples (Schwartz 2017; Bellegarde 2018). This idea fitted perfectly with Canada's progressive trade agenda. For Chrystia Freeland, then Canada's minister of Foreign Affairs, the inclusion of an indigenous chapter was a priority (see Schwartz 2017, p. 1). In the end, USMCA includes an exception for indigenous peoples rights. Article 32.5 says:

> Provided that such measures are not used as a means of arbitrary or unjustified discrimination against persons of the other Parties or as a disguised restriction on trade in goods, services, and investment, this Agreement does not preclude a Party from adopting or maintaining a measure it deems necessary to fulfill its legal obligations to indigenous peoples.[2]

In other words, USMCA cannot be an obstacle for the three states parties to take action to fulfill their obligations toward indigenous peoples. The mere inclusion of an exception when a complete chapter was desired could appear as a disappointing result. But it is not seen this way, at least in Canada. For the national chief of the Assembly of First Nations, Perry Bellegarde: "… the result is ground-breaking for Indigenous peoples and their rights. In the most inclusive international trade agreement for Indigenous peoples to date, the United States-Mexico-Canada Agreement (USMCA) will serve to help protect Indigenous peoples' rights when it comes to their enterprises and goods" (2018).

Such an enthusiastic assessment is probably due to what preexisted in NAFTA. The only explicit mentions of indigenous rights were found in the Schedules of Canada and the United States, in Annex II. This annex includes reservations for futures measures related to investment and services. In the Canadian reservation, for instance, Canada reserved its right to adopt or maintain any measure denying investors or service providers any rights or preferences provided to "aboriginal peoples." The scope of application of Article 32.5 is incomparably greater than that of the reservations found in NAFTA.

If Article 32.5 of USMCA certainly represents a big step forward in the recognition of indigenous rights in PTAs, it can hardly be qualified as a novelty. Article 29.6 of the CPTPP, in favor of the Maori People of New Zealand, predates the entry in force of USMCA and its terms are more precise and generous. Article 29.8 of the CPTPP also requires each party "to respect, preserve and promote traditional knowledge and traditional cultural expressions."

CULTURAL INDUSTRIES (ARTICLE 32.6)

The general exception for cultural industries that appeared in NAFTA Annex 2106 and before in the United States–Canada Free Trade Agreement (USCFTA) at Article 2005 is maintained in USMCA. The expression "cultural industry" was defined in those previous agreements at a time when the digital world was not as present in our lives as it is today. Yet, the definition has remained the same, but the Canadian government assures that the exception "continues" to apply to the "online environment" (Canada 2020). It is worth noting that Mexico also secured a cultural exception, at the end of this Chapter on services, in Annex 15-E. This exception sums up what Mexico has described in its Annexes I and II related to investment and cross-border trade in services. In Chapter 16 of this book, Gilbert Gagné analyzes the cultural industries exception in detail.

THE PROVISIONS RELATED TO INFORMATION: DISCLOSURE, PROTECTION AND ACCESS (ARTICLES 32.7, 32.8, AND 32.9)

USMCA "does not require a Party to furnish or allow access to information, the disclosure of which would be contrary to its law," to the public interest, or which would prejudice commercial interests, public or private (art. 32.7). This non-disclosure exception is a copy of Article 29.7 of the CPTPP. It already existed in NAFTA, while differently phrased, in Article 2105.

Acknowledging the huge place the digital environment now takes in our personal and professional lives, and the increasing need to protect all the personal data we enter and diffuse on the web, the USMCA parties have agreed on the terms of Article 32.8, which is somewhere between soft law and hard law. According to this provision, "each Party shall adopt or maintain a legal framework that provides for the protection of personal information." While leaving to each government the choice of the legal approach, USMCA requires each party to "take into account principles and guidelines of relevant international bodies." The parties also shall publish information on the protections they provide, and shall endeavor to adopt non-discriminatory practices in the protection against violations of personal information and to foster cooperation between government agencies on matters involving personal information protection.

Article 32.9 is definitely hard law. It prescribes that a non-discriminatory treatment must be given to the request of any natural person, originating from one of the parties, to obtain access to records held by a central government.

The Non-Market Country Free Trade Agreement (FTA) Clause (Article 32.10)

Among the unprecedented and original provisions of USMCA is Article 32.10 that requires each party to "inform the other Parties of its intention to commence free trade agreement negotiations with a non-market country" "at least 3 months prior to commencing negotiations" (art. 32.10.2). In many ways, Article 32.10 forces a USMCA party intending to enter into a PTA with a non-market country to obtain the full approval of the other parties.

Paragraph 3 provides that "[u]pon request of another Party, a Party intending to commence free trade negotiations with a non-market country shall provide as much information as possible regarding the objectives for those negotiations." When the said negotiations have concluded, the duty to inform and disclose all available information is total and absolute:

> As early as possible, and no later than 30 days before the date of signature, a Party intending to sign a free trade agreement with a non-market country shall provide the other Parties with an opportunity to review the full text of the agreement, including any annexes and side instruments, in order for the Parties to be able to review the agreement and assess its potential impact on this Agreement. If the Party involved requests that the text be treated as confidential, the other Parties shall maintain the confidentiality of the text (art. 32.10.4)

Once the other two parties have analyzed the content and the effects of the PTA to be signed by a USMCA party with a non-market country, they are allowed to terminate USMCA on six months' notice and replace it with a bilateral agreement as between them (art. 32.10.5).

The Canadian and Mexican USMCA negotiators tried to minimize the importance and the meaning of this clause by arguing that a withdrawal clause already existed in NAFTA (Wingrove 2018; Perezcano 2019, p. 13; McDaniel 2019, p. 5). This downplaying of Article 32.10 is a bit misleading. The non-market country clause allows expelling a country from USMCA, something NAFTA never provided for. A former Canadian diplomat who harshly condemns this article even says that Canada could "get kicked-out" of USMCA if it signed with China a PTA that would not please the United States (Stephens 2018).

The definition of "non-market country," as worded in Paragraph 1 of Article 32.10, is also unusual.

> For the purposes of this Article:
> **non-market country** is a country:
> (a) that on the date of signature of this Agreement, a Party has determined to be a non-market economy for purposes of its trade remedy laws; and
> (b) with which no Party has signed a free trade agreement.

What first strikes when reading this paragraph is that the definition of a non-market country is largely left to each USMCA party. Yet, it happens that the United States has a definition of what a "non-market economy country" (NME country) is, for purposes of anti-dumping and countervailing duty laws. To date, 11 countries have been designated as NMEs by the US Department of Commerce (US Department of Commerce 2020). China, Vietnam and nine other countries that are former republics of the Union of Soviet Socialist Republics or former countries of the Eastern Bloc appear on that list. The second surprising element of this definition is the exclusion of countries with which a party belongs to a PTA. This criterion excludes Vietnam, which is, with Canada, Mexico and eight other countries, a party to the CPTPP.

All commentators and observers agree that Article 32.10 targets China, aims at isolating it and building a front against it (Perezcano 2019, p. 13). As Canada and China had begun exploratory talks toward a PTA in September 2016, and as Mexican and Chinese leaders seem to enjoy a good relationship since the BRICS Summit held in China in September

2017, the US administration probably felt the need to prevent its neighboring countries to sign PTAs with what has become the largest rival for the US economy (Gantz 2020, p. 222).

While unprecedented, the advent of such a clause in USMCA is not that surprising. For the last 20 years, since the accession of China to the World Trade Organization (WTO) in 2001, the US administrations, either Republican or Democrat, have expressed many grievances about Chinese economic and trade policies. Subsidies, state-owned enterprises, currency, intellectual property and heavy-handed government control over strategic industries, are the main questions about which the US and other countries contend that Chinese practices are inconsistent with the global trading system. Long before Trump took office, the US underlined the need to address NME practices, and more specifically Chinese practices, at the WTO (McDaniel 2019, p. 5). As it appeared difficult if not impossible to conduct this struggle before the WTO bodies, the Trump administration believed trade wars and regionalism would be efficient manners to compel China to implement some changes in its commercial policy. Accordingly, besides Article 32.10, USMCA contains a few provisions designed to combat Chinese practices in different fields like currency manipulation, state-owned enterprises or data localization rules (Lilly 2019, p. 18).

The debate over the consistency of Chinese commercial practices with global trade rules goes far beyond the terms of USMCA and will probably remain partly unsolved for a long time, but the question of the impact of Article 32.10 now arises. For Canada, this provision is an obstacle to its objective of trade diversification (Stephens 2018). Even for the US, this "China clause" might prove counterproductive and could undermine its ability to negotiate its own PTAs (Ciuriak 2019, p. 5). Interestingly, within USMCA parties, the US was the first to conclude a partial and provisory trade agreement with China in January 2020 as a sign of appeasement in the tariff war that opposes the two mega-economies (US–China Economic and Trade Agreement). Since the signature of this agreement occurred before the USMCA's entry in force, it will be of the highest interest to see if the parties to the USMCA still consider China as a "non-market country" under the language of paragraph 1.b of Article 32.10.

Specific Provision on Cross-Border Trade in Services, Investment and State-Owned Enterprises and Designated Monopolies for Mexico (Article 32.11).

This provision is certainly the most difficult to read and interpret in UCSMA. Indeed, most commentators avoid analyzing its convoluted phrasing. As of this writing, David Gantz seems to be the only scholar, besides some US law firms, to dare interpreting this text (Gantz 2020, pp. 107–10).

Some elements of context need be provided in order to fully understand the meaning and impact of Article 32.11. Mexico is very jealous of its sovereignty over the hydrocarbons on its territory. Annex 602.3 of NAFTA and Chapter 8 of USMCA are eloquent illustrations of it. For a long time, the Mexican state had a heavy-handed control over all aspects of extraction, exploitation, distribution and sale of petroleum on Mexican soil. During the life of NAFTA, Mexico began to liberalize this economic sector of activity. The most recent and important wave of liberalization began in 2013 under President Peña-Nieto. The new regulatory context attracted foreign investments in the Mexican hydrocarbons sector. But there is no consensus about this reform among Mexican political leaders and a new president and administration could call for a rollback. Article 32.11 draws the contours of what could be a new reform, acceptable to the US.

The 2013 Peña-Nieto reform is included in the reservations listed by Mexico in Annex I of the CPTPP. The other parties to the CPTPP, including Canada, are bound by these reservations. These set the terms under which a foreign investment originating from a CPTPP party is accepted and treated in Mexico. Article 32.11 refers to these reservations without naming them (Gantz 2020, p. 108). Therefore, Article 32.11 recognizes that, for purposes of Chapter 14 on investment, this chapter on services, and Chapter 22 on state-owned enterprises and designated monopolies, Mexico reserves its right to adopt or maintain a measure with respect to specific sectors not included already in Annexes I, II and IV of USMCA. But should Mexico adopt a new measure, its application would be restricted in light of any other least restrictive measure found in *any other trade and investment agreement ratified prior to the USMCA,* read here *the CPTPP.*

Foreign Investment Review in Canada / Exclusion from Dispute Settlement Chapter (Article 32.12)

A foreign investor who wishes to establish a new business in Canada or to acquire direct or indirect control of an existing Canadian business is subject to the Investment Canada Act. This act allows the Canadian government to screen the envisaged foreign investment to make sure it is likely to produce a "net benefit" to the Canadian economy. In view of the origin of the investor, the type of investment, the value of the investment and the sector of activity involved, the foreign investor may have to submit a notification or an application for review of the investment. If an economic review is required, the investment shall be analyzed under the criteria provided for in the act and Canadian regulations. Many departments of the Canadian government might be involved in such review, depending on the proposed investment. In the end, the Canadian government may, after review, reject the foreign investment.

In other times, this Canadian review system was much more restrictive and severe than it is now. The 1973 original version of the act and the prescription of results Canada imposed following the economic review were found inconsistent with the GATT by a panel in the now famous Foreign Investment Review Agency (FIRA) case. Today, with regard to WTO law, Canada complies with the Agreement on Trade-Related Investment Measures (TRIMs).

In most of the PTAs it concludes, Canada obtains from its counterparts to exempt the investment decisions reviewed under the Investment Canada Act from the investor-state and the state-to-state dispute settlement mechanisms. This was the case under Annex 1138.2 of NAFTA. In the USMCA, since Canada is not bound by the investor-state dispute settlement mechanism of Chapter 14, Article 32.12 is slightly different. It is not inserted in the investment chapter, but in the general provisions chapter. It exempts the Canadian investment decisions reviewed under the Investment Canada Act from the state-to-state dispute settlement mechanism of Chapter 31.

The Review and Term Extension Clause (Article 34.7)

Article 2205 of NAFTA provided for the withdrawal of a party six months after it notified the other parties of its intention to withdraw. In January 2017, the newly sworn in President Trump, convinced that NAFTA was the "worst trade deal ever signed by any country," threatened to take profit of this provision if Canada and Mexico did not engage in trade negotiations in order to review NAFTA (White House Archives 2017). One can disagree with the assessment of NAFTA thrown by the President, one can also disapprove of the way he initiated the trade relations between his administration and the Canadian and Mexican governments, but it remains true that some chapters of NAFTA had fallen into obsolescence or disuse (Bélanger and Ouellet 2011).

Like the vast majority of trade agreements in force in the world, NAFTA did not provide for its termination or any kind of mandatory revision. The NAFTA Free Trade Commission, created to "supervise the implementation" of the agreement, "oversee its further elaboration" and "consider any matter that may affect the application" of the agreement (art. 2001.2), did not succeed at keeping the interpretation and the application of NAFTA up to date and fit to the North American economy that had undergone significant transformations for a quarter of a century.

When the renegotiation of NAFTA began in August 2017, the inclusion of a "mechanism for ensuring that the Parties assess the benefits of the Agreement on a periodic basis" was a US objective (USTR 2017, p. 17). Rapidly, this general objective was fleshed out and the United States demanded a five-year sunset clause (US House 2018; Bahri and Lugo 2020, pp. 5, 8). As US Trade Representative Robert Lighthizer explained before the Committee on Ways and Means of the US House of Representatives, this clause was aimed at giving the US President the capacity to assess the economic effects of the agreement after a reasonable period of time and see if the terms of the trade relations between the three North American countries have to be rebalanced. A viewing[3] of his testimony and the questions asked by the representatives clearly reveals that this proposal did not spark enthusiasm among the members of the committee (US House 2018; McDaniel 2019, p. 3). Fortunately, the Mexican delegation came with a better idea that turned out to be an acceptable compromise for the US side.

Like NAFTA, USMCA contains a withdrawal mechanism at Article 34.6. But it contains much more. USMCA is the first PTA concluded by the United States (Gantz 2020, pp. 223–24; Lester and Manak 2018a, p. 164) and by Canada (and, as far as we could verify, by Mexico) that provides for its termination. In Article 34.7, paragraph 1, the parties agree that:

> This Agreement shall terminate 16 years after the date of its entry into force, unless each Party confirms it wishes to continue this Agreement for a new 16-year term, in accordance with the procedures set forth in paragraphs 2 through 6.

The Free Trade Commission, established under Article 30.1, is mandated to drive those procedures. A joint review of the operation of USMCA shall be conducted by the Commission on the sixth anniversary of its entry into force (art. 34.7.2). As part of this joint review, each party shall confirm if it wishes to extend the term of USMCA for another 16-year period. If so, the term of USMCA is automatically extended for another 16 years and the Commission shall conduct a new joint review no later than at the end of the next six-year period (art. 34.7.3).

If a party does not confirm its wish to extend the term of USMCA for another 16-year period, the Commission shall conduct a joint review every year for the remainder of the term of USMCA. At any time between the conclusion of a review and the expiry of USMCA, the parties may convene to extend the term of USMCA for another 16 years (art. 34.7.4). Under this "Review and Term Extension" clause, USMCA should be in force for at least 16 years. The six-yearly review should give the parties the opportunity to assess, review and, if needed, modernize USMCA without facing a short expiry deadline, benefitting from a 10-year buffer period.

When compared to what the US administration had brought at the table of negotiation, Article 34.7 can be seen as a win for Canada and Mexico (Bahri and Lugo 2020, p. 8). But a majority of observers believe the inclusion of such a provision remains a source of uncertainty and will have a detrimental effect on investors' and business operators' confidence (Villareal and Fergusson 2020, p. 39; Gantz 2020, p. 225–227; Anderson 2020, p. 162). Some go further and qualify this clause as a "ticking time bomb," creating "artificial deadlines" (Lester and Manak 2018a, p. 165; 2018b), imposed by the populist trade skeptics of the Trump administration (Anderson 2020, p. 162).

It is difficult today to foresee the impact of Article 34.7 on the trade and investment flows between Canada, US and Mexico. It is also perilous to try to predict how the USMCA parties will take advantage of the leeway given by this provision to review and adapt the terms of their PTA. But one thing is clear. One must not be naïve. In no way does this clause protect Canada and Mexico from political pressures like the ones imposed by the US administration in January 2017 to force an unsolicited and unplanned renegotiation of NAFTA.

CONCLUDING REMARKS

Oftentimes, the exceptions, general provisions and review clause are invoked in periods of tensions between trading partners. Their use can radically change the state of the relations between PTA partners. The articles of the USMCA discussed in this chapter have very specific aims and meanings because the negotiation and "legal scrub" of those articles were conducted under the auspices of three particular administrations. It will be of the highest interest to see if and how succeeding administrations use and invoke those articles.

NOTES

1. The RCEP groups 15 Asia–Pacific countries, notably China and Japan, the two largest Asian economies, for the first time in a same PTA.
2. A footnote attached to Article 32.5 specifies that, for Canada, the legal obligations include those recognized in the 1982 Constitution Act and in the self-government agreements concluded with indigenous peoples.
3. To view, see https://www.c-span.org/video/?c4720040/user-clip-us-trade-policy-agenda.

REFERENCES

Anderson, Greg. 2020. *Freeing Trade in North America*. Montreal: McGill-Queen's University Press.

Bahri, Amrita, and Monica Lugo. 2020. Trumping Capacity Gap with Negotiation Strategies: The Mexican USMCA Negotiation Experience. *Journal of International Economic Law* 23 (1): 1–23.

Bélanger, Louis, and Richard Ouellet. 2011. Ruling the North American Market: NAFTA and Its Extensions. In *Inter-American Cooperation at a Crossroads*, ed. Gordon Mace, Andrew F. Cooper, and Timothy M. Shaw, 187–203. Basingstoke: Palgrave Macmillan.

Bellegarde, Perry. 2018. By including Indigenous Peoples, the USMCA Breaks New Ground. *Maclean's*, October 4. https://www.macleans.ca/opinion/by-including-indigenous-peoples-the-usmca-breaks-new-ground/.

Ciuriak, Dan. 2019. From NAFTA to USMCA and the Evolution of US Trade Policy. *Verbatim*, June 25. https://www.cdhowe.org/sites/default/files/attachments/research_papers/mixed/Verbatim-Ciuriak-2019-June%2025.pdf.

Gantz, David A. 2020. *An Introduction to the United States-Mexico-Canada Agreement: Understanding the New NAFTA*. Northampton: Edward Elgar.

Lester, Simon, and Inu Manak. 2018a. The Rise of Populist Nationalism and the Renegotiation of NAFTA. *Journal of International Economic Law* 21 (1): 151–169.

Lester, Simon, and Inu Manak. 2018b. *New NAFTA's Sunset Clause Is a Ticking Time Bomb.* Cato Institute, November 7. https://www.cato.org/publicati ons/commentary/new-naftas-sunset-clause-ticking-time-bomb.

Lilly, Meredith. 2019. A Canadian Perspective on the Future of North America's Economic Relationship. *In The Future of North America's Economic Relationship—From NAFTA to the New Canada-United States-Mexico Agreement and Beyond —Special Report*, 15–19. Waterloo, ON: Centre for International Governance Innovation.

McDaniel, Christine. 2019. A US Perspective on the Future of North America's Economic Relationship. In *The Future of North America's Economic Relationship—From NAFTA to the New Canada-United States-Mexico Agreement and Beyond —Special Report*, 3–6. Waterloo, ON: Centre for International Governance Innovation.

Perezcano, Hugo. 2019. Trade in North America: A Mexican Perspective on the Future of North America's Economic Relationship. In *The Future of North America's Economic Relationship—From NAFTA to the New Canada-United States-Mexico Agreement and Beyond—Special Report*, 7–14. Waterloo, ON: Center for International Governance Innovation.

Schwartz, Risa. 2017. *Toward a Trade and Indigenous Peoples' Chapter in a Modernized NAFTA.* CIGI Paper No. 144. https://www.cigionline.org/pub lications/toward-trade-and-indigenous-peoples-chapter-modernized-nafta.

Stephens, Hugh. 2018. USMCA's Fine Print Giving U.S. the Right to Veto Canada–China Trade Deal Is a Major Setback. *The Globe and Mail,* October 2. https://www.theglobeandmail.com/business/commentary/art icle-usmcas-fine-print-giving-us-the-right-to-veto-canada-china-trade/.

Villareal, M. Angeles, and Ian F. Fergusson. 2020. *NAFTA and the United-States-Mexico-Canada Agreement.* Congressional Research Service. Report R44981, Updated March 2. https://crsreports.congress.gov/product/pdf/R/R44981/18.

Wingrove, Josh. 2018. USMCA China Clause Latest Blow to Trudeau's Asia Ambitions. *BNN Bloomberg,* October 4. https://www.bnnbloomberg.ca/nafta-s-china-clause-is-latest-blow-to-trudeau-s-asia-ambitions-1.1147743.

OFFICIAL DOCUMENTS

Canada. 2020. *Cultural Industries Summary.* https://www.international.gc.ca/trade-commerce/trade-agreements-accords-commerciaux/agr-acc/cusma-aceum/culture.aspx?lang=eng.

Comprehensive and Progressive Agreement for Trans-Pacific Partnership (CPTPP), Signed March 8, 2018, Entered into Force December 30, 2018. https://www.international.gc.ca/trade-commerce/trade-agreements-accords-commerciaux/agr-acc/tpp-ptp/text-texte/toc-tdm.aspx?lang=eng.

Economic and Trade Agreement Between the Government of the United States of America and the Government of the People's Republic of China (US–China Economic and Trade Agreement), Signed January 15, 2020. https://ustr.gov/sites/default/files/files/agreements/phase%20one%20a greement/Economic_And_Trade_Agreement_Between_The_United_States_And_China_Text.pdf.

General Agreement on Tariffs and Trade (GATT), Signed October 20, 1947, Entered into Force January 1, 1948. https://www.wto.org/english/docs_e/legal_e/gatt47_e.pdf.

General Agreement on Trade in Services (GATS), Signed April 15, 1994, Entered into Force January 1, 1995. https://www.wto.org/english/docs_e/legal_e/26-gats.pdf.

North American Free Trade Agreement (NAFTA), Signed December 17, 1992, Entered into Force January 1, 1994. https://www.international.gc.ca/trade-commerce/trade-agreements-accords-commerciaux/agr-acc/nafta-alena/fta-ale/index.aspx?lang=eng.

Office of the United States Trade Representative (USTR). 2017. *Summary of Objectives for the NAFTA Renegotiation*, November update. https://ustr.gov/sites/default/files/files/Press/Releases/Nov%20Objectives%20Update.pdf.

Russia – Measures concerning Traffic in Transit. WTO Doc. WT/DS512/R (Panel Report). Adopted April 5, 2019. https://docs.wto.org/dol2fe/Pages/SS/directdoc.aspx?filename=q:/WT/DS/512R.pdf&Open=True.

United States – Canada Free Trade Agreement (USCFTA), Signed January 2, 1988, Entered into Force January 1, 1989. http://www.international.gc.ca/trade-agreements-accords-commerciaux/assets/pdfs/cusfta-e.pdf.

United States. House of Representatives (US House). Committee on Ways and Means. 2018. *Hearing on U.S. Trade Policy Agenda*. March 21. https://docs.house.gov/meetings/WM/WM00/20180321/108050/HHRG-115-WM00-Transcript-20180321.pdf.

United States-Mexico-Canada Agreement (USMCA), Signed November 30, 2018, Entered into Force July 1, 2020. https://ustr.gov/trade-agreements/free-trade-agreements/united-states-mexico-canada-agreement/agreement-between.

US Department of Commerce. 2018a. *The Effects of Imports of Steel on the National Security—An Investigation Conducted under Section 232 of the Trade Expansion Act, as Amended*. January 11. https://www.commerce.gov/sites/default/files/the_effect_of_imports_of_steel_on_the_national_sec urity_-_with_redactions_-_20180111.pdf.

US Department of Commerce. 2018b. *The Effects of Imports of Aluminum on the National Security: An Investigation Conducted under Section 232 of the Trade Expansion Act, as Amended.* January 11. https://www.commerce.gov/sites/default/files/the_effect_of_imports_of_aluminum_on_the_national_security_-_with_redactions_-_20180117.pdf.

US Department of Commerce. 2020. *Countries Currently Designated by Commerce as Non-Market Economy Countries.* https://www.trade.gov/nme-countries-list.

White House Archives. 2017. *Remarks by President Trump in Meeting with Manufacturing CEOs.* February 23. https://trumpwhitehouse.archives.gov/briefings-statements/remarks-president-trump-meeting-manufacturing-ceos/.

CHAPTER 16

The Treatment of Cultural Products and the Cultural Exemption Clause

Gilbert Gagné

Culture or, more precisely, the treatment of cultural products in international trade has long been debated. Alongside visual, performing and literary arts, cultural products (including goods and services) encompass newspapers, magazines, books, movies, video and music recordings, radio and television and now multimedia. To the extent that such products reflect the cultural identity of specific communities, issues have arisen as to whether or the extent to which they should be exempted from trade disciplines. The latter mainly relate to national treatment, which requires states to treat imported products no less favorably than domestic products with regard to internal taxes and regulations. The ensuing "trade and culture debate" belongs to the wider "trade and" or trade-linkage debate. Involving other fields, such as intellectual property, the environment, labor standards, also considered in this book, this debate revolves around

G. Gagné (✉)
Department of Politics and International Studies, Bishop's University, Sherbrooke, QC, Canada
e-mail: gilbert.gagne@ubishops.ca

© The Author(s), under exclusive license to Springer Nature Switzerland AG 2022
G. Gagné and M. Rioux (eds.), *NAFTA 2.0*, Canada and International Affairs,
https://doi.org/10.1007/978-3-030-81694-0_16

the relationship between economic and non-economic values in global governance. The growing salience of "trade and" problems is attributable to more issues being viewed as trade related as their associated regulations impact trade and an increasing number of areas becoming subject to international agreements (Leebron 2002).

The trade and culture debate is one, however, for which the states parties to the North American Free Trade Agreement (NAFTA), now NAFTA 2.0, have had starkly contrasting views. As the nucleus of global entertainment, the United States has long championed the liberalization of the cultural sector and sought to prevent restrictions of cultural exports, in recent years particularly in new or digital platforms. On the other hand, concerned about the impact of such exports from its giant and culturally close neighbor on its identity and insistent on the pursuit of cultural policies to foster its national culture, Canada has sought to exempt cultural industries from trade agreements. Cultural policy instruments usually fall into two main categories: financial measures, such as subsidies; and regulatory measures, such as those reserving the ownership and/or management of cultural enterprises to nationals, or in the form of national content quotas in broadcasting. Mexico, for its part, while seeking cultural liberalization commitments, also acknowledges restrictions or conditions allowing for the conduct of cultural policies (Gagné 2016, 2020; Goff 2019; Jaramillo 2019, pp. 603–07).

These positions of the three North American partners have been reflected in the obligations they have undertaken in various forums, notably as a result of the Uruguay Round of multilateral trade negotiations and the NAFTA negotiations, both taking place in the early 1990s, and, recently, in the negotiations of the United States—Mexico–Canada Agreement (USMCA) or NAFTA 2.0. In turn, their respective perspectives have made the United States and Canada the main protagonists of the trade and culture debate. The debate culminated in 2005 with the adoption of the Convention on the Protection and Promotion of the Diversity of Cultural Expressions (Cultural Diversity Convention) within the United Nations Educational, Scientific and Cultural Organization. Chiefly sponsored by Canada and France, despite US opposition, the Convention notably enshrines in international law states' right to implement cultural policies and, in so doing, aims to counterbalance obligations and commitments under the World Trade Organization (WTO) and preferential trade agreements (PTAs) (see Vlassis 2015).

The concerns over cultural products in trade agreements essentially revolve around services. In fact, most cultural, notably audiovisual, products take the form of services. These are associated with key measures of states' cultural policies, such as domestic content regulations in the media. Cultural goods are less often subject to special treatment in trade agreements. Indeed, as we will see, when Canada secured an exemption for cultural industries in the United States–Canada Free Trade Agreement (USCFTA) in 1987, it abolished its tariffs on US cultural goods (books, records, magazines, films and tapes). Furthermore, unlike services, regulated by the General Agreement on Trade in Services (GATS) and in which few countries have made commitments relating to the cultural sector, cultural goods come under the general disciplines of the General Agreement on Tariffs and Trade (GATT). Unlike the GATT, market access and national treatment are not general obligations under the GATS and only apply if and to the extent that specific commitments are listed in a country's schedule. Beyond goods and services, the fields of investment and electronic commerce or digital trade are also most relevant as regards the cultural sector. To a lesser degree, the chapters and/or provisions on subsidies, telecommunications, intellectual property, government procurement, and domestic regulations, must also be considered.

Negotiations of trade agreements covering services may take place following two approaches or a combination of the two. Under the bottom-up or positive-list approach, used within the WTO, only sectors and measures specifically included are subject to either full or partial liberalization. By contrast, following the top-down or negative-list approach, used for the NAFTA and USMCA negotiations, sectors and measures not specifically excluded are liberalized by default. Thus, what is mainly relevant are the exceptions or reservations that states parties have secured for the sake of cultural policies. In this respect, with the high-profile exception of cultural products, not many sectors are singled out for special treatment in PTAs with any regularity (Chase 2015, pp. 218, 230). Aside from a blanket exemption, as secured by Canada, such exceptions figure in two types of annexes. Exceptions in annexes I allow the maintenance and renewal of measures in a given area. Yet, following the "standstill" clause, any renewed or revised measure could not be more trade restrictive than the existing one; while, under the "ratchet" mechanism, any subsequent liberalizing measure is to be automatically bound. As for exceptions in annexes II, also known as reservations for future measures, these are broader, since states parties can not only maintain existing, but adopt new or more restrictive, measures in a sector or sub-sector. The key obligations contained in the investment and services chapters are subject to the exceptions or reservations secured by states parties under such annexes.

Following these introductory considerations, the chapter is divided into two sections. Section I concentrates on the provisions relating to the cultural sector in the NAFTA. This is accompanied by elements pertaining to the negotiation and implementation of Canada's cultural exemption. As for Section II, it deals with the treatment of cultural products in the USMCA and, notably, the changes brought to the cultural exemption clause. A conclusion sums up the main findings of the chapter.

The North American Free Trade Agreement

The negotiations for the NAFTA took place between June 1991 and August 1992. Compared with the USCFTA, the NAFTA had more ambitious provisions on services and investment and was the first PTA with specific chapters on telecommunications and intellectual property. The whole chapter on cross-border trade in services and the key obligations of the investment chapter[1] did not apply to "subsidies or grants provided by a Party or a state enterprise, including government-supported loans, guarantees and insurance" (NAFTA, arts 1108.7.b and 1201.2.d). Thus, the NAFTA hardly constrained states parties in their ability to use financial instruments to promote their cultural industries.

Intellectual property rights are understood as exclusive rights granted to creators, inventors and/or owners to control the use made of their productions and/or properties. Those most relevant for cultural products are copyrights and related rights, aimed at ensuring the remuneration of artists and creators for their works. Each party to the NAFTA should, at a minimum, have acceded to the 1971 Geneva Convention for the Protection of Producers of Phonograms Against Unauthorized Duplication of their Phonograms and the 1971 Berne Convention for the Protection of Literary and Artistic Works. Each party should also have ensured the effective protection and enforcement of intellectual property rights under its domestic law. On copyrights, similarly to the WTO Agreement on Trade-Related Aspects of Intellectual Property Rights, the NAFTA provided for a minimal protection of 50 years following the publication of a work (NAFTA, arts 1705 and 1706).

Besides the commitments and exceptions pertaining to cultural products taken by the United States and Mexico as part of the NAFTA negotiations, the latter owed much to the provisions already included in the USCFTA. The United States sought to renegotiate the exemption of the cultural sector secured at Canada's behest (Cameron and Tomlin 2000, p. 160). For the Canadian government, however, this issue was settled and not to be reopened. The USCFTA's cultural exemption was to be carried over into the NAFTA, thus preserving the *status quo* (Robert 2000, pp. 87–89). Article 2106 of the NAFTA stipulates that "Annex 2106 applies to the Parties specified in that Annex with respect to cultural industries." In turn, Annex 2106 provides that the USCFTA governs rights and obligations between Canada and any party with regard to cultural industries, except for Article 302 on tariff elimination.

During the negotiations for the USCFTA, Canada insisted on exempting cultural industries and was ready to jeopardize the whole PTA unless this sector was excluded from the treaty (Doern and Tomlin 1991, p. 200; Acheson and Maule 1999, pp. 76–77; see also Ritchie 1997, pp. 121–37). Thus, under the USCFTA (art. 2005.1), "[c]ultural industries are exempt from the provisions of this Agreement, except as specifically provided." These specific provisions pertained to: the elimination of tariffs for cultural goods (art. 401); the requirement that any US investor having to divest him/herself of assets in Canada because of ownership restrictions in cultural industries is to receive fair market value (art. 1607.4); amendments to Canadian law so as to ensure authorizations from, and payments to, US copyright holders for retransmission of program signals (art. 2006); and the removal of the requirement for a Canadian magazine or newspaper to be printed or typeset in Canada in order for advertisers to deduct expenses for advertising space (USCFTA, art. 2007). The exemption was accompanied by a party's right to retaliate, with "measures of equivalent commercial effect in response to actions that would have been inconsistent with this Agreement but for paragraph 1" (USCFTA, art. 2005.2).

As issues relating to Canada's cultural industries were discussed within the NAFTA negotiations, the Canadian government envisaged securing reservations for each chapter covering cultural matters, as will later be done in some Canadian PTAs (see Goff 2019; Gagné 2020). Nonetheless, Canada resolved to keep a cultural exemption incorporating the whole trade agreement, as in the USCFTA. By specifically referring to the latter agreement, Canada then ensured that new obligations under the NAFTA would not affect Canadian cultural industries. Canada could adopt measures departing from NAFTA obligations, if these are not included in the USCFTA, as for intellectual property and cultural services, such as broadcasting, without being subject to retaliation by the United States or Mexico (Robert 2000, pp. 51–52, 92–93).

The definition of cultural industries was slightly modified, from the CUSFTA to the NAFTA, to refer to *persons*, and not anymore to *enterprises*, engaged in any of the following activities:

a. the publication, distribution, or sale of books, magazines, periodicals, or newspapers in print or machine-readable form but not including the sole activity of printing or typesetting any of the foregoing;
b. the production, distribution, sale, or exhibition of film or video recordings;
c. the production, distribution, sale, or exhibition of audio or video music recordings;
d. the publication, distribution, or sale of music in print or machine-readable form; or
e. radiocommunications in which the transmissions are intended for direct reception by the general public, and all radio, television and cable broadcasting undertakings and all satellite programming and broadcast network services (USCFTA, art. 2012; NAFTA, art. 2107).

As in the USCFTA, performing arts (e.g., theatre, opera, dance), visual arts and museums were not included, and, thus, not exempted from NAFTA provisions.

Much has been written about the "conditional" cultural exemption under the NAFTA regime. The retaliatory clause has been criticized for making Canadian authorities apprehensive, if not unwilling, to adopt or even maintain existing cultural policy measures, out of fear of US reaction. Tensions peaked during the second half of the 1990s, as result of certain Canadian cultural policy initiatives and decisions, some of which developing into overt trade disputes (Taras 2000; Gagné 2003/2004, pp. 37–38, 45; see also Ritchie 1997, pp. 224–38; Acheson and Maule 1999, pp. 185–348). The United States has much leeway as to the conditions of retaliation, although no actual case of retaliation has taken place. The US government could determine the economic sectors subject to trade sanctions and, as happened during the periodicals dispute, target various unrelated sectors, sensitive for Canadian interests, the selection of which it could modify any time, with a view to maximize pressure on Canada.

As it seeks extensive liberalization, the United States had relatively few reservations pertaining to cultural products in the NAFTA, all under Annex II. The US government preserved the right to adopt or maintain any measure relating to investment in, or the provision of, telecommunications transport networks and services, as well as radiocommunications, the latter referring to all communications by radio, including broadcasting. This reservation did not apply to enhanced or value-added services or to the production, sale or licensing of radio or television programming. Two other reservations provided that equivalent treatment may be accorded to persons of any country that limit ownership by US persons in an enterprise engaged in the operation of a cable television system or the publication of daily newspapers primarily written for audiences and distributed in that country (NAFTA, annex II-US).

Unlike Canada, Mexico significantly liberalized its cultural sector under the NAFTA, but secured a certain number of exceptions. Reminiscent of the provision of the USCFTA pertaining to retransmission rights (art. 2006), documentation showing the granting of licenses by copyright holders was required for the *Secretariá de Gobernación* to authorize the import in any form of radio or television programming for broadcast or cable distribution within Mexico (NAFTA, annex I-MX, pp. 9–10). Unless otherwise decided by the same Secretariat, the use of the Spanish language was mandated for the broadcast or cable distribution of radio or television programming, while radio or television announcers or presenters must have been Mexicans to perform in the country. A majority of the time of each day's live broadcast programs should also have featured Mexican nationals (NAFTA, annex I-MX, p. 12). The use of Spanish language or subtitles was as well required for advertising broadcasted or otherwise distributed in Mexican territory. Advertising included in programs transmitted directly from outside Mexico may not have been distributed in such programs when retransmitted in Mexican territory (NAFTA, annex I-MX, p. 13).

In the case of cable television, investors of another party or their investments may only have owned, directly or indirectly, up to 49% of the ownership interest in an enterprise in this sub-sector. The latter exception was to be discussed by the parties five years after NAFTA's entry into force (NAFTA, annex I-MX, p. 14). A concession to construct and/or to operate a cable television system could only have been granted to Mexican nationals and enterprises (NAFTA, annex I-MX, p. 15). A quota of up to 30% of the screen time of every theatre, assessed on an annual basis, may have been set for films produced by Mexican persons, either within or outside Mexico's territory (NAFTA, annex I-MX, p. 16). Foreign governments and state enterprises or their investments were prevented to invest, directly or indirectly, in Mexican enterprises engaged in communications, transportation, and other general means of communication (NAFTA, annex I-MX, p. 19). Investors of another party or their investments may have owned, directly or indirectly, 100% of the ownership interest in an enterprise in Mexico engaged in the simultaneous printing and distribution within Mexico of a daily newspaper published outside Mexican territory, but only up to 49% in the case of the printing or publication of a newspaper written primarily for a Mexican audience and distributed in the country (NAFTA, annex I-MX, p. 41).

Mexico took relatively few reservations for future measures, however. It reserved the right to adopt or maintain any measure regarding investment in, or provision of, broadcasting, multipoint distribution systems, uninterrupted music, and high-definition television services. This reservation did not apply to measures concerning the production, sale or licensing of radio or television programming (NAFTA, annex II-MX).

Notwithstanding NAFTA, and now USMCA, provisions, cultural industries have remained subject to multilateral disciplines. It is particularly the case under the GATT, regulating trade in goods, within which the only exception applying to cultural products relates to cinematographic quotas (art. IV). Even if Canada has not undertaken any commitments on cultural services within the GATS, cultural products often have both goods and services features, which may make them subject to diverging rules. This was illustrated by the US complaint to the WTO in 1996 against Canada's measures for the protection of periodicals, which were found to contravene international trade obligations. The main issue at stake pertained to the loss of advertising revenues for Canadian periodicals in favor of US split-run magazines. WTO authorities ruled that in cases where measures affect the furniture of a service (advertising) associated to a specific good (periodical), the links between GATS and cultural services, on the one hand, and GATT and cultural goods, on the other, can only be determined case by case, taking into consideration the nature and the effects of the measure(s) at issue (Canada - Periodicals; see Gagné 1999).

THE UNITED STATES-MEXICO-CANADA AGREEMENT

After US President Trump threatened to either renegotiate or break the NAFTA, the renegotiation took place from August 2017 to September 2018. The ensuing USMCA was signed on November 30, 2018, and, following a Protocol of Amendment reached in December 2019, entered into force on July 1, 2020. The exceptions under Annexes I and II continue to subtract states parties from the key obligations of the investment and services chapters (USMCA, arts 14.12.1-2 and 15.7.1-2) and, consequently, are still prime determinants of their ability to pursue cultural policies. The investment and services chapters also essentially reiterate that their respective key disciplines do not apply to "subsidies or grants provided by a Party, including government-supported loans, guarantees and insurance" (USMCA, arts 14.12.5.b and 15.2.3.d).

As the US government was eager to "upgrade" the NAFTA and ensure "digital freedom," the USMCA includes a chapter relating to electronic commerce or to trade in digital products. The latter notion is understood as "a computer program, text, video, image, sound recording, or other product that is digitally encoded, produced for commercial sale or distribution, and that can be transmitted electronically." Interestingly, it is specified in a footnote that this definition does not reflect parties' views of digital products as goods or services (USMCA, art. 19.1). For greater certainty, a measure affecting the supply of a service delivered or performed electronically is subject to the provisions and exceptions under the investment and services chapters (USMCA, art. 19.2.4). The chapter prohibits the imposition of customs duties, fees, or other charges on or in connection with the international exchange of digital products transmitted electronically; but not of internal taxes, fees, or other charges, as long as these are consistent with the USMCA (art. 19.3). There is also a requirement for the non-discriminatory treatment of digital products, subject to an exception for parties' subsidies or grants (USMCA, art. 19.4). Finally, the chapter on digital trade must be considered in conjunction with the liberalizing measures in telecommunications, computer and related services, as well as high technology products.

The audiovisual, computer and telecommunications sectors tend to converge. Digital technologies blend the market segments of telecommunications, centered on transmission and networks, and of audiovisuals, centered on programming and contents, so to combine the availability of contents with network accessibility. The actors in the telecommunications sector, then, are to play an increasing role in the dissemination of digital cultural contents, notably through the Internet access services they provide (Gagné 2016, pp. 52–54). As is the case for intellectual property, parties to the USMCA ought to ensure a proper regulatory oversight of the telecommunications sector under their domestic law. Within the intellectual property chapter, as concerns cultural products, each party affirms that it has ratified or acceded to the 1971 Berne Convention, the 1996 World Intellectual Property Organization (WIPO) Copyright Treaty and the 1996 WIPO Performances and Phonograms Treaty (USMCA, art. 20.7). On copyrights and related rights, the USMCA (art. 20.62) extends the term of protection of a work, performance or phonogram to the life of an author and 70 years after his/her death, or no less than 75 years from first authorized publication or 70 years from creation.

Despite the "resolute plan" of the United States Trade Representative to strip Canada's cultural exemption (Siripurapu 2018), within the exceptions and general provisions chapter, Article 32.6 of the USMCA relates to cultural industries and contains five paragraphs (McGregor 2018; Gagné 2020, pp. 306–07). The first paragraph repeats the definition of such industries, as found in the NAFTA. Concerned by technological shifts toward digital platforms, Canadian cultural stakeholders might have preferred an updated or expanded definition. Yet, the United States would have resisted this, while a uniform definition might be preferable across the multiple Canadian PTAs (Goff 2019, p. 564). In a second paragraph, the general cultural exemption now reads: "This Agreement does not apply to a measure adopted or maintained by Canada with respect to a cultural industry, except as specifically provided in Article 2.4 (Treatment of Customs Duties) or Annex 15-D (Programming Services)."

The Annex 15-D services relate to: (1) the simultaneous substitution of signals, under which Canada is to rescind the Canadian Radio-television and Telecommunications Commission's regulations that stopped the simultaneous substitution of US with Canadian advertisements, therefore allowing Canadians to watch US commercials, during Super Bowl broadcasts, the latter to receive treatment no less favorable than other US programs retransmitted in Canada; (2) the requirements for authorizations from copyright holders for retransmission of program signals (largely echoing USCFTA art. 2006); and (3) US home shopping programming services to be authorized for distribution in Canada. With respect to the latter annex, as in the USCFTA, the Canadian cultural exemption is accompanied by some commitments. Yet, in view of the whole of Canada's cultural policy measures, these are fairly limited, and, unlike Geist (2018), their scope should not be overblown.

The retaliatory clause is reconducted in paragraph 4: "Notwithstanding any other provision of this Agreement, a Party may take a measure of equivalent commercial effect in response to an action by another Party that would have been inconsistent with this Agreement but for paragraph 2 or 3." In this regard, a new provision, under paragraph 3, reads: "With respect to Canadian goods, services, and content, the United States and Mexico may adopt or maintain a measure that, were it adopted or maintained by Canada, would have been inconsistent with this Agreement but for paragraph 2." Thus, the other USMCA partners are henceforth entitled to adopt or maintain cultural policy measures, in view of similar Canadian measures in place. Interestingly, this could trigger the use of the retaliatory clause by Canada.

There is finally a new paragraph pertaining to dispute settlement. It provides that a "dispute regarding a measure taken under paragraph 4 shall be settled exclusively under [the USMCA] unless a Party seeking to establish a panel ... has been unable to do so within 90 days of the date of delivery of the request for consultations ...." (USMCA, art. 32.6.5.a). On delivery of the request to establish an arbitral panel, the latter *is* established (USMCA, art. 31.6.4). Here, the Protocol of Amendment removed the possibility, initially carried over from the NAFTA, for parties to block the establishment of panels (Gantz and Puig 2019). Arguably, this change, limited to the dispute settlement chapter, should have led to a reformulation of the relevant section of paragraph 5, as it renders moot the possible inability to establish a panel. Besides, a panel under paragraph 5 shall have jurisdiction and may make findings only with regard to whether an action to which another party replies is a measure adopted or maintained with respect to a cultural industry and whether a party's retaliatory action is of "equivalent commercial effect" to the other party's relevant action. This limited jurisdiction raises questions, notably in regard to whether a panel could rule if a measure, although related to a cultural industry, is consistent with the USMCA and, thus, cannot lead to retaliation.

There are still few exceptions taken by the US government relating to cultural industries in the USMCA. Compared with the NAFTA, these tend to be formulated differently and in more detail, following an evolution across successive US PTAs. Under Annex I, in the field of radio-communications, consisting of all communications by radio, including broadcasting, the United States reserves the right to restrict ownership of radio licenses in accordance with its statutory and regulatory provisions on foreign participation (USMCA, annex I-US, p. 12). Under Annex II, with respect to Canada, the US government reserves the right to: (a) adopt or maintain any measure according differential treatment to persons of other countries due to application of reciprocity measures or through international agreements involving sharing of the radio spectrum, guaranteeing market access or national treatment with regard to the one-way satellite transmission of direct-to-home (DTH) and direct broadcasting satellite (DBS) television services and digital audio services; and (b) prohibit a person of a party from offering DTH or DBS television and digital audio services into US territory unless that person establishes that the party of which it is a person: (i) permits US persons to obtain a license for such services in that party in similar circumstances; and (ii) treats the supply of audio or video content originating in the party no more favorably than the supply of audio or video content originating in a non-party or any other party (USMCA, annex II-US, p. 1). In the case of the latter prohibition, a similar one, not specifically aimed at Canada, pertains to the owning or operating of a cable television system in the United States (USMCA, annex II-US, p. 2). Finally, the US government has reserved its right to adopt or maintain any measure not inconsistent with its market access commitments under the GATS (USMCA, annex II-US).

While Canada's few commitments regarding the cultural sector figure in Annex 15-D of the USMCA's services chapter, Annex 15-E sums up the cultural *exceptions* taken by Mexico and contained in Annexes I and II of the agreement. Annex 15-E begins with a preamble that echoes the Cultural Diversity Convention and reads:

> Recognizing that culture is an important component of the creative, symbolic and economic dimension of human development,
>
> Affirming the fundamental right of freedom of expression and the right to plural and diverse information,
>
> Recognizing that states have the sovereign right to preserve, develop and implement their cultural policies, to support their cultural industries for the purpose of strengthening the diversity of cultural expressions, and to preserve their cultural identity.

Under Annex I, for broadcasting (radio and free-to-air television), sole concessions and frequency band concessions are to be granted only to Mexican nationals or enterprises constituted under Mexican laws and regulations. An investor of a party or its investments may participate up to 49% in a concessionaire enterprise supplying broadcasting services. This maximum shall apply according to the reciprocity existent with the country in which the investor or trader who ultimately controls such foreign investment, directly or indirectly, is constituted. In any case, a favorable opinion of the National Commission on Foreign Investments is required for the granting of such concessions involving foreign investment. Under no circumstances may a concession, the rights conferred therein, facilities, auxiliary services, offices or accessories and properties affected thereto, be assigned, encumbered, pledged or given in trust, mortgaged, or transferred totally or partially to any foreign government or state. Concessions for indigenous social use are to be granted to Mexican indigenous people and communities, with the objective to promote, develop and preserve languages, cultures, knowledge, traditions, identity and internal rules that, under principles of gender equality, enable the integration of indigenous women in the accomplishment of the purposes for which the concession is granted. The state should guarantee that broadcasting promotes the values of national identity. Broadcasting concessionaires shall use and stimulate local and national artistic values and expressions of Mexican culture, according to the characteristics of their programming. Daily programming with personal performances shall include more time covered by Mexicans (USMCA, annex I-MX, pp. 10–11).

Investors of another party or their investments may only own, directly or indirectly, up to 49% of the ownership interest in an enterprise established or to be established in Mexican territory engaged in the printing or publication of daily newspapers written primarily for a domestic audience and distributed in the territory of Mexico (USMCA, annex I-MX, p. 16). Cinema exhibitors should reserve 10% of the total screen time to the projection of national films (USMCA, annex I-MX, p. 49). Finally, under Annex II, Mexico has taken limited market access commitments with respect to audiovisual services (USMCA, annex II-MX, pp. 20–23).

Conclusion

Canada has secured a cultural exemption in all its PTAs. In those with the United States, that is, the USCFTA, NAFTA and USMCA, a general exemption has been assorted with provisions for retaliation against cultural policy measures. A key question in the NAFTA renegotiation was whether Canada's exemption of cultural industries would apply to trade in digital products. In an unprecedented rebuff of the US digital trade agenda, Canada's overall cultural exemption has been maintained. To the extent that the Canadian government, as the vanguard of cultural exception/diversity, made the preservation of its near complete ability to pursue cultural policies a *sine qua non* condition for its participation in the USMCA, the United States has seemingly relented. Yet, this may have been rendered easier since the retaliatory clause has also been kept in place (Gagné 2019, p. 624).

The Canadian blanket, yet conditional, cultural exemption, as maintained in the USMCA, is not without some concerns. One has to do with whether the definition of cultural industries, dating back to the USCFTA, is neutral from a technological standpoint so as to encompass digital platforms and notably the Internet. If the websites of broadcasters and newspapers could be covered by the definition, it might be different for Internet-only services, which would then fall outside the cultural exemption (Acheson and Maule 1999, p. 76; Geist 2016; Guèvremont and Otašević 2017, p. 58). For most analysts, however, the definition of cultural industries inherited from the USCFTA seems broad enough to include digital media and, hence, not particularly problematic. On the other hand, the retaliatory clause may continue to act as a strong disincentive for Canadian public authorities to adopt cultural policy measures, especially in the digital field. Finally, the Canadian cultural exemption should normally be strengthened with provisions to settle cultural trade disputes exclusively under the USMCA; rather than under the WTO, within which no such broad exemption exists.

As a champion of trade liberalization, the United States has few restrictions in its PTAs, including for the cultural sector. Under the NAFTA, it kept its latitude in the field of radiocommunications, while other reservations provided for reciprocity in the case of cable television and newspapers ownership. The US government, under the USMCA, still has restrictions for ownership of broadcasting licenses. With regard to

Canada, it has secured exceptions for MFN treatment in the case of satel-lite television and digital audio services, as well as for reciprocal treatment in the offering of such services in the United States, and, for USMCA parties, in cable television.

Under the NAFTA, Mexico had reservations with respect to the use of the Spanish language in radio and television. It was also the case for the resort to nationals in the majority of broadcast programs and as announcers or presenters. There were also restrictions with regard to: the ownership of, and concessions for, cable television enterprises/services; theatrical screen quotas; and the printing or publication of daily newspa-pers for a Mexican audience. Reservations for future measures included the right to adopt or maintain any measure relating to investment in, or provision of, broadcasting, multipoint distribution systems, uninterrupted music, and high-definition television services. Mexico has maintained much of the same restrictions under the USMCA; except for those regarding cable television, which had been dropped, while the theatrical screen quotas had been reduced. As result of US discontent with restric-tions pertaining to the Spanish language, Mexico reformulated them to emphasize cultural diversity, notably the ability to help indigenous cultures and languages (Siripurapu 2018).

Thus, from NAFTA 1.0 to 2.0, the treatment of cultural products has evolved, notably with provisions dealing with digital trade and the exten-sion in time of copyrights. Yet, with respect to the reservations secured by states parties, not much has changed overall. Besides provisions for the reciprocal maintenance or adoption of cultural policy measures by other partners and for dispute settlement exclusively under the USMCA, the essential of Canada's outright cultural exemption has been reconducted, including for the digital field. If a little more numerous and formulated somehow differently, the exceptions taken by the United States have not varied significantly in scope and remain very limited. As for Mexico, despite a new emphasis on cultural diversity and identity, the scope of its exceptions has actually narrowed.

NOTES

1. These obligations pertain to national treatment, most-favored-nation (MFN) treatment, and senior management and boards of directors. Under MFN, any trade advantage a country gives to another must be extended, immediately and unconditionally, to all other countries. While national

treatment corresponds to the internal dimension of the non-discrimination principle, central in the international trading regime, MFN is the external one. The third obligation forbids or limits restrictions based on nationality for the senior management and boards of directors of enterprises.

References

Acheson, Keith, and Christopher Maule. 1999. *Much Ado About Culture: North American Trade Disputes*. Ann Arbor: University of Michigan Press.

Cameron, Maxwell A., and Brian W. Tomlin. 2000. *The Making of NAFTA: How the Deal Was Done*. Ithaca, NY: Cornell University Press.

Canada – Certain Measures Concerning Periodicals. WTO Doc. WT/DS31/R (Panel Report). WTO Doc. WT/DS31/AB/R (Appellate Body Report). Adopted July 30, 1997.

Chase, Kerry A. 2015. Audiovisual Goods and Services in Preferential Trade Agreements. In *Trade Cooperation: The Purpose, Design and Effects of Preferential Trade Agreements*, edited by Andreas Dür and Manfred Elsig, 218–245. Cambridge: Cambridge University Press.

Convention on the Protection and Promotion of the Diversity of Cultural Expressions, Adopted October 20, 2005, Entered into Force March 18, 2007. https://en.unesco.org/creativity/convention/what-is/convention-text.

Doern, G. Bruce, and Brian W. Tomlin. 1991. *Faith and Fear: The Free Trade Story*. Toronto: Stoddart.

Gagné, Gilbert. 1999. Libéralisation et exception culturelle: Le différend canado-américain sur les périodiques. *Études Internationales* 30 (3): 571–588.

Gagné, Gilbert. 2003/2004. Cultural Sovereignty, Identity, and North American Integration: on the Relevance of the U.S.-Canada-Quebec Border. *Québec Studies* 36: 29–49.

Gagné, Gilbert. 2016. *The Trade and Culture Debate: Evidence from US Trade Agreements*. Lanham, MD: Lexington Books.

Gagné, Gilbert. 2019. Trade and Culture: The United States. *International Journal of Cultural Policy* 25 (5): 615–628.

Gagné, Gilbert. 2020. The Evolution of Canada's Cultural Exemption in Preferential Trade Agreements. *Canadian Foreign Policy Journal* 26 (3): 298–312.

Gantz, David A., and Sergio Puig. 2019. The Scorecard of the USMCA Protocol of Amendment. *EJIL: Talk!*, December 23. https://www.ejiltalk.org/the-sco recard-of-the-usmca-protocol-of-amendment/.

Geist, Michael. 2016. *The Trouble with the TPP, Day 29: Cultural Policy Innovation Uncertainty*. February 11. http://www.michaelgeist.ca/2016/02/the-trouble-with-the-tpp-day-29-cultural-policy-innovation-uncertainty/.

Geist, Michael. 2018. *The Full "Culture Exception" That Isn't: Why Canada Caved on Independent Cultural Policy in the USMCA*. October 11. http://www.michaelgeist.ca/2018/10/usmcaculture/.

General Agreement on Tariffs and Trade (GATT), Signed October 20, 1947, Entered into Force January 1, 1948. https://www.wto.org/english/docs_e/legal_e/gatt47_e.pdf.

General Agreement on Trade in Services (GATS), Signed April 15, 1994, Entered into Force January 1, 1995. https://www.wto.org/english/docs_e/legal_e/26-gats.pdf.

Goff, Patricia. 2019. Canada's Cultural Exemption. *International Journal of Cultural Policy* 25 (5): 552–567.

Guèvremont, Véronique, and Ivana Otašević. 2017. *Culture in Treaties and Agreements: Implementing the 2005 Convention in Bilateral and Regional Trade Agreements*. Paris: UNESCO. https://en.unesco.org/creativity/sites/creativity/files/dce-policyresearch-book1-en-web.pdf.

Jaramillo, Grace. 2019. Latin America: Trade and Culture at a Crossroads. *International Journal of Cultural Policy* 25 (5): 602–614.

Leebron, David W. 2002. Linkages. *American Journal of International Law* 96 (1): 5–27.

McGregor, Janyce. 2018. Canada to Apply USMCA Cultural Exemption to Trade in Digital Media. *CBC News*. October 17. https://www.cbc.ca/news/politics/usmca-nafta-cultural-exemption-1.4865113.

North American Free Trade Agreement (NAFTA), Signed December 17, 1992, Entered into Force January 1, 1994. https://www.nafta-sec-alena.org/Home/Legal-Texts/North-American-Free-Trade-Agreement.

Protocol of Amendment to the United States-Mexico-Canada Agreement (USMCA), Signed December 10, 2019. https://ustr.gov/sites/default/files/files/agreements/FTA/USMCA/Protocol-of-Amendments-to-the-United-States-Mexico-Canada-Agreement.pdf.

Ritchie, Gordon. 1997. *Wresting With the Elephant: The Inside Story of the Canada–US Trade Wars*. Toronto: Macfarlane, Walter & Ross.

Robert, Maryse. 2000. *Negotiating NAFTA: Explaining the Outcome in Culture, Textiles, Autos, and Pharmaceuticals*. Toronto: University of Toronto Press.

Siripurapu, Anshu. 2018. Seade: Mexico Demanded Cultural Exemption in USMCA after Canada Got One. *World Trade Online*. October 11. https://insidetrade.com/daily-news/seade-mexico-demanded-cultural-exemption-usmca-after-canada-got-one.

Taras, David. 2000. Swimming Against the Current: American Mass Entertainment and Canadian Identity. In *Canada and the United States: Differences that Count*, 2nd ed., edited by David M. Thomas, 192–208. Peterborough, ON: Broadview Press.

United States – Canada Free Trade Agreement (USCFTA), Signed January 2, 1988, Entered into Force January 1, 1989. http://www.international.gc.ca/trade-agreements-accords-commerciaux/assets/pdfs/cusfta-e.pdf.

United States-Mexico-Canada Agreement (USMCA), Signed November 30, 2018, Entered into Force July 1, 2020. https://ustr.gov/trade-agreements/free-trade-agreements/united-states-mexico-canada-agreement/agreement-between.

Vlassis, Antonios. 2015. *Gouvernance mondiale et culture: De l'exception à la diversité*. Liège: Presses Universitaires de Liège.

CHAPTER 17

Conclusion—NAFTA's Impacts: Can the USMCA Do Better?

Michèle Rioux, Sandra Polaski, and Gilbert Gagné

North America has been a significant and influential experiment in regional integration for the last 28 years, that is, since the entry into force of the North American Free Trade Agreement (NAFTA). That

M. Rioux (✉)
Department of Political Science, Centre for the Study of Integration and Globalization, Université du Québec À Montréal, Montreal, QC, Canada
e-mail: rioux.michele@uqam.ca

S. Polaski
Global Economic Governance Initiative, Boston University, Boston, MA, USA

Independent Mexico Labor Expert Board, Washington, DC, USA

G. Gagné
Department of Politics and International Studies, Bishop's University, Sherbrooke, QC, Canada
e-mail: gilbert.gagne@ubishops.ca

Research Group on Continental Integration, Université du Québec À Montréal, Montreal, QC, Canada agreement was built on the United States–Canada Free Trade Agreement (USCFTA), that entered into force in 1989. This preferential trade agreement (PTA) allowed Canada to secure its access to the US market in a context of rising US protectionism. In the broader context of a lengthy Uruguay Round at the multilateral level, the USCFTA attracted a lot of attention, including from Mexico, which sought to negotiate a similar trade agreement with the United States. NAFTA was then negotiated as a trilateral agreement. This occurred at the very early stages of a new wave of globalization and integration of world production. It aimed to achieve competitiveness gains for North America, which was facing challenges in this regard. The new NAFTA model proved important because of the size of the region, and it was replicated in other trade deals, spreading beyond North America.

The negotiation in 2017–2018 of a new North American agreement occurred in a very different context. By then, many other bilateral and regional trade agreements had been negotiated by the United States, Canada and Mexico, with further innovations beyond NAFTA. In parallel, global value chains had become highly integrated, with a strong Asian component. In a way, the United States–Mexico–Canada Agreement (USMCA) represents a catching up with the rest of the trading world, that had by then outpaced and overridden NAFTA.

If NAFTA became outdated, at its inception it innovated in many aspects. It established a template for trade agreements on new issues such as investment, intellectual property, services, business-related mobility, as well as labor and the environment. It was also a new model of regional integration, contrasting sharply with the model underlying the European Union (EU). Building the EU was a gradual integration process, starting with the creation of a customs union and eventually evolving very elaborate supranational legal and political institutions over time, leading to a single market, a single currency and many areas of common policy-making. This model of deep integration required a strong sense of common interests across the layers of governance from the local, the national and the EU levels of regulation.

By contrast, NAFTA did not aim to establish a North American community of interests.[1] Regional integration as defined by NAFTA essentially relied on a market-led approach, aiming at cross-border investment and production integration, with no ambition to create a shared community and supranational institutions (Gutiérrez Haces 1995; Morales 1999). From the US perspective, NAFTA aimed to improve the competitiveness of US firms by extending their production platform across the region. For Canada and Mexico, the key interests were to secure their access to the US market and to put an end to unilateral US trade measures. They also shared the US ambition to create a North American-wide production platform, which involved relocating low-tech and labor-intensive production to Mexico, particularly in auto, electronic and other industries. NAFTA's proponents argued that North American producers would be more competitive globally, consumers would benefit from lower prices and jobs would be created.

In this concluding chapter, we take stock of the actual impact of NAFTA on the three countries over its 26 years' existence, summarizing its economic and social effects. We put emphasis on employment since North American integration was intended to bring more and better employment opportunities. These impacts, particularly on employment, are also crucial in order to understand the dissatisfaction with the agreement that led to its renegotiation. We then evaluate whether its successor, the USMCA, is likely to address these concerns and produce a stable and prosperous North American economic space.

NAFTA's Economic and Social Impacts

It is not simple or straightforward to tally the overall effects of NAFTA on its three states parties' economies, jobs and overall welfare. The trade agreement contains myriad provisions that directly and indirectly touch the economies, sometimes in ways that push in different directions. Further, the effects of the trade agreement coexist with cyclical changes, changes in exchange rates and the prices of key commodities, which may be unrelated or tangentially related to NAFTA. The agreement also coexisted or interacted with changes in technology and in national policies toward employment and wages, among other confounding factors. Yet, with the accumulation of an historical record over time, it is possible to identify broad patterns with some confidence.

At the level of overall economic welfare, most studies conclude that the impact of NAFTA was very small.[2] A highly regarded study that takes into account the extensive trade in intermediate goods between the parties finds that the agreement led to an increase of economic welfare of 1.3% in Mexico, 0.08% in the United States, and a decrease of 0.06% in Canada (Caliendo and Parro 2015). That is to say, only Mexico experienced an overall impact exceeding 1% of its Gross Domestic Product

(GDP) when all effects are taken into account. A review of studies of impacts on the United States by the US International Trade Commission (ITC) in 2016 concludes that "the literature has shown small increases in U.S. welfare and GDP as a result of NAFTA... consistent with the findings from pre-2002 literature showing that even large trade liberalizations lead to gains of less than 0.5 percent of GDP" (USITC 2016). A 2003 report by the US Congressional Budget Office (CBO) concluded that the effect of NAFTA on overall US GDP after about a decade was "probably no more than a few billion dollars, or a few hundredths of a percent," a figure consistent with the Caliendo and Parro study (USCBO 2003).

It is at the sectoral level within each country that the contours of NAFTA's effects become discernible. There are winners and losers from trade, as expanded exports increase production and employment while expanded imports decrease them, all else being equal. To understand the effect of trade on a country's economic activities, incomes and social well-being, it is essential to know which sectors or groups gained or lost and to what degree they were affected. We begin with Mexico because the overall impact of NAFTA on that economy was much greater than on the United States or Canada and, therefore, the economic and social impacts were also more extensive.

Mexico

NAFTA was expected to bring employment and improve working conditions in Mexico and lead to convergence in North America in this domain. The Mexican economy and employment were already changing when NAFTA came into force, due to unilateral trade liberalization and policies adopted by the government in the 1980s. NAFTA led to further adjustments, induced by changes in tariffs and quotas and patterns of production that were facilitated by the agreement. A balance of payments crisis and devaluation of the peso in 1994–1995 complicated the effects of the NAFTA in its early years.[3]

The largest early impact of NAFTA was on Mexican agricultural labor, particularly smallholder farmers. Agriculture engaged 8.1 million Mexicans at the end of 1993, just before NAFTA came into force. Employment in the sector began a downward trend, with a loss of 1.3 million jobs over the next decade (Vicario et al. 2003). While not all of that reduction can be attributed to NAFTA, other forces that affected trade, such as the sharp devaluation of the peso during 1994–1995, pushed in the opposite direction, toward greater growth of Mexican exports than imports.[4] Imports of grains from the United States, particularly corn, increased dramatically. The rural poor bore the brunt of early adjustment to NAFTA, with little government support (Polaski 2004).

Over the following decades, agricultural exports gradually grew, based mainly on exports of fruits, vegetables and tree nuts, for which Mexico has a climatic advantage and involving cross-border investment and supply chains. This expansion began to absorb labor and agricultural employment stopped its decline and started to grow modestly from 2008 (Zahniser et al. 2018). As of 2019, about 6.5 million workers were employed in Mexican agriculture, with about 3.5 million self-employed farmers and 3 million hired agricultural workers, of whom 2 million were employed in regions that produce primarily for Mexican consumers and 1 million in states that produce primarily for export (UC Davis Rural Migration Blog 2019). Employment on export farms generally provides somewhat better pay than farms serving domestic markets, but there are health, safety and other workplace issues due to the production practices (Gonzalez 2019; Escobar et al. 2019).

With regard to manufacturing, the maquiladora sector, which produces only for export, added about 800,000 jobs between 1994 and 2001, when employment in the sector hit a peak of 1.3 million jobs (Polaski 2004). Employment in the non-maquila manufacturing sector, which produces for both domestic and export markets, contracted as a result of the peso crisis and then recovered, adding about 100,000 jobs to peak at about 1.47 million by 2000. Both manufacturing sectors then lost jobs for several years, due in part to a US recession and to growing competition from China, which joined the World Trade Organization (WTO) in 2001 and competed with Mexico for both the US export and domestic markets (Gallagher et al. 2008). The modest growth of employment in export manufacturing is partly explained by the production model enabled by NAFTA, in which component parts are imported, processed or assembled, then re-exported, crossing the border multiple times. This limits forward and backward linkages and weakens job creation (Moreno-Brid et al. 2005). As NAFTA neared its end in 2019, about 2.73 million workers were employed in manufacturing for export, out of an economically active population of 57.6 million (INEGI).

In Mexico's service sectors, NAFTA had little direct effect on employment because most of its services are not traded and those that are, such as financial services, are not very labor intensive. Nevertheless, the service sector is key to an overall understanding of the Mexican labor market, because it is here that most Mexicans find employment, with the share of total employment in the service sector increasing from 51% immediately before NAFTA took effect to 63% in 2020 (INEGI). Much of this growth reflected absorption of labor from the agricultural sector, whose share of employment decreased from 26% of employment in 1993 to 13% in 2020.

The service sector is the epicenter of the growth in informal employment, which includes self-employment, work in microenterprises and other forms of employment that do not provide benefits such as health care and pensions. Due to the exodus of labor from small-scale agriculture and sluggish employment growth in the manufacturing sector, work was found or created in low-paying service jobs, such as domestic work, street vending, personal services and repairs. Informal employment grew to 50% of all employment in Mexico in 1995 and 1996, following the peso crisis (Vicario et al. 2003). After economic growth resumed in the late 1990s, the informal sector shrank somewhat to about 46% of Mexican jobs, but has subsequently expanded again and currently accounts for about 57% of the workforce (ILO 2014; INEGI).

A recent phenomenon in Mexico is the growth of contract labor in the formal sector, with workers hired on a short-term basis or through intermediaries. Contract labor provides less secure employment, often with lower wages and not covered by labor regulations and social security laws (Bensusán and Sánchez 2021). One study finds that regions in Mexico exposed to more import competition expanded use of contract workers (Trachtenberg 2019).

Mexican wages declined sharply during the peso crisis of 1994–1995, recovered slightly, and then largely stagnated, despite increases in productivity (Shaiken 2014). This reflects a number of factors. The labor supply continues to exceed demand in most categories of labor in Mexico. Mexican workers also compete with unskilled and semi-skilled labor in other countries in increasingly integrated global production chains, as firms make production and sourcing decisions based in part on labor costs in various countries. Mexican wage policy and institutions have also been biased against wage increases (Polaski 2004). The government policy was to hold down minimum wage, both before and during the NAFTA period, a policy that changed with the new Mexican government in late

2018. Unionization and collective bargaining, among the main institutional mechanisms for determining wages, have also been repressed in Mexico through weak labor laws and corruption.[5] As a result of Mexican wage policy and labor market forces, Mexican wages failed to converge with those of the United States and Canada, contrary to the prediction of trade theory and of NAFTA's proponents (Gandolfi et al. 2015).

United States

The extremely modest overall effects of NAFTA on the US economy—estimated by most credible studies at a few hundredths of a percent—can be explained by several factors. The US economy is much larger than those of Mexico and Canada and less dependent on trade due to the huge domestic market. US tariffs were generally low before NAFTA and most tariff reductions were small. The minor overall impact of the agreement is reflected in very small effects on aggregate employment, but with larger differences in wages and across sectors and regions. The USITC's 2016 literature review of NAFTA's impacts found little to no change in total US employment but noticeable changes in wages in the footwear, textiles, and plastics industries (USITC 2016). A study of manufacturing employment in the United States found that it "did fall off a cliff—but not until after 2001, seven years after NAFTA went into effect" (Blecker and Esquivel 2013). The sharp decline coincided with the full phasing in of NAFTA provisions, a recession in the United States, China's accession to the WTO and a rapid increase in offshoring of production.

A new generation of studies that exploits data on local labor markets reveals more about the diversity and intensity of impacts. A seminal study looks at each industry's exposure to Mexican imports and each local labor market's dependence on the most vulnerable industries (Hakobyan and McLaren 2016). The authors find that the most affected industries and localities faced "dramatically lower wage growth for blue-collar workers in the most affected industries and localities" and that these negative wage effects extended from manufacturing to service sector workers as well. They conclude that the "distributional effects are much larger than aggregate welfare effects estimated by other authors."

The United States provided income and other support to workers who lost jobs due to the agreement under the NAFTA Trade Adjustment Assistance (NAFTA TAA) program. The US Department of Labor certified petitions covering 757,000 workers as having lost jobs due to

NAFTA through 2001 (Kessler 2017). From 2002, the NAFTA TAA was combined with the broader TAA program covering jobs lost due to all trade agreements. While workers displaced by NAFTA after that date continued to qualify for benefits, the Department of Labor no longer published separate figures for NAFTA-related claims and so a tally for the entire 26 years of NAFTA is not available from the government. A database compiled by Public Citizen, a non-governmental organization critical of US trade policy, shows that about one million workers were certified as losing their jobs to NAFTA through 2019 (Public Citizen 2020).

Canada

As noted above, the leading general equilibrium study of NAFTA found that economic welfare decreased in Canada by 0.06%; a small impact offset by a deterioration of terms of trade (Caliendo and Parro 2015). A significant factor explaining Canada's experience is the composition of its major exports. For much of the NAFTA period, primary sector exports including crude oil and other energy products were the largest component of the country's exports to the United States, its largest trading partner (Villarreal and Fergusson 2017). The share of energy exports affected Canadian employment negatively at some points over the last decades by driving up the Canadian currency and thus hurting Canadian manufacturing exports (Villarreal and Fergusson 2014; Meyer and Fergusson 2021).

At the sectoral level, the impact of NAFTA on Canada combined with the effects of its predecessor, the USCFTA. NAFTA incorporated its provisions and in addition liberalized trade between Canada and Mexico, although the latter continues to account for a relatively small share, about 3–4%, of Canada's total trade. A seminal study of the impacts of USCFTA and NAFTA from 1989 through 1996 found that in industries most affected by Canadian tariff cuts employment fell by 12% over those years, while in the export-oriented industries that experienced the largest US tariff cuts there was no increase in employment (Trefler 2004). These outcomes reflected in part the closure of US-owned Canadian factories that had been established behind the former tariff walls, and in part the decline of other less productive factories faced with new cross-border competition. Overall, there was a 5% loss of manufacturing employment. Labor productivity improved and wages rose slightly, by about 3% over the eight years covered by the study (Trefler 2004; see also Villarreal and Fergusson 2014).

NAFTA led to more tightly integrated production and value chains across North America for a number of important products, particularly automobiles and auto parts. This has benefited Mexico more than Canada. In addition to the attraction of Mexico's much lower wages, the periodic appreciation of the Canadian currency also influenced investment decisions in favor of Mexico over Canada (Rubin 2017; Meyer and Fergusson 2021). As the currency began to depreciate with the end of the commodities boom in 2013, manufacturing recovered somewhat but represents a declining share of Canadian employment, with about 1.6 million workers today out of total employment of 17.2 million (Meyer and Fergusson 2021; Statistics Canada 2020).

CAN THE USMCA DO BETTER?

As noted above, most official and economic analysis of NAFTA concludes that its impact on the three countries' GDP and overall economic welfare was extremely small, a fraction of a percent for the US and Canada and just over 1% for Mexico. And yet the agreement generated intense and sustained political controversy that finally led to its denunciation by then US President Donald Trump and its renegotiation. To understand this seeming puzzle, we have looked at the winners and losers from NAFTA. The winners were corporations, which gained a continent-wide production platform that included a large expansion of available labor, much of it at far lower wages, with guaranteed access for their goods and services into the three countries' markets. They also gained important protections for their rights as cross-border investors and for their corporate intellectual property. The main losers were workers in import-competing industries in Canada and the United States and small-scale farmers in Mexico, whose losses were often deep and long-lasting. At a fundamental level, these were the logical consequences of the original design of NAFTA as a regional integration of markets, investment and production aimed at increasing the competitiveness of the private sector in the three countries.

Does the USMCA change that basic model? This book has explored the changes that were made to NAFTA in the new USMCA across the range of topics covered by the agreement. Abstracting from the wealth of detail covered in the preceding chapters, it is possible to discern an overall pattern.

First, the North American integration model launched by NAFTA is preserved under the USMCA. Cross-border trade, investment and production continue to be at the heart of the new agreement. In some cases, the rights of producers and the enforcement of those rights have been strengthened, for example with respect to intellectual property. Some sectors that were covered in NAFTA have gained additional cross-border rights, for example, the financial sector. The digital technology sector gained extensive new rights under the USMCA.[6] The one aspect of protection for corporations and investors that has been scaled back is the investor-state dispute settlement mechanism, which had generated opposition as a threat to state sovereignty and governments' ability to regulate in the public interest (Gagné and Morin 2006).

Second, with regard to workers and labor markets, the USMCA contains far stronger obligations concerning labor rights and strengthened enforcement mechanisms to ensure compliance. These changes reflect the recognition that NAFTA and other trade agreements can have harsh distributional effects and that Mexican wages had not converged toward US and Canadian wages. Whether the new labor approaches will be effective in constraining anti-labor behavior by employers and fostering an upward convergence of wages and living standards between Mexico and its northern neighbors remains to be seen. In terms of rebalancing private production interests and the public interest, some moderate strengthening of environmental obligations and enforcement are also included in the USMCA.

The rebalancing of corporate and public interests is a consequence of the sharp political reaction against the negative distributional impacts of NAFTA. It might seem ironic that the first phase of the labor revisions was negotiated by US and Mexican administrations that were largely anti-labor in their political orientation. It was the need for ratification by a pro-labor US Congress that explains this seeming anomaly. Further pro-labor and environmental changes were required by the US Congress as a condition for ratification and readily agreed by a new pro-labor Mexican government.

Overall, the USMCA is probably best seen as an update and slight rebalancing of the existing North American integration model rather than a new model. The update responds to the emergence of China and Asia as the center of many global production chains. The negotiation of the

Trans-Pacific Partnership (TPP), which preceded the USMCA, was a first attempt at such an update, designed to expand the NAFTA production platform to include a number of Asian countries. The TPP also allowed the countries to negotiate new trade-related regulatory issues with the strategic goal of setting the rules for global production chains not only in North America but in Asia as well. After the United States withdrew from the TPP, the negotiation of the USMCA presented a second chance to update the regulatory issues for North American production and trade and in some matters to go further. The additional behind-the-border regulatory provisions of USMCA further blur the relationship between national sovereignty and transnational trade governance. There can be debate as to whether this reflects a convergence of regulation and governance models across the three countries or the hegemonic diffusion of the US regulatory model.

WHERE TO FROM HERE?

The inception of the USMCA has coincided with a pandemic that has upended the economies of the three countries. The relative weight of the North American economy is likely to shrink somewhat as the Asian economies recover faster and new trade and investment agreements within Asia and between China and the EU are negotiated. The initial steps to translate the terms of the USMCA into new practices will be made by center-left governments in each of the three North American countries, suggesting that the rebalancing aspects may be given additional attention and importance during the implementation process.

This book has compared the NAFTA and the USMCA. The similarities are important. The USMCA is building on the North American integration model and is strongly business oriented. Yet, there are more progressive and inclusive commitments as the democratic legitimacy of NAFTA was much questioned and debated. This partly explains why the ratification process and participation at all levels have proved more important than nearly 30 years ago. Also, the motivation to increase competitiveness has now focused on regulatory cooperation across North American global value chains on issues such as intellectual property, investment, industrial and production standards. The new digital trade provisions export the permissive US policy toward Internet platforms' responsibility, tolerance of their market concentration and disregard for data privacy issues. The USMCA, as envisioned by its negotiators and stakeholders, may be open to contestation and reinterpretation. There is a sunset clause that might open the possibility for termination or deepening of the agreement.

All of these elements suggest that North American economic integration will continue to be a contested work in progress. As for now, the USMCA offers avenues but it might no longer be at the center of the world economic initiatives. The USMCA is much less likely to prove a model to be followed than the NAFTA was in the 1990s. If the book cannot conclude on this question, it has opened the debate on the significance and impact of the USMCA as compared to NAFTA. The book has also brought to light the tensions and unfinished business that might structure future North American integration, as well as its role and importance in the world economy.

Notes

1. There were some, like Pastor (2011), who supported the creation of a North American community.
2. "Welfare" is the term used by economists employing computable general equilibrium models to describe the aggregate effects of trade agreements including changes in prices, wages, etc.
3. A description of the peso crisis and its relation to NAFTA can be found in Polaski (2004, pp. 18–19).
4. During this period, Mexico was also liberalizing trade with other partners, so the entire impact cannot be ascribed to NAFTA. But an evaluation shows that Mexico reduced its agricultural tariffs much more for the United States than for other trading partners (WTO 2003).
5. It is a widespread practice for employers to conclude "protection contracts" with corrupt or non-existent trade unions, precluding efforts by workers or more legitimate unions to bargain for wage increases. See: Bouzas (2007); Alcalde and Bensusan (2013).
6. The US Trade Representative website states that "The new Digital Trade chapter contains the strongest disciplines on digital trade of any international agreement, providing a firm foundation for the expansion of trade and investment in the innovative products and services where the United States has a competitive advantage" (USTR n.d.).

REFERENCES

Alcalde, Arturo, and Graciela Bensusan. 2013. *El sistema de justicia laboral en México: Situación actual y perspectivas.* Friedrich Ebert Stiftung México, No. 1, June. http://library.fes.de/pdf-files/bueros/mexiko/10311.pdf.

Bensusán, Graciela, and Landy Sánchez (eds.). 2021. *Estudio sobre la Subcontratación en México: Tendencias, modalidades y regulación.* El Colegio de México.

Blecker, Robert A., and Gerardo Esquivel. 2013. Trade and the Development Gap. In *Mexico and the United States: The Politics of Partnership*, ed. Peter H. Smith and Andrew Selee, 83–110. Boulder, CO: Lynne Rienner.

Bouzas, José Alfonso (ed.). 2007. *Contratación Colectiva de Trabajo en México: Informe a la Organización Regional Interamericana de Trabajadores (ORIT).*

Caliendo, Lorenzo, and Fernando Parro. 2015. Estimates of the Trade and Welfare Effects of NAFTA. *Review of Economic Studies* 82 (1): 1–44. https://academic.oup.com/restud/article/82/1/1/1547758.

Escobar, Agustin, Philip Martin, and Omar Stabridis. 2019. *Farm Labor and Mexico's Export Produce Industry.* Washington, DC: Wilson Center, October. https://www.wilsoncenter.org/sites/default/files/media/documents/public ation/farm_labor_and_mexico_export_produce_industry.pdf. Accessed April 30, 2020.

Gagné, Gilbert, and Jean-Frédéric Morin. 2006. The Evolving American Policy on Investment Protection: Evidence from Recent FTAs and the 2004 Model BIT. *Journal of International Economic Law* 9 (2): 357–382.

Gallagher, Kevin, Juan Carlos Moreno-Brid, and Roberto Porzecanski. 2008. The Dynamism of Mexican Exports: Lost in (Chinese) Translation? *World Development* 36 (8): 1365–1380.

Gandolfi, Davide, Timothy Halliday, and Raymond Robertson. 2015. *Trade, Migration, and the Place Premium: Mexico and the United States.* Washington, DC: Center for Global Development, Working Paper 396, March. https://www.cgdev.org/publication/trade-migration-and-place-premium-mexico-and-united-states-working-paper-396.

González, Humberto. 2019. What Socioenvironmental Impacts Did 35 Years of Export Agriculture Have in Mexico? (1980–2014): A Transnational Agri-food Field Analysis. *Journal of Agrarian Change* 20 (1): 163–187. https://online library.wiley.com/doi/full/10.1111/joac.12343.

Gutiérrez Haces, Maria Teresa. 1995. From Protectionism to Free Trade: Mexico's Problematic Transition. *Critical Sociology* 21 (2): 53–57. https://doi.org/10.1177/089692059502100205.

Hakobyan, Shushanik, and John McLaren. 2016. Looking for Local Labor Market Effects of NAFTA. *The Review of Economics and Statistics* 98 (4): 728–741. https://doi.org/10.1162/REST_a_00587.

Instituto Nacional de Estadística y Geografía (INEGI). https://www.inegi.org. mx/sistemas/bie/.

International Labor Organization (ILO). 2014. *Informal Employment in Mexico: Current Situation, Policies and Challenges*. ILO Regional Office for Latin America and the Caribbean. https://www.ilo.org/wcmsp5/groups/public/---americas/---ro-lima/documents/publication/wcms_245889.pdf.

Kessler, Glenn. 2017. The Trump Administration's Claim That the U.S. Government 'Certified' 700,000 Jobs Lost by NAFTA. *The Washington Post*, August 18. https://www.washingtonpost.com/news/fact-checker/wp/2017/08/18/the-trump-administrations-claim-that-the-u-s-government-certified-700000-jobs-lost-by-nafta/.

Meyer, Peter J., and Ian F. Fergusson. 2021. *Canada–U.S. Relations*. Congressional Research Service, Report 96–397, Updated February 10. https://fas.org/sgp/crs/row/96-397.pdf.

Morales, Isidro. 1999. NAFTA: The Governance of Economic Openness. *The Annals of the American Academy of Political and Social Science* 565 (1): 35–65. https://doi.org/10.1177/000271629956500103.

Moreno-Brid, Juan Carlos, Jesus Santamaria, and Juan Carlos Rivas. Valdivia. 2005. Industrialization and Economic Growth in Mexico after NAFTA: The Road Travelled. *Development and Change* 36 (6): 1095–1119.

North American Free Trade Agreement (NAFTA), Signed December 17, 1992, Entered into Force January 1, 1994. https://www.nafta-sec-alena.org/Home/Legal-Texts/North-American-Free-Trade-Agreement.

Office of the United States Trade Representative (USTR). n.d. *United States-Mexico-Canada Trade Fact Sheet: Modernizing NAFTA into a 21st Century Trade Agreement*. https://ustr.gov/trade-agreements/free-trade-agreements/united-states-mexico-canada-agreement/fact-sheets/modernizing.

Pastor, Robert. 2011. *The North American Idea: A Vision of a Continental Future*. New York: Oxford University Press.

Polaski, Sandra. 2004. Jobs, Wages and Household Income. In *NAFTA's Promise and Reality: Lessons from Mexico for the Hemisphere*, ed. John J. Audley, Demetrios G. Papademetriou, Sandra Polaski, and Scott Vaughan, 11–37. Washington: Carnegie Endowment for International Peace. https://carnegieendowment.org/pdf/files/NAFTA_Report_ChapterOne.pdf.

Public Citizen. 2020. *Trade Adjustment Assistance Database*. https://www.citizen.org/article/trade-adjustment-assistance-database/.

Rubin, Jeff. 2017. *How Has Canadian Manufacturing Fared Under NAFTA? A Look at the Auto Assembly and Parts Industry*. Waterloo, ON: Centre for International Governance Innovation, CIGI Paper No. 138, August 8. https://www.cigionline.org/publications/how-has-canadian-manufacturing-fared-under-nafta-look-auto-assembly-and-parts-industry.

Shaiken, Harley. 2014. The Nafta Paradox. *Berkeley Review of Latin American Studies*, Spring: 37–43. https://clas.berkeley.edu/research/trade-nafta-paradox.

Statistics Canada. 2020. *Employment by Industry*. https://www150.statcan.gc.ca/t1/tbl1/en/tv.action?pid=1410020101.

Trachtenberg, Danielle. 2019. *Local Labor-Market Effects of NAFTA in Mexico: Evidence from Mexican Commuting Zones*. Inter-American Development Bank, IDB Working Paper Series No. IDB-WP-01078. November. https://publications.iadb.org/publications/english/document/Local_Labor-Market_Effects_of_NAFTA_in_Mexico_Evidence_from_Mexican_Commuting_Zones_en.pdf.

Trans-Pacific Partnership (TPP), Signed February 4, 2016. https://www.international.gc.ca/trade-commerce/trade-agreements-accords-commerciaux/agr-acc/tpp-ptp/text-texte/toc-tdm.aspx?lang=eng.

Trefler, Daniel. 2004. The Long and Short of the Canada–U.S. Free Trade Agreement. *American Economic Review* 94 (4): 870–895. https://www.aeaweb.org/articles?id=10.1257/0002828042002633.

United States – Canada Free Trade Agreement (USCFTA), Signed January 2, 1988, Entered into Force January 1, 1989. http://www.international.gc.ca/trade-agreements-accords-commerciaux/assets/pdfs/cusfta-e.pdf.

United States, Congressional Budget Office (USCBO). 2003. *The Effects of NAFTA on U.S.-Mexican Trade and GDP*. May. https://www.cbo.gov/sites/default/files/108th-congress-2003-2004/reports/report_0.pdf. Accessed April 21, 2020.

United States International Trade Commission (USITC). 2016. *Economic Impact of Trade Agreements Implemented Under Trade Authorities Procedures, 2016 Report*. June. Publication Number: 4614, Investigation Number: 332–555. https://www.usitc.gov/publications/332/pub4614.pdf.

United States-Mexico-Canada Agreement (USMCA), Signed November 30, 2018, Entered into Force July 1, 2020. https://ustr.gov/trade-agreements/free-trade-agreements/united-states-mexico-canada-agreement/agreement-between.

University of California (UC) Davis Rural Migration Blog. 2019. Workers on Mexico's Export Farms. November 19. https://migration.ucdavis.edu/rmn/blog/post/?id=2367. Accessed April 24, 2020.

Vicario, Maria Elena, Sandra Polaski, and Dalil Maschino. 2003. *North American Labor Markets: A Comparative Profile*. Washington, DC: Secretariat of the North American Commission for Labor Cooperation.

Villarreal, M. Angeles, and Ian F. Fergusson. 2014. *NAFTA at 20: Overview and Trade Effects*. Congressional Research Service, Report R42965, April 28. http://nationalaglawcenter.org/wp-content/uploads/assets/crs/R42965.pdf.

Villarreal, M. Angeles, and Ian F. Fergusson. 2017. *The North American Free Trade Agreement (NAFTA)*. Congressional Research Service, Report R42965, May 24. https://fas.org/sgp/crs/row/R42965.pdf.

World Trade Organization (WTO). 2003. *World Trade Report 2003*. Geneva: World Trade Organization. https://www.wto.org/english/res_e/booksp_e/anrep_e/world_trade_report_2003_e.pdf.

Zahniser, Steven, J. Edward Taylor, Thomas Hertz, and Diane Charlton. 2018. Farm Labor Markets in the United States and Mexico Pose Challenges for U.S. Agriculture. US Department of Agriculture, Economic Research Service, EIB No. 201, November. https://www.ers.usda.gov/webdocs/publications/90832/eib-201.pdf?v%3D1521.2. Accessed April 28, 2020.

INDEX